Combat Asthma Through Diet

Combat Asthma Through Diet

A collection of 50 low-allergen recipes to beat the symptoms of asthma, eczema and hayfever and to improve your health

BRIGID McCONVILLE

southwater

This edition is published by Southwater, an imprint of Anness Publishing Ltd, Hermes House, 88–89 Blackfriars Road, London SE1 8HA; tel. 020 7401 2077; fax 020 7633 9499

www.southwaterbooks.com; www.annesspublishing.com

If you like the images in this book and would like to investigate using them for publishing, promotions or advertising, please visit our website www.practicalpictures.com for more information.

© Anness Publishing Ltd 2002, 2009

A CIP catalogue record for this book is available from the British Library.

UK agent: The Manning Partnership Ltd;
tel. 01225 478444; fax 01225 478440; sales@manning-partnership.co.uk
UK distributor: Grantham Book Services Ltd;
tel. 01476 541080; fax 01476 541061; orders@gbs.tbs-ltd.co.uk
North American agent/distributor: National Book Network;
tel. 301 459 3366; fax 301 429 5746; www.nbnbooks.com
Australian agent/distributor: Pan Macmillan Australia;
tel. 1300 135 113; fax 1300 135 103; customer.service@macmillan.com.au
New Zealand agent/distributor: David Bateman Ltd; tel. (09) 415 7664; fax (09) 415 8892

Publisher: Joanna Lorenz
Managing Editor: Linda Fraser
Senior Editor: Susannah Blake
Copy Editor: Rosie Hankin
Editorial Reader: Jonathan Marshall
Recipes: Brian Glover, Christine Ingram, Lucy Knox, Jane Milton, Jennie Shapter, Marlena Spieler, Kate Whiteman
Designer: Oakley Design Associates
Photographers: Martin Brigdale, Gus Filgate, David King, William Lingwood, Sam Stowell

ETHICAL TRADING POLICY

Because of our ongoing ecological investment programme, you, as our customer, can have the pleasure and reassurance of knowing that a tree is being cultivated on your behalf to naturally replace the materials used to make the book you are holding. For further information about this scheme, go to www.annesspublishing.com/trees

Previously published as *Kitchen Doctor: Asthma Cooking for Health*

NOTES

For all recipes, quantities are given in both metric and imperial measures and, where appropriate, in standard cups and spoons.
Follow one set of measures, but not a mixture, because they are not interchangeable.
Standard spoon and cup measures are level. 1 tsp = 5ml, 1 tbsp = 15ml, 1 cup = 250ml/8fl oz.
Australian standard tablespoons are 20ml. Australian readers should use 3 tsp in place of 1 tbsp for measuring small quantities.
American pints are 16fl oz/2 cups. American readers should use 20fl oz/2.5 cups in place of 1 pint when measuring liquids.
Electric oven temperatures in this book are for conventional ovens. When using a fan oven, the temperature will probably need to be reduced by about 10–20°C/20–40°F. Since ovens vary, you should check with your manufacturer's instruction book for guidance.
The nutritional analysis given for each recipe is calculated per portion (i.e. serving or item), unless otherwise stated. If the recipe gives a range, such as Serves 4–6, then the nutritional analysis will be for the smaller portion size, i.e. 6 servings.
Measurements for sodium do not include salt added to taste.

Medium (US large) eggs are used unless otherwise stated.

Main front cover image shows Chicken Breasts with Chilli Salsa – for recipe, see page 39.

PUBLISHER'S NOTE

Although the advice and information in this book are believed to be accurate and true at the time of going to press, neither the authors nor the publisher can accept any legal responsibility or liability for any errors or omissions that may be made.

contents

asthma, eczema and hayfever

AROUND THE WORLD – especially in the West – more and more people are suffering from asthma, eczema and hayfever, conditions that may be caused by intolerance or allergy to substances we eat, drink, touch or inhale. In the US it is thought that up to 15 million people have symptoms of asthma, and in the UK one in eight children and one in thirteen adults are affected. However, Australia tops the international league with one in three children having asthma symptoms.

ASTHMA SYMPTOMS

The symptoms of asthma vary from person to person and may be accompanied by extreme anxiety, sweating and increased pulse rate. You may not suffer from all these symptoms at any one time and their severity may vary at different times:
- A long-lasting cough, often worse at night or after exercise
- Wheezing (the whistling sound produced as air is expelled from the lungs) – this may be very quiet and sometimes can only be heard with the aid of a stethoscope
- Shortness of breath
- Difficulty breathing out
- Tightness of the chest

The following symptoms are likely to occur in a severe attack:
- Breathing becomes increasingly shallow and fast
- The lips and face may turn blue as oxygen levels in the blood diminish
- The skin may become pale and feel clammy

WARNING:
Severe asthma attacks can kill. If someone is suffering from a severe attack, call an ambulance immediately, then place the patient in the recovery position until medical attention arrives.

If you are prone to severe asthma attacks, make sure that you always keep your inhaler with you.

A MODERN PROBLEM
There is no simple answer as to why more people are suffering. Allergies are common in the developed world, but rare in countries without our industries, pollution and medicines. It could be that over thousands of years, the human body has developed the ability to defend itself against natural compounds, but we have fewer defences against the many new and artificial substances.

Above: *Air pollution in the developed world is thought to be one of the major contributing factors in causing asthma.*

Left: *In some parts of the world as many as one in three children suffer from asthma.*

ABOUT ASTHMA

If you – or perhaps a member of your family – are one the world's many asthma sufferers, you will know that the symptoms can vary from mild wheezing and coughing to a terrifying inability to breathe, which can be life threatening. For this reason it is vital to follow your doctor's recommendations at all times and – whatever else you may try in terms of self help – to keep any vital medications always at hand.

Technically, asthma is an inflammatory condition in which the muscles in the walls of your lungs' tiny airways go into spasm. At much the same time that the spasms occur, the linings of the airways swell up and thick mucus is produced. All this makes it difficult for you to get air in and out of your lungs. A variety of factors such as cold air, exercise, infections or common allergens including house dust mites and pollen may trigger an attack.

THE CAUSES AND SYMPTOMS OF ECZEMA

Like asthma, eczema is linked to allergies and shows up as patches of dry, scaly skin, which may crack, itch, become reddened, swell and/or weep. These are often located in the creases of joints around the body. Damaged skin is more open to infection so there may also be pimples or pus. Symptoms

can range from mildly irritating to almost unbearable, and may change according to the time of day or the season of the year. Sufferers of eczema also often find symptoms become worse when under pressure or suffering from emotional stress.

Above: *For sufferers of hayfever, late spring and early summer can prove to be a misery as they react to the grass and flower pollen in the air. Sneezing, a running nose and itchy, inflamed eyes are all common symptoms.*

URTICARIA

This skin condition, which often occurs in people with asthma and eczema, is also known as hives or nettlerash. It is usually, though not always, triggered by an allergic reaction to a particular food such as cow's milk, eggs, shellfish, strawberries or nuts, or to food additives such as the food colourant tartrazine.

Urticaria can also be caused by certain medicines such as aspirin and penicillin, or by insect stings, pollen and dander, which are small particles or scales of animal hair or feathers. For some people, stress or tension can make urticaria worse.

If you develop urticaria, white or yellow itchy lumps surrounded by a red area of inflammation develop on the skin. You may also suffer swelling – called angio-oedema – of the face, lips, eyelids, tongue or throat. This is often due to food allergy or intolerance and can come on within seconds of food entering the mouth.

Urticaria is usually an irritating but harmless condition. However, if you suffer an attack of angio-oedema and the swelling begins to spread to your throat, contact your doctor immediately as there is a slight risk of suffocation.

HAVING HAYFEVER

If you – or your child – has hayfever, you will know exactly how maddening this particular allergy can be. Just when the sun has come out and everyone else seems to be enjoying themselves outside in the fresh air, you can't stop sneezing, your nose is running and your eyes are red, weeping and itchy. You may also be wheezing, have shortness of breath and a dry throat.

Hayfever is an allergic reaction to air-borne pollen from grasses and flowers, and it can affect the nose, throat and eyes. The condition is seasonal, and occurs mainly in late spring and early summer, though the exact timing of when symptoms develop will depend on which type of specific pollen you are allergic to.

how food can cause allergy and intolerance

YOUR DIET can have an important part to play in allergies. A nutritious diet can help keep your immune system in tip-top condition, warding off the bugs that can trigger asthma and make hayfever and eczema worse. If your allergies are triggered by certain foods, you can try to find out what these are – and then avoid them. But, to understand how food triggers your symptoms, it helps to know about allergic responses.

IMMUNE SYSTEM OVERREACTION

Allergic reactions are rather like your body's response to any foreign substance – be they germs or splinters. Normally, your body responds with a range of defences, called antibodies, to fight off any invaders (antigens). Familiar signs of this fight in your body include swelling, redness and fever – all healthy indications that your immune system is at work.

If you are prone to allergies however, your immune system overdoes it, recognising usually harmless substances, such as pollen or foods, as enemies and attempting to fight them off. Once your body has mistaken these harmless substances for the enemy, it remembers what happened the last time and sets up a system for making the antibodies quickly, in case the invader returns.

It is this overreaction by the body's natural defence mechanisms to a foreign body that causes a range of symptoms anywhere in the body. As well as the symptoms of asthma, eczema and hayfever, allergy can cause other unpleasant reactions such as vomiting and diarrhoea, headaches and migraine, tiredness, wakefulness at night and irritability.

ANTIBODIES AT WORK

The main antibody that causes these allergic symptoms is immunoglobulin E (IgE). It becomes active chiefly in the blood, the mucous membranes of the nose, throat and mouth, and in the skin. When the enemy invader shows up in the body, IgE reacts with the antigen and sets off a release

of various chemicals. The best known of these chemicals is histamine, and it (together with other chemicals produced by cell tissue) causes the familiar, immediate symptoms of allergy, from itchy skin, running nose and sneezing, and itchy eyes to tiredness, headaches and irritability. Histamine is produced by the body whenever it is injured

Above: Eating a balanced diet is essential for good health, but some common foods can also be the cause of allergies.

or under attack from infection. It causes the blood vessels to increase in size so that blood can quickly get to damaged tissue in order to repair it.

ANAPHYLACTIC SHOCK

This massive allergic reaction is a rare but potentially life-threatening event during which the blood vessels suddenly swell, causing a dramatic drop in blood pressure. This in turn leads to a lack of oxygen in the brain. Without sufficient oxygen, the brain cannot control blood pressure, which can cause it to fall even further. Once into this downward spiral, your body cannot recover of its own accord.

As blood pressure continues to fall the sufferer may become drowsy and confused, and might finally lose consciousness.

Anaphylaxsis can be triggered by a variety of allergens, the most common of which are foods (especially peanuts, some other nuts, eggs, cow's milk and products made from it, and shellfish); certain drugs such as penicillin; the venom of stinging insects such as bees, wasps and hornets, latex and paint.

The symptoms – which may appear very suddenly and without any warning – can include:
• Sweating, faintness and nausea
• Panting and rapid pulse rate
• Pale, cold, clammy skin
• Hives may appear on the skin

If you are with someone who is going into anaphylactic shock, call an ambulance immediately. Meanwhile lie them down – on their side if already unconscious – wrap them in a coat or blanket and do not give them anything to eat or drink.

If you know that you or your child is at risk of anaphylaxis, your doctor will prescribe medication for use in the event of an allergic reaction. This may include a pre-loaded injection of adrenaline (epinephrine), and antihistamines and hydrocortisone may also be given.

Above: *Although milk is considered healthy and nutritious, particularly for children, it can also be the cause of food allergy and intolerance in others.*

ALLERGY AND INTOLERANCE: TELLING THE DIFFERENCE

The dividing line between allergy and intolerance is rather blurred, so much so that intolerance is sometimes referred to as "pseudo-allergy". Intolerance can be difficult to "prove" and so traditionally the medical profession has been sceptical of its existence, and therefore its treatment. Intolerance, like allergy, occurs when the body's immune system overreacts to foreign substances, but the process is much slower and the symptoms are not so obvious.

With allergy, the response is usually quick and noticeable almost immediately – or at least within 72 hours. Intolerance, on the other hand, tends to reveal itself much more slowly. If a person is allergic to cats, for instance, you will probably be able to tell there is a cat in the room (or even that a cat has been in the room) because the person's eyes and nose will start to run within just a few minutes. In contrast, an intolerance to a commonly eaten food such as wheat can take

months or even years to develop. Because of this very slow response, it is often much more difficult to work out what is causing the symptoms of intolerance than it is to discover the cause of an allergic reaction.

The mechanism of intolerance may be different from that of allergy, too. During an allergic reaction, the body fights an invader and produces the chemical histamine. With intolerance, the body does not necessarily produce a histamine reaction.

When a person has an intolerance to a substance, it may be an ingredient of food – such as gluten in cereals, proteins in cheese or fish, or caffeine in coffee, tea, cola drinks and chocolate – which directly harms or irritates the body. Another reason for intolerance may be that a person lacks the physical ability to cope with certain foods. For example, people who have an intolerance to dairy products usually have a shortage of the enzyme lactase. Without this enzyme, the lactose in dairy products cannot be digested properly.

SYMPTOMS OF INTOLERANCE

One complication of identifying intolerance is that some of the common symptoms of intolerance overlap with those of certain allergies, for instance, tiredness, migraine, nausea and vomiting. Symptoms of intolerance include:
• Aching muscles
• Mouth ulcers
• Water retention
• Gastric and duodenal ulcers
• Wind and bloating, IBS (irritable bowel syndrome) and constipation
• Rheumatoid arthritis
• Anxiety and depression
• Hyperactivity in children and ADD (attention deficit disorder)

why people suffer from allergies

THE WHOLE SUBJECT of allergy and intolerance is a contentious one – especially when it comes to identifying causes. This is partly because we don't know all the answers to how and why allergies and intolerances occur, and partly because health practitioners can take very different approaches in treatment.

HEREDITY

Is it in your genes? Heredity seems to play a part in who gets allergies, although these can show up in different forms within the same family. For instance, if one of your parents suffers from hayfever, you may get asthma and your child might develop eczema.

Research shows that if one of your parents has an allergy, you have a 20–30 per cent chance of developing one. If both your parents have allergies, you have a 40–60 per cent chance of having one. If both your parents have the same allergy, you have a 70 per cent chance of developing that allergy. However, a third of children with allergies are born to parents who aren't aware of any allergic symptoms in themselves.

Below: *Allergies often run in families yet, in over one third of these, sufferers develop symptoms their parents didn't have.*

OTHER FAMILY INFLUENCES

The family influence is more than genetics. Some recent studies into childhood illnesses suggest that the more people are exposed to infections, the less likely they are to develop allergies. The same may be true for dust and dirt. There is evidence that children with older siblings – and who are introduced that way to more infections – suffer less from allergy than first born children.

While allergies and intolerances seem to run in families, children will inherit only a tendency to allergy. Whether or not a full-blown allergy develops depends very much on their diet and environment, not only in the sensitive weeks and months after birth, but also before birth while the child is still in the womb. To help reduce the chances of your child developing allergic conditions, follow the guidelines given in the advice box on early preventive measures.

OUR POLLUTED ENVIRONMENT

There is no definitive proof, but the emerging consensus is that environmental pollution even in moderation is a significant trigger for common allergies like asthma. Toxins from the air could be compromising our immunity as well as irritating our airways.

Not only the air we breathe, but also our water and our food often contain chemicals, such as pesticides, additives and artificial flavourings. We also come into regular contact with many other toxins including heavy metals from petrol fumes, mercury in some tooth fillings, and chemicals in cosmetics and detergents.

Inside the home

Protected by insulation and double glazing, our modern homes may be warm and dry but they are poorly ventilated and they trap:

- Fumes given off by solvent-based paints, varnishes, cleaning fluids and glues
- Formaldehyde from soft furnishings
- Nitrogen oxide and carbon monoxide from gas appliances
- A range of pollutants in cigarette smoke

Outside the home

We talk about getting a "breath of fresh air", but consider the following:

- Exhaust fumes and heavy industry mean we are ingesting about 1000 times as much lead as our prehistoric ancestors
- Ozone, a chemical cocktail containing hydrocarbons and nitrogen oxides, is beginning to pose a major health problem in some cities. This gas is thought to be responsible for causing increased asthma attacks, headaches, eye irritation, coughs and other respiratory problems
- Pollen in the air can bring on an allergic response in hayfever sufferers and an asthma attack in allergic asthmatics

EARLY PREVENTIVE MEASURES

- Pregnant women should avoid eating peanuts or any foods that contain peanuts. Babies exposed to peanuts while still in the womb may be more likely to develop this allergy
- Breastfeeding mothers should also avoid eating peanuts. Check that peanut oil (sometimes labelled arachis oil or groundnut oil) is not an ingredient of nipple or skin cream
- Breastfeed your baby for at least six months (longer if possible) and give your baby nothing but breastmilk for the first four to six months. Breastfeeding affords the best possible protection against all sorts of illnesses, including allergy
- Avoid the common allergy-causing foods while you are breastfeeding, as whatever you eat or drink finds its way into breast milk
- If there is a history of allergy in your family, do not give your child peanuts to eat until he or she is about five years old. Meanwhile, avoid using any commercial infant creams that contain peanut oil
- Introduce solids slowly, in small quantities and one at a time. Avoid wheat, rye, barley, fish, soya, citrus fruits and sesame seeds until your baby is at least six months old
- If allergies run in your family, avoid cow's milk products until your child is one year old

INSIDE YOUR BODY
Antibiotics and vaccines

The relatively recent worldwide increase in allergies appears to coincide both with the increased use of antibiotics and the administration of childhood vaccinations. Many complementary practitioners believe that the vaccination of children actually reduces their body's need to activate an immune response early in life and that this may increase allergic tendencies.

Stress

We can also be made more susceptible to allergies by stress. While we may not experience more stress than our ancestors, our modern sedentary way of life causes stress to build up inside us. Instead of running or fighting when faced with stress – as nature intended – we are more often than not stuck behind a desk or the wheel of a car. Yet stress causes the release of two hormones: adrenaline (epinephrine) and cortisol (or hydrocortisone). Adrenaline speeds up the body, uses up nutrients and can lead to deficiencies in vitamin B$_6$ (pyridoxine), amino acids and zinc. All these changes can lead to a weakening of the immune system.

Cortisol, known as the body's natural steroid, is an immune suppressant. You might think that suppressing the immune response would be no bad thing when dealing with allergies or intolerances but, unfortunately, when cortisol diminishes the body goes into rebound, creating an even stronger inflammatory response.

Foods

There is some evidence that the symptoms of asthma, eczema and hayfever may be triggered by a particular food. Allergic reaction to certain foods is often immediate and severe, with vomiting, rashes, eczema, asthma, or even anaphylactic shock. Food intolerance produces a less acute and much slower reaction, and is often triggered by foods that are eaten frequently – and which the sufferer craves.

Left: It is best for pregnant women to avoid any foods or products containing peanuts.

Foods that may trigger asthma and eczema in some people include cow's milk and other dairy products, alcohol, yeasts (and foods that may contain yeasts, such as dried fruit) and seafood.

Leaky gut syndrome

Another possible cause of food intolerance is leaky gut syndrome. Your small intestine is a kind of sieve that should allow only the breakdown products of digestion into your bloodstream (for instance amino acids and peptides, broken down from proteins). Larger particles of protein, carbohydrate and fat are usually sieved out so that they don't get into the blood. This is because your body may react to these larger particles as the enemy, and trigger an attack response from your immune system.

However, in leaky gut syndrome, this sieve mechanism breaks down and fails to work so that foods that have not been digested fully are absorbed into the bloodstream. This syndrome may have a number of causes, ranging from foods that inflame the bowels to certain drugs and yeasts that can actually make tiny holes in the walls of the gut.

Below: Take time to relax, as a build up of stress can make you susceptible to allergies.

finding the common food triggers

IT CAN BE A LONG and complicated process to find out which foods, amongst other things, are setting off your allergic reactions. However, it is often possible to identify your personal food culprits and find foods to alleviate your symptoms. There is a wide range of elimination diets to try, some more arduous than others. Remember that children, in particular, should maintain a balanced diet, so consult a nutritionist first.

FOOD ELIMINATION DIETS

The "food group" exclusion diet

Allergies and food intolerance can be caused by a specific group of foods, such as dairy products, grains or citrus fruits. To find out if one of these groups of foods is causing your allergic reactions, pick one group and cut out foods belonging to it. For example, if the group is grain, eliminate wheat, rice, rye, corn, millet etc. If the group is dairy, then eliminate all cow's milk products. Other food groups are animal protein (meat, fish, eggs, cheese) and vegetable protein (wholegrain cereals, lentils, beans, tofu, soya).

Keep up this diet for six weeks. If you see no improvement, you are looking in the wrong direction. If you do see an improvement, carry on for three months before trying to reintroduce the foods.

The "favourite foods" exclusion diet

This diet works on the principle that an allergic response can often develop to the foods you eat most.

Cut out your five favourite foods, plus the five foods that you eat most (these are quite likely to overlap), from your diet for a minimum period of at least six weeks.

If you see no improvement, these foods are unlikely to be the source of the problem. If you do see an improvement, keep up the diet for three months, then reintroduce foods you dropped from your diet one at a time to see if your body reacts.

If you respond allergically to the reintroduced food, keep off it for another six weeks then try again. If you still respond allergically, keep off the food for about three months before you try again.

Above: *Red wine, bread, cheese, chocolate and milk are all commonly eaten foods that can cause allergic responses.*

The "lamb and pears" diet

Exclude all foods except lamb and pears from your diet for seven to ten days. Very few people have an allergic response to lamb or pears. If you wish, substitute two other foods that you don't normally eat, for instance mackerel and courgettes (zucchini). Gradually reintroduce other foods to your diet and note your response.

The "Stone Age" diet

A number of scientists believe that we took a wrong turn in our diets about 10,000 years ago when we ceased to be hunter-gatherers and began to rely on agriculture.

This diet avoids all "recent" foods such as cereals, dairy produce, sugar, food additives, coffee, tea and alcohol. Instead, you follow a restricted diet of fresh meat, fish, fruit, vegetables and nuts.

Below: *Grains such as corn, wheat and rice may cause allergic reactions. You need to eliminate them from your diet to find out if they are the cause of your symptoms.*

Below: *Citrus fruits are one of the common triggers for allergies and intolerance. Try cutting out this group of foods to see if it makes an improvement to your condition.*

Above: *If you feel that you need to take drastic action to find out which foods are triggering your symptoms, try eating only lamb and pears for a week as very few people are allergic to these two foods.*

The rotation diet

If you are mildly allergic or intolerant towards different foods, achieving a healthy balanced diet can be difficult. By eating each of these foods in rotation, only once every four days (or longer), you can maintain a healthy diet and reduce your allergic response.

DIAGNOSTIC TESTS

If you don't want to try an elimination diet – or if this hasn't worked – there are a number of diagnostic tests that may be helpful in identifying your triggers:

Skin tests

Patch testing This is often used to detect the allergens responsible for eczema. Tiny patches saturated in a number of different substances – from plant extracts to solvents – are stuck to the skin on your back and left for two to three days. When the patches are removed, areas of redness or swelling indicate allergy.

The "pin prick" test In this test, small or dilute amounts of suspected allergens are pinpricked under the skin. If the person is allergic, their skin will begin to itch and a raised red weal will develop. The bigger the weal, the more allergic they are.

Blood tests

ELISA (enzyme-linked immunosorbent assay) and RAST (radioallergosorbent) These tests are used to measure the amount of IgE produced in the blood by allergic reactions. Only a small sample of blood is taken for testing.

FACT (food allergy cellular test) This is useful in complex cases where many allergens may be involved as it tests not only for IgE but also for IgG4 (an immunoglobulin that is produced against certain foods and other allergens) and leukotrienes (chemicals that are released by white blood cells that have recognized an invader).

ALCAT (antigen allergy cellular test) This test is designed to measure the activity of white blood cells.

OTHER TESTS

Bio-resonance testing This is based on the Eastern belief that there are energy channels – or meridians – throughout the body. Bio-resonance machines are specialized computers that send small electric currents around your body to measure your energy field and detect abnormalities. Used by complementary practitioners to indicate allergens, the machine may also be used to "switch off" the allergic response.

Gut permeability test This test may be suggested by a complementary practitioner if leaky gut syndrome is suspected. You will be given a drink containing many different sized molecules. Your urine is then collected over a period of about six hours and the size of the molecules present in the urine are measured. If there are very large molecules present – or if there are too many of one particular kind of molecule getting through the gut wall – then leaky gut syndrome can be confirmed.

Kinesiology A small quantity of the suspect allergen is placed on your abdomen. The kinesiologist then pushes against your arm (usually) to test for muscle weakness. This is believed to show whether a substance has a negative effect on you. (This test has not been proven but some people find that it can be very effective.)

Below: *Fresh vegetables, fish and fruit are the basis of the "Stone Age" diet.*

how to alleviate your symptoms

IF YOU OR YOUR CHILD have asthma, eczema or hayfever, there are many things you can do to make life better. Identifying and avoiding potential allergens in your diet is important, but there are many more things that you can do to reduce your exposure to other allergens.

Above: If you have allergy-related asthma or eczema, improving your diet by eating locally produced, organic vegetables may help to alleviate your symptoms.

EAT LOCAL FOODS IN SEASON

If our modern diet – rich in imported exotic fruits and vegetables – is the cause of many allergy-related problems, it makes sense to return to a more natural diet that relies on locally grown produce, eaten in season.

Include at least five portions of fruit and vegetables a day. Eat tomatoes, lettuce and other salad vegetables – preferably organic – in the summer when they are home-produced.

KEEP HEALTHY AND HAPPY

Whatever your allergy, the symptoms are likely to be less severe if you are in good health. A strong immune system staves off infections – such as colds and flu – which can trigger asthma attacks in some people. Follow these golden rules:

- Sleep well. Most adults need eight hours, children far more. Drink chamomile tea at bedtime.

- Get plenty of exercise. Even 20 minutes a day can improve your health. Holistic forms of exercise such as yoga and t'ai chi can help you keep fit physically, mentally and emotionally.
- Have a good breakfast. Organic porridge provides instant energy and also slow-release energy to keep you going. Some complementary practitioners believe unrefined oats also have a calming effect on your system, which may benefit your heart and encourage healthy circulation.
- Avoid excessive alcohol consumption. This can cause serious depression, lower immunity to infections, raise blood pressure and disrupt sleep.
- Don't smoke. Cigarettes are full of poisons that can do your body nothing but harm – let alone the implications smoking has for asthma.
- Drink up to eight glasses of water a day if you can. This helps to dilute any allergens in your system and may reduce the immune over-response.
- Enjoy yourself. Go out, see friends and have a good time.

Above: Lavender oil is one of the many aromatic essential oils that can be used to help you relax or sleep.

AROMATHERAPY

Essential oils have been used for thousands of years for healing and promoting a general feeling of relaxation and wellbeing. Use aromatic lavender oil in your bath or put a few drops on your pillow at bedtime to help you to sleep. If you are pregnant or breastfeeding, consult your doctor before using any essential oils.

RELAXATION IS IMPORTANT

There are many different ways to relax – from listening to music to lying in a flotation tank. Find one that is right for you and make a regular habit of it. Stress can increase and prolong the symptoms of allergy, and can trigger attacks of asthma and eczema so try to counteract it by making time to relax.

Left: A glass of chamomile tea before bedtime will help you sleep better, which in turn will keep you healthy and well.

MEDITATION

Take 20 minutes out of your day to meditate and switch off. Find somewhere comfortable and warm to sit or lie down (you may prefer to meditate in the dark), then slowly breathe in through your nose and out through your mouth. Count each out breath and once you reach ten, start again from one. Repeat this cycle of ten breaths over and over again. Then count the in breaths in cycles of ten. After a while, stop counting and just watch the breath, concentrating on its flow. Then focus your attention on the point at which each breath first enters your body and be aware of how it feels. With practice, you will be able to exclude all distracting thoughts, feelings and worries and feel very relaxed indeed.

HOW TO AVOID ALLERGENS

Another crucial aspect of self-help for people with allergies such as asthma, eczema and hayfever is avoiding whatever makes them worse. Here are some ideas on dealing with common culprits.

Dust mite faeces

These are in every home and are one of the main causes of asthma. Reduce them by taking the following measures:

- Remove curtains, carpets and as many other soft furnishings as you can from your home.
- Cover mattresses, pillows and duvets (filled with man-made fibres) with special barrier covers.
- To kill dust mites, wash all bedding regularly at above 55°C (131°F)
- Vacuum floors and soft furnishings every day.
- Dust mites love warm, moist conditions, so keep your home cool, dry and well aired. Use an extractor fan when bathing or cooking, and always try to dry laundry outdoors.
- Soft toys are dust mite havens, so wrap them in a plastic bag and put them in the freezer for a couple of hours. The low temperature will kill any dust mites.

Above: *Practising a relaxation technique such as meditation can help to alleviate the symptoms of eczema and asthma.*

Pollen and mould spores

These are the big culprits in hayfever. Use the information and tips below to help lessen your symptoms:

- If your hayfever symptoms are at their worst in late spring and early summer, grass pollen is likely to be the culprit.
- The grass pollen count varies throughout the day and tends to be highest in late afternoon and early evening, especially in cities. A high count can persist through the night.
- Hayfever sufferers often notice an increase in their symptoms before a thunder storm and as heavy rain begins.
- The pollen count tends to be lowest on dull, damp days.
- Keep your windows – especially in the bedroom – closed during the day. You can open the bedroom window again when you go to bed. Windy weather can blow grass and tree pollens many miles – and through your open windows.
- Try to keep your car windows closed when driving.
- Stay indoors, if possible, with the windows closed on high pollen count days.

- Wear sunglasses when the pollen count is high and bathe your eyes to remove pollen.
- Avoid hanging clothes to dry in the garden on high pollen count days as they will collect pollen.
- If you are allergic to tree pollens avoid areas of uncut, flowering grass, or flowering woodland.
- If you are allergic to mould spores, keep away from woodland in the autumn.
- Change your clothes and shower when you come indoors.
- Pets can collect pollen on their fur as they move through flowering grass. Ask a non-hayfever sufferer to brush them before they come inside.
- Get someone else to mow the lawn.
- Opt for a low allergy garden. Avoid grasses, hedges, trees, mould-producing mulches and heavily scented pollinated flowers. Go for paved or gravelled areas with pot plants and ground-cover plants (to cut down on pollen-producing weeds).

EASING ECZEMA

Eczema – and other allergy – sufferers are likely to benefit from taking the following steps:

- Wear natural fabrics such as cotton or linen that allow your skin to keep dry, cool and yeast free
- Use old-fashioned cleaning methods – soap and water, soda crystals, damp dusting – rather than modern chemical-based cleaning products
- Avoid wearing bright or dark-coloured clothing because deep dyes may cause allergic rashes on sensitive skin
- Make your garden organic, especially if you grow fruit and vegetables. This will help to reduce your "chemical load"
- Avoid using solvent-based paints, varnishes and other DIY products, especially in bedrooms or if you are pregnant

using modern medical treatments

IF YOU SUFFER FROM ALLERGIES, you may well be very grateful for any medication your doctor has prescribed. For people with asthma in particular, drugs can be a life-saver. However, orthodox medical treatments for allergies are not cures; they are designed to suppress the symptoms and relieve discomfort. The underlying condition will not be eliminated, but it should be controlled.

DRUG TREATMENTS FOR ASTHMA

In orthodox medicine, there are two basic kinds of treatment for asthma. The first type, known as "relievers" or bronchodilators, work by relaxing the muscles around the airways when they constrict. Relievers can be taken as a rescue when you experience symptoms, or when you expect symptoms to appear.

This type of medication is usually taken from an inhaler, and may include the drugs salbutamol and tarbutaline. Reliever drugs act in a similar manner to adrenaline (epinephrine), the substance your body naturally produces to increase your heart rate or to open your airways.

The second type of medication given to asthma sufferers is known as "preventers". These drugs are designed to treat any inflammation of the airways and thus stop asthma symptoms from developing. Because they are designed to suppress the symptoms not cure the condition, preventers have to be used regularly to be effective. Non-steroidal drugs such as sodium cromoglycate, are often prescribed for children. For adults, inhaled steroid drugs (such as beclomethasone or budesonide) are more often prescribed.

Asthma sufferers may need extra medication at times, particularly if they react badly to stress or environmental factors such as cold air or dust mites.

CREAMS AND DRUG TREATMENTS FOR ECZEMA

Eczema is common in families with a history of allergies, including asthma and hayfever. Orthodox treatment involves treating the symptoms usually with topical steroid creams in combination with soothing lotions. Topical steroids work by controlling and damping down inflammation in the skin. They alleviate the itching and remove the urge to scratch the affected area, which allows the skin to heal.

Some corticosteroid medication (such as prednisolone and prednisone) may be given orally, however, there is a risk of side effects with these drugs.

Topical steroids can be very effective in the short term. But the more they are used, the less effective they can become – and the side-effects may become unacceptable. Old-fashioned pastes and ointments,based on coal tar, can also be effective in treating eczema, although many people find that the smell and the messiness of these preparations is unacceptable.

Occasionally, doctors will also prescribe a course of antibiotics if the skin becomes infected. Finally, ultraviolet light (UVA) treatment used in combination with the drug psoralen is known as PUVA. This treatment can sometimes be effective for long-term eczema sufferers.

Eczema sufferers will be aware of the changing seasons and the need for increased medication at some times of the year.

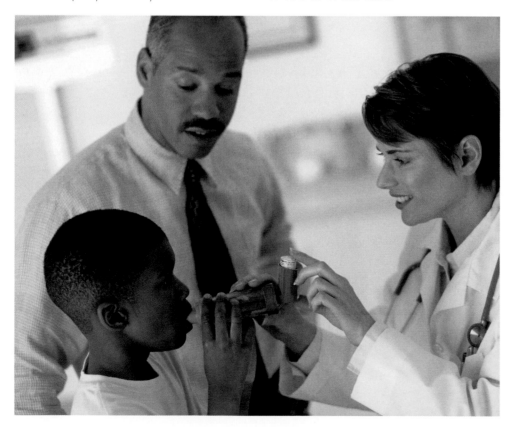

Left: *A young boy is taught to use an inhaler to improve his breathing during an asthma attack. By pumping the drug into a bottle, the sufferer is able to inhale the dosage normally.*

PROS AND CONS OF CONVENTIONAL TREATMENTS

Pros:

- Are life-saving in extreme cases such as asthma or anaphylactic shock
- Give immediate, or very quick, relief of symptoms
- May stop symptoms developing
- Allow allergy sufferers to manage their own condition with as little change to their lifestyle as possible
- Adverse reactions to conventional drug treatments are rare

Cons:

- May have side-effects, such as drowsiness or loss of appetite
- Alleviate the symptoms, but do not address the underlying causes of the allergy
- Often necessitate increasing doses of medication – the more the treatment is used the less effective it is likely to become
- The use of steroid drugs over a long period of time may cause a range of problems, which is of particular concern when treating young children

DRUG TREATMENTS FOR HAYFEVER

The best way to treat an allergy is to avoid the substance causing the allergic reaction but this can be difficult in the case of airborne pollen. Treatment for hayfever depends very much on your doctor. Some practitioners prefer one-dose antihistamine tablets, which have no sedative side effects, but act on the whole body. Others prefer local, targeted treatments, including nasal corticosteroids and nasal antihistamines (for a very blocked nose) or eye drops containing antihistamine and decongestant (for very puffy eyes). Preventive drops are made from sodium cromoglycate, which most doctors consider safe.

Desensitizing injections may also be considered by your doctor if your hayfever is very severe. However these have to be taken all year round – not just when the symptoms are unbearable – and entail regular visits to the hospital or clinic. Now that the trigger for hayfever has been identified as part of a protein called profilin, a new treatment for the condition may eventually be forthcoming.

Depending on the time of year, hayfever suffers will need varying levels of medication during different seasons.

Below: *There are specially designed inhalers for asthmatic babies.*

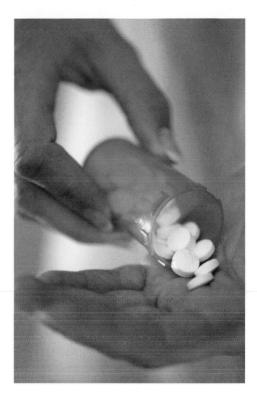

Above: *Many hayfever sufferers control their symptoms with antihistamine tablets, which are convenient and can greatly improve their allergic response.*

Below: *Hayfever sufferers often find soothing eye drops can alleviate the discomfort of itchy, puffy eyes caused by their allergic reaction to pollen.*

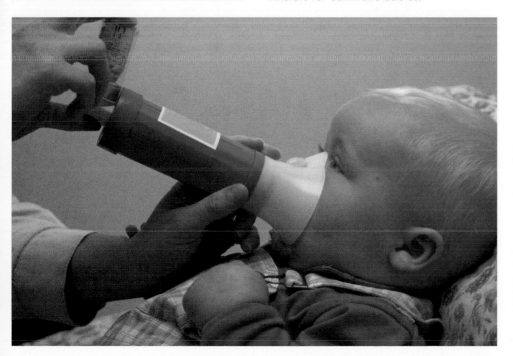

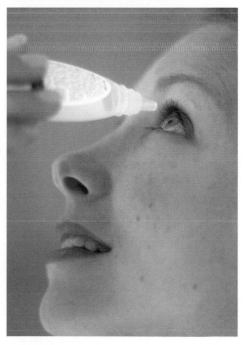

complementary treatments

ALL OVER THE WESTERN WORLD, people are turning increasingly to complementary therapies. This does not necessarily mean giving up conventional medicines and many practitioners would urge you to adopt an "integrated" approach. An increasing number of doctors now accept that complementary therapies can help with asthma, eczema and hayfever. However, do try to discuss the therapy you are considering with your doctor before beginning treatment.

SPOILT FOR CHOICE

One of the problems often faced by people who want to try a complementary therapy is that there are so many of them, all apparently using different methods. So how do you decide which therapy suits you best? Here is a brief outline of some of the therapies that are most effective in treating asthma, eczema and hayfever.

PROS AND CONS OF COMPLEMENTARY TREATMENTS

Pros:
- Complementary therapies are holistic, addressing not just your symptoms but every aspect of your health – physical, mental, emotional and spiritual
- You may find a therapy that eliminates the cause of your allergy
- There are rarely any side effects with complementary treatment

Cons:
- Complementary therapy works to restore the body's natural balance – it is not a quick fix
- It may be weeks or months before benefits become evident
- Treatments work most effectively as part of a healthy lifestyle that includes exercise and balanced diet
- They can be expensive
- There may not be a qualified practitioner in your area

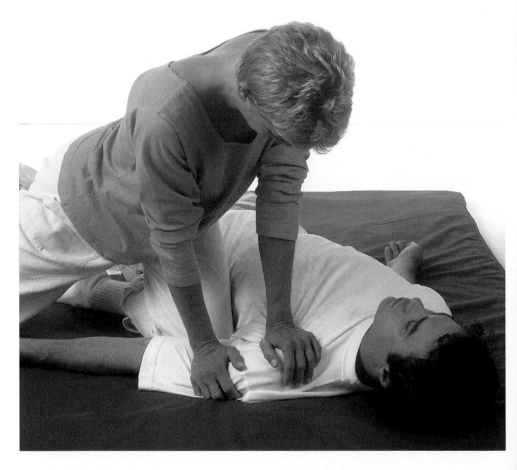

HOMEOPATHY

The principle of this complementary healing system is to "treat like with like". Patients are treated with tiny doses of substances that would cause the symptoms of their illness in a healthy person. Homeopaths believe this will stimulate your body's own healing process, as opposed to treating symptoms alone, which may bring only temporary relief. Homeopathic practice involves a full assessment of your physical and mental health,

Above: *Some people find that alternative therapies such as Shiatsu help to improve their respiratory function by promoting relaxation and deeper breathing.*

and may also include specific allergy or intolerance testing. Once you have established any substances or foods that may trigger your allergy, your practitioner will discuss further treatment, from desensitization to treatment with established homeopathic remedies.

Above: *Raw fruits and vegetables in juice form are often prescribed by naturopaths to boost the immune system.*

NATUROPATHY

Modern naturopathy seeks to treat and avert disease by bolstering the body's own defence systems, primarily through a healthy diet and sensible lifestyle. Following a detailed consultation, your naturopath will advise on diet, exercise and other treatment for your condition. Naturopaths regard a healthy diet – based on raw, organic food – as the best form of medicine. This is often combined with other treatments to stimulate your body's vital force, rather than to suppress your symptoms. Raw fruits and vegetables in juice form are also often prescribed.

NUTRITIONAL THERAPY

The use of food, vitamin, mineral and other supplements to cure and prevent disease is an increasingly scientific and complex field. Research shows that a heavily processed "junk food" diet is linked to asthma – as well as many other health problems.

Treatment begins with a detailed questionnaire about your medical history, symptoms, diet and lifestyle. The practitioner may also undertake a number of tests to pinpoint any dietary problems, allergies or intolerances. Treatment programmes consist of nutritional advice, a short-term diet tailored to suit your condition and a course of supplements that may include vitamins, minerals or herbs.

ACUPUNCTURE

One of the best known and most respected complementary therapies, acupuncture is part of a comprehensive system of traditional Chinese medicine dating back thousands of years. Acupuncture involves using very fine needles that are inserted at strategic points (acupoints) on the body to stimulate the vital flow of energy and correct imbalances which may be causing symptoms.

Following very careful observation and questioning, your practitioner will seek to restore balance and harmony through meridians in your body. You may feel a slight pinprick as the needle is inserted, and a sensation of tingling or numbness. Initially the needles are left in for only six to ten minutes, building to 20 to 25 minutes in later sessions. For those who find the prospect of needles too alarming, there are other forms of therapy related to acupuncture, sometimes known as "acupuncture without needles", which include Shiatsu massage, acupressure and laser and ultrasound acupuncture. These therapies are based on the same principles as acupuncture, stimulating key points to balance your energies.

Above: *Complementary therapists will recommend avoiding heavily processed and "junk" foods and opting for fresh, healthy, nutritious foods.*

Above: *Yoga can be used to reduce stress and improve breathing technique.*

BREATHING TREATMENTS

Many Eastern philosophies of health regard breathing as the central factor in staying well. Of the breathing techniques currently offered by complementary practitioners, the best known is remedial yoga. Yoga breathing, in particular, has the benefit of moving blocked energy in the body. Yoga breathing can also be valuable in treating allergic conditions, because it helps reduce the effects of stress.

Other, more recent, breathing treatments that are beneficial to health include:

- Oxygenesis: an easy-to-learn technique, developed in California, which enables individuals to learn the ideal breathing pattern for themselves.
- The Buteyko Method: developed by Dr Konstantin Buteyko, this therapy is based on the theory that many illnesses – including asthma and allergies – are caused by overbreathing. Practitioners claim the Buteyko Method can rapidly "cure" asthma and allergies with special breathing exercises.

healing through diet

CAN THE "WRONG" FOODS TRIGGER asthma, make eczema worse, or aggravate hayfever? Can the "right" foods improve general health and these conditions in particular? By and large the medical experts say "no", although a balanced diet is always recommended. Yet sufferers often disagree. Many people say that by identifying "culprit" ingredients and eating beneficial foods, they have managed to control their condition.

Above: *Onions are one of many foods that can reduce allergy symptoms – they are particularly helpful for asthma sufferers.*

FOOD CULPRITS AND HELPERS

While the experts continue to argue about cause and effect, it is well established that in some people, certain foods cause typical allergic reactions such as wheezing, nausea, hives, bloating, diarrhoea or vomiting. Food allergies affect about one in 50 people in the West, but babies, because their digestive and immune systems are not yet mature, are more susceptible – although many grow out of them in time.

Most of those who do suffer in this way are only allergic to one, or a limited number of foods, commonly cow's milk, eggs, wheat, soya, nuts, fish and shellfish. (Nut allergies are the commonest cause of anaphylaxsis.) Food allergies often show up as hives (urticaria), while eczema is often an allergic reaction to wheat, milk or eggs.

So if you suspect you have a food allergy, or that certain foods are making your symptoms worse, ask to see an allergy specialist who can give you an accurate diagnosis of the foods that may be causing you problems. (Remember that DIY dietary restrictions can be harmful – especially for children – so seek the advice of a qualified dietician or nutritionist). Once you have identified a food culprit, get into the habit of reading labels on food packages to be sure that you are avoiding your triggers. Unfortunately, allergy is so complex that it is unlikely that foods will be your only triggers – so don't stop taking prescribed medication.

ATHSMA FOOD CULPRITS

- Dairy products
- Eggs
- Fish and shellfish
- Nuts, especially peanuts
- Yeast (and products containing yeast, such as dried fruits, wine and beer)

Food additives such as monosodium glutamate (flavour enhancer), aspartame (sweetener), tartrazine E102 (food colourant), and the preservatives E210–E227 can act as irritants (rather than allergens) to asthma suffers.

ASTHMA FOOD HELPERS

- A good diet protects against colds and viruses that can trigger asthma
- Eat plenty of fresh fruit and vegetables
- Onions – which have anti-inflammatory properties – are likely to be good for those with asthma; try to eat one a day
- Vitamin C, bromelain and quercetin are often recommended by naturopaths for their anti-inflammatory properties

ECZEMA FOOD CULPRITS

- Wheat
- Cow's milk
- Eggs
- Artificial colourants

ECZEMA FOOD HELPERS

- Supplements of vitamin B, zinc, essential fatty acids and evening primrose oil can improve skin quality.

HAYFEVER

Some nutritionists suggest altering your diet a few weeks before your particular hayfever season begins. For instance, if you are allergic to grass pollen, avoid foods that are species of grass, such as wheat-based foods (bread, pasta, cakes and biscuits) and other gluten grains (rye, barley, and oats). Start

Below: *Fresh fruits such as kiwis and blackcurrants are rich in vitamin C and will help to relieve the symptoms of asthma.*

four weeks before your symptoms usually appear and continue throughout that pollen season. Use other starches — such as potatoes, beans and gram flour (which is made from chick peas) — instead.

On the same plant family principle, if you are allergic to birch pollen, you may well be also allergic to apples and some other fruits (including peaches, apricots and nectarines).

Some nutritionists argue it can help to avoid dairy products during the summer.

Below: *Wine and ripe cheeses are thought to exacerbate the symptoms of asthma, eczema and hayfever.*

Left: *Bread and pasta made with wheat, eggs, and fruit drinks that contain food colouring are thought to trigger excema in some people.*

(this may work for those with asthma, too) because these foods can make inflammation worse. Live yogurt can be an exception.

Nettle leaf tea, reishi mushrooms and eyebright are often used as anti-hayfever herbs. The homeopathic hayfever remedy, Pollenna, can also help.

ADVICE FOR ASTHMA, ECZEMA AND HAYFEVER SUFFERERS

- All of these conditions have been linked to a deficiency of "good fats", so a supplement of GLA may help
- Avoid histamine-loaded foods such as wine, beer, ripe cheeses, salami, pickled food, mackerel and tuna. Vitamin C and the supplement quercetin can help to eliminate histamines
- Drink plenty of fresh water
- Avoid salt
- Eat plenty of fresh fruit and vegetables
- Vitamin and minerals supplements which may be useful include vitamin B complex, vitamin C, zinc and magnesium

Below: *If you suffer from hayfever, you may find that a cup of nettle leaf tea will alleviate the symptoms.*

HELPING YOUR CHILD TO LIVE WITH ASTHMA, ECZEMA OR HAYFEVER

- Food elimination diets are tricky for children because common culprits like milk have essential nutrients. In addition, most babies with asthma don't have food triggers: viruses and cigarette smoke are the common culprits. However, if there is a strong family history of food allergy in your family, if your baby has both eczema and asthma, and symptoms showed up when you introduced a particular weaning food, discuss this with your doctor. It may be wise to try removing that food
- Soya milk may not be a useful alternative to cow's milk; children fed on soya milk instead of dairy milk are just as likely to develop asthma
- Breastfeeding mothers need to avoid foods to which they are allergic — and to avoid creams and lotions that may contain peanut oil (such as cracked nipple creams)
- When weaning, introduce foods and drinks (avoiding fizzy drinks) one at a time, and watch for allergic symptoms
- Avoid eggs and cow's milk until babies are one year old, and, if there is a family history of allergy to fish, nuts, peanuts or wheat flour, avoid these, too
- Rotate foods: allergies may develop from eating the same foods daily
- Don't give children peanuts until they are five years old
- Encourage your child to eat more fruit and vegetables. Try making fresh fruit salads. Serve sticks of vegetables such as carrot, red pepper and cucumber. Make easy-to-eat soups from puréed vegetables and pulses. Create thick smoothies using fresh fruits, and use both fruits and vegetables to make delicious drinks. Add grated vegetables such as carrots and courgettes (zucchini) to pasta sauces. Serve diluted fruit juices rather than drinks like orange squash or lemonade

appetizers

and soups

With a wide range of different recipes to try, dishes to help beat asthma, eczema or hayfever certainly don't have to be boring. All the recipes in this chapter are ideal to start a meal or, to eat as a light lunch, simply serve with crusty bread or crackers. Take your pick from dips, such as spicy pumpkin to boost the immune system or guacamole to relieve congestion. Or opt for a bowl of nourishing soup – roasted garlic and squash soup with tomato salsa is full of vitamin C to help fight histamines and spicy black eyed bean soup is a good source of B vitamins, which can help improve the skin.

smoky aubergine and pepper salad

THIS WONDERFULLY AROMATIC SALAD contains plenty of garlic, which is thought to aid the respiratory system. Sweet red peppers provide a useful supply of immune-boosting vitamin C.

INGREDIENTS

Serves four

2 aubergines (eggplant)
2 red (bell) peppers
3–5 garlic cloves, chopped, or more to taste
2.5ml/½ tsp ground cumin
juice of ½–1 lemon, to taste
45–60ml/3–4 tbsp extra virgin olive oil
1–2 pinches of cayenne pepper
coarse sea salt
chopped fresh coriander (cilantro), to garnish
thinly sliced ciabatta bread, to serve (optional)

free from

✓ nuts
✓ dairy
  wheat
✓ seafood
✓ eggs
  yeast
  citrus
✓ alcohol

VARIATION

Other grilled (broiled) or barbecued vegetables would be good served with this salad – try wedges of red onion.

1 Place the aubergines and peppers directly over a medium-low gas flame, under a grill (broiler) or on a barbecue. Turn the vegetables frequently until they are deflated and the skins are evenly charred.

2 Put the aubergines and peppers in a plastic bag or in a bowl and seal tightly. Leave to cool for 30–40 minutes.

3 Peel the vegetables, roughly chop the flesh and reserve the juices. Put the flesh in a bowl with the juices, and add the garlic, cumin, lemon juice, olive oil, cayenne pepper and salt. Mix well. Tip the mixture into a serving bowl and garnish with coriander. Serve with bread, unless avoiding wheat or yeast.

NUTRITION NOTES

Per portion:	
Energy	128Kcal/530kJ
Fat	9.3g
saturated fat	1.2g
Carbohydrate	9.1g
Fibre	4.4g
Calcium	29.6mg

spicy pumpkin dip

PUMPKIN IS AN EXCELLENT CHOICE for those suffering from asthma and eczema because it rarely causes allergies. It is also rich in betacarotene, which is thought to help the immune system.

INGREDIENTS

Serves six

45–60ml/3–4 tbsp olive oil
1 onion, finely chopped
3–4 garlic cloves, roughly chopped
675g/1½lb pumpkin, peeled
   and diced
5–10ml/1–2 tsp ground cumin
5ml/1 tsp paprika
1.5–2.5ml/¼–½ tsp ground ginger
1.5–2.5ml/¼–½ tsp curry powder
75g/3oz chopped canned tomatoes or
   diced fresh tomatoes and 15–30ml/
   1–2 tbsp tomato purée (paste)
½–1 red jalapeño or serrano chilli,
   chopped, or cayenne pepper,
   to taste
pinch of sugar
salt
chopped coriander (cilantro), to garnish

1 Heat the olive oil in a frying pan, add the onion and half the garlic and fry for about 5 minutes, stirring occasionally, until the onion is softened. Add the diced pumpkin to the pan, then cover and cook for about 10 minutes, stirring once or twice, or until the pumpkin is half-tender.

2 Add the spices to the pan and cook for 1–2 minutes. Stir in the tomatoes, chilli, sugar and salt and cook over a medium-high heat until the liquid has evaporated.

3 When the pumpkin is tender, mash to a coarse purée. Add the remaining garlic and taste for seasoning. Serve at room temperature, sprinkled with the coriander.

NUTRITION NOTES

Per portion:

Energy	82Kcal/338kJ
Fat	6g
saturated fat	0.8g
Carbohydrate	5.5g
Fibre	1.4g
Calcium	42mg

VARIATION

Use butternut squash, or any other winter squash, in place of the pumpkin.

free from
✓ nuts
✓ dairy
✓ wheat
✓ seafood
✓ eggs
✓ yeast
✓ citrus
✓ alcohol

guacamole

A RICH AND CREAMY DIP that provides vitamin C, which is essential for good health. Garlic and chillies are thought to help relieve congestion so may be beneficial for hayfever sufferers.

INGREDIENTS

Serves six
2 large, ripe avocados
2 red chillies, seeded
1 garlic clove
1 shallot
30ml/2 tbsp extra virgin olive oil, plus
    extra to serve
juice of 1 lemon
salt and ground black pepper
flat leaf parsley leaves, to garnish
vegetable crudités, such as cucumber,
    carrot, red pepper and celery,
    to serve

1 Cut the avocados in half and carefully remove the stones.

2 Scoop out the avocado flesh into a large mixing bowl, then using a fork or potato masher, mash the avocado flesh until smooth.

3 Finely chop the seeded chillies, garlic and shallot, then stir them into the mashed avocado with the olive oil and lemon juice. Season to taste.

4 Spoon the mixture into a small serving bowl. Drizzle over a little extra olive oil and scatter with a few flat leaf parsley leaves. Serve the dip immediately.

COOK'S TIP
This dish can be prepared with any other green vegetable that is in season, such as Swiss chard, fennel or Chinese leaves (Chinese cabbage).

NUTRITION NOTES

Per portion:	
Energy	146Kcal/604kJ
Fat	15.1g
saturated fat	1.9g
Carbohydrate	1.6g
Fibre	2.1g
Calcium	9.9mg

free from
✓ nuts
✓ dairy
✓ wheat
✓ seafood
✓ eggs
✓ yeast
  citrus
✓ alcohol

spiced marinated herrings

THESE DELICIOUS MARINATED OILY FISH provide a valuable source of essential fatty acids, which can help improve skin quality for those suffering from eczema.

INGREDIENTS

Serves four

2–3 herrings, filleted
1 onion, sliced
juice of 1½–2 lemons
25ml/1½ tbsp sugar
10–15 black peppercorns
10–15 allspice berries
1.5ml/¼ tsp mustard seeds
3 bay leaves, torn
salt

1 Place the herrings in a shallow dish, cover with cold water and soak for about 5 minutes, then drain. Place in a shallow dish and pour over enough cold water to cover. Leave to soak for 2–3 hours, then drain. Pour over enough fresh cold water to cover and leave to soak overnight.

2 Hold the soaked herrings under cold running water and rinse them very thoroughly, both inside and out.

3 Cut each herring into bitesize pieces, then place the pieces in a glass bowl or shallow dish.

4 Sprinkle the onion over the fish, then add the lemon juice, sugar, peppercorns, allspice, mustard seeds, bay leaves and salt. Add enough water to just cover. Cover the bowl and chill for 2 days to allow the flavours to blend before serving.

NUTRITION NOTES	
Per portion:	
Energy	233Kcal/971kJ
Fat	13.5g
saturated fat	2.2g
Carbohydrate	9.9g
Fibre	0.4g
Calcium	76.9mg

free from
✓ nuts
✓ dairy
✓ wheat
 seafood
✓ eggs
✓ yeast
 citrus
✓ alcohol

skewered lamb with red onion salsa

THESE LITTLE KEBABS are a perfect choice of appetizer for people avoiding potential allergens because lamb is one of the least allergenic foods known.

2 Cover the bowl with clear film and set aside in a cool place for a few hours, stirring once or twice.

3 Spear the lamb cubes on four small skewers – if using wooden skewers, soak them first in cold water for 30 minutes to prevent them from burning.

4 To make the salsa, put the sliced onion, tomato, red wine vinegar and basil or mint leaves in a small bowl and stir together until thoroughly blended. Season to taste with salt, garnish with mint, then set aside while you cook the lamb skewers.

5 Cook on a barbecue or under a preheated grill (broiler) for 5–10 minutes, turning frequently, until the lamb is well browned but still slightly pink in the centre. Serve hot, with the salsa.

INGREDIENTS

Serves four
225g/8oz lean lamb, cubed
2.5ml/½ tsp ground cumin
5ml/1 tsp paprika
15ml/1 tbsp olive oil
salt and ground black pepper

For the salsa
1 red onion, very thinly sliced
1 large tomato, seeded and chopped
15ml/1 tbsp red wine vinegar
3–4 fresh basil or mint leaves, coarsely torn
small mint leaves, to garnish

free from
✓ nuts
✓ dairy
✓ wheat
✓ seafood
✓ eggs
  yeast
✓ citrus
  alcohol

1 Place the lamb cubes, cumin, paprika and olive oil in a bowl. Season with salt and pepper and stir well.

NUTRITION NOTES	
Per portion:	
Energy	136Kcal/564kJ
Fat	7.8g
saturated fat	2.6g
Carbohydrate	4.1g
Fibre	0.7g
Calcium	29.1mg

shallot skewers with mustard dip

SHALLOTS ARE THOUGHT TO HAVE anti-inflammatory properties that can help combat the symptoms of asthma. These tasty skewers make an ideal start to a meal.

INGREDIENTS

Serves six

1kg/2¼lb small new potatoes, or larger
    potatoes halved
200g/7oz shallots, halved
30ml/2 tbsp olive oil
15ml/1 tbsp sea salt

For the dip

4 garlic cloves, crushed
2 egg yolks
30ml/2 tbsp lemon juice
300ml/½ pint/1¼ cups extra virgin
    olive oil
10ml/2 tsp wholegrain mustard
salt and ground black pepper

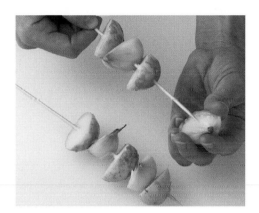

3 Par-cook the potatoes in their skins in boiling water for 5 minutes. Drain well and then thread them on to short skewers alternating them with the shallots.

4 Brush the skewers with oil and sprinkle with salt. Barbecue or grill for about 10 minutes, turning occasionally. Serve with the mustard dip.

NUTRITION NOTES

Per portion:

Energy	592Kcal/2453kJ
Fat	51.7g
saturated fat	7.4g
Carbohydrate	28.7g
Fibre	2.4g
Calcium	29.6mg

1 Prepare a barbecue or preheat the grill (broiler). Place the garlic, egg yolks and lemon juice in a food processor or blender and process for a few seconds until smooth.

2 Keep the motor running and add the oil gradually, pouring it in a thin stream, until the mixture forms a thick, glossy cream. Stir in the mustard and season. Chill until ready to use.

COOK'S TIP

If eggs trigger your condition, then try serving these skewers with a fresh tomato salsa.

free from

✓ nuts
✓ dairy
✓ wheat
✓ seafood
  eggs
  yeast
  citrus
  alcohol

spinach and rice soup

THIS NUTRITIOUS SOUP makes a substantial appetizer or a healthy lunch or supper for sufferers of asthma, eczema and hayfever. For those with an intolerance or allergy to dairy products, simply omit the shavings of cheese.

2 Either chop the spinach finely using a large kitchen knife or place in a food processor and process the leaves to a fairly coarse purée.

3 Heat the oil in a large pan and gently cook the onion, garlic and chilli for 4–5 minutes until softened. Stir in the rice until well coated, then pour in the stock and reserved spinach liquid. Bring to the boil, lower the heat and simmer for 10 minutes.

INGREDIENTS

Serves four

675g/1½lb fresh spinach leaves, washed
30ml/2 tbsp extra virgin olive oil
1 small onion, finely chopped
2 garlic cloves, finely chopped
1 small fresh red chilli, seeded and
    finely chopped
225g/8oz/generous 1 cup risotto rice
1.2 litres/2 pints/5 cups fresh stock
salt and freshly ground black pepper
shavings of pared Parmesan or Pecorino
    cheese, to serve (optional)

1 Place the spinach in a large pan with just the water that clings to its leaves after washing. Add a large pinch of salt. Heat gently until the spinach has wilted, turning it occasionally with a wooden spoon, then remove the pan from the heat and drain, reserving any liquid from the pan.

free from
✓ nuts
  dairy
✓ wheat
✓ seafood
✓ eggs
  yeast
✓ citrus
✓ alcohol

COOK'S TIP
Risotto rice gives this soup a lovely creamy texture, but you could use long grain rice instead.

NUTRITION NOTES

Per portion:

Energy	296Kcal/1232kJ
Fat	7.5g
saturated fat	1.1g
Carbohydrate	49g
Fibre	4.8g
Calcium	335.9mg

4 Add the spinach, with salt and pepper to taste. Cook for 5–7 minutes, until the rice is tender. Check the seasoning. Serve in heated bowls, topped with the shavings of cheese, if you like.

roasted garlic and squash soup

BUTTERNUT SQUASH is rich in immune boosting betacarotene, while tomatoes provide a good supply of vitamin C, which can help to fight histamines. Garlic is a natural decongestant and may help to alleviate the symptoms of hayfever.

INGREDIENTS

Serves four

2 garlic bulbs, outer papery skin removed
75ml/5 tbsp olive oil
a few fresh thyme sprigs
1 butternut squash, halved and seeded
2 onions, chopped
5ml/1 tsp ground coriander
1.2 litres/2 pints/5 cups fresh chicken stock
45ml/3 tbsp chopped fresh oregano
salt and ground black pepper

For the salsa

4 large ripe tomatoes, halved and seeded
1 red pepper, halved and seeded
1 large fresh red chilli, halved and seeded
30–45ml/2–3 tbsp extra virgin olive oil

1 Preheat the oven to 220°C/425°F/ Gas 7. Place the garlic bulbs on a piece of foil and pour over half the oil. Add the thyme, then fold over the foil to enclose the garlic. Place on a baking sheet with the squash, then brush the squash with 15ml/ 1 tbsp of the remaining olive oil. Add the tomatoes, pepper and chilli for the salsa.

2 Roast for 25 minutes, then remove the tomatoes, pepper and chilli. Reduce the oven temperature to 190°C/375°F/Gas 5 and cook the squash and garlic for 20–25 minutes more, or until the squash is tender.

3 Heat the remaining oil in a pan add the onions and coriander and cook for 10 minutes, or until the onion has softened.

4 Skin the pepper and chilli and process in a food processor or blender with the tomatoes and the olive oil. Season to taste.

5 Squeeze the roasted garlic out of its papery skin into the onions and scoop the squash out of its skin, adding it to the pan. Add the stock, 5ml/1 tsp salt and plenty of black pepper. Bring to the boil and simmer for 10 minutes. Then stir in half the fresh oregano. Leave the soup to cool slightly, then process in a food processor or blender (in batches if necessary) or press the soup through a fine sieve.

6 Reheat the soup over a medium heat without allowing it to boil, then taste for seasoning before ladling it into warmed bowls. Top each portion with a spoonful of salsa and sprinkle over the remaining chopped fresh oregano.

NUTRITION NOTES

Per portion:

Energy	202Kcal/835kJ
Fat	14.3g
saturated fat	2g
Carbohydrate	15.4g
Fibre	2.6g
Calcium	142.9mg

free from
✓ nuts
✓ dairy
✓ wheat
✓ seafood
✓ eggs
✓ yeast
✓ citrus
✓ alcohol

spicy black-eyed bean soup

A FILLING AND SATISFYING SOUP which is a good source of low-fat protein and fibre. Beans provide complex B vitamins, which can improve skin quality, and onions, with their natural anti-inflammatory properties, are believed to help those with asthma.

INGREDIENTS

Serves four

175g/6oz/1 cup black-eyed beans (peas)
15ml/1 tbsp olive oil
2 onions, chopped
4 garlic cloves, chopped
1 medium-hot or 2–3 mild fresh
    chillies, chopped
5ml/1 tsp ground cumin
5ml/1 tsp ground turmeric
250g/9oz fresh or canned
    tomatoes, diced
600ml/1 pint/2½ cups fresh chicken, beef
    or vegetable stock
25g/1oz fresh coriander (cilantro) leaves,
    roughly chopped
pitta bread, to serve (optional)

1 Put the black-eyed beans in a pan, cover with cold water, bring to the boil, then cook for 5 minutes. Remove from the heat, cover and leave to stand for 2 hours. Drain the beans, return them to the pan, cover with fresh cold water, then simmer for 35–40 minutes, or until the beans are tender. Drain and set aside.

2 Heat the oil in a pan, add the onions, garlic and chilli and cook for about 5 minutes, or until the onion is soft. Stir in the cumin, turmeric, tomatoes, stock, half the coriander and the beans and simmer for 20–30 minutes. Stir in the remaining coriander and serve at once with pitta bread, if you are not allergic to wheat or yeast.

free from

✓ nuts
✓ dairy
  wheat
✓ seafood
✓ eggs
  yeast
✓ citrus
✓ alcohol

VARIATION

If you like, substitute other beans such as haricot or cannellini beans for the black-eyed beans.

COOK'S TIP

If you are in a hurry and don't have time to soak and cook the black-eyed beans, then use a 400g/14oz can instead. Simply drain and rinse the beans thoroughly in cold water, then add to the soup in step 2.

NUTRITION NOTES

Per portion:

Energy	202Kcal/854kJ
Fat	4.2g
saturated fat	0.5g
Carbohydrate	31g
Fibre	9.1g
Calcium	140.5mg

a potage of lentils and garlic

THIS NOURISHING SOUP makes a perfect addition to a healthy diet and is an ideal lunch or supper dish. Maintaining a healthy diet helps to protect against colds and viruses that can trigger asthma.

INGREDIENTS

Serves four

30ml/2 tbsp olive oil
1 onion, chopped
2 celery sticks, chopped
1–2 carrots, sliced
8 garlic cloves, chopped
1 potato, peeled and diced
250g/9oz/generous 1 cup red lentils
1 litre/1¾ pints/4 cups fresh vegetable
   or chicken stock
2 bay leaves
1–2 lemons, halved
2.5ml/½ tsp ground cumin, or
   to taste
cayenne pepper, to taste
salt and ground black pepper
lemon slices and chopped fresh flat leaf
   parsley leaves, to serve

1 Heat the oil in a large pan. Add the onion and cook for about 5 minutes, or until softened, stirring occasionally. Stir in the celery, carrots, half the garlic and all the potato. Cook for a few minutes, stirring once or twice, until the vegetables begin to soften.

2 Add the lentils and stock to the pan and bring to the boil. Reduce the heat, cover and simmer for about 30 minutes, or until the potato and lentils are tender.

3 Add the bay leaves, remaining chopped garlic and half the lemons to the pan and cook the soup for a further 10 minutes. Remove the bay leaves from the pan. Squeeze the juice from the remaining lemons, then stir into the soup, to taste.

4 Pour the soup into a food processor or blender and process until smooth. (You may need to do this in batches.) Tip the soup back into the pan, stir in the cumin, cayenne pepper, and season with salt and pepper.

5 Ladle the soup into bowls and top each portion with lemon slices and a sprinkling of flat leaf parsley.

NUTRITION NOTES

Per portion:	
Energy	321Kcal/1357kJ
Fat	7g
saturated fat	0.8g
Carbohydrate	49g
Fibre	5.3g
Calcium	122.3mg

free from

✓ nuts
✓ dairy
✓ wheat
✓ seafood
✓ eggs
✓ yeast
  citrus
✓ alcohol

chicken and leek soup with prunes

THIS TASTY, WHOLESOME SOUP is packed with fresh vegetables essential for a healthy immune system. Try and use organic produce if possible.

3 Add the chicken fillets and cook for a further 30 minutes until they are just cooked. Leave until cool enough to handle, then strain the stock. Reserve the chicken fillets and the meat from the chicken carcass. Discard all the skin, bones, cooked vegetables and herbs. Skim as much fat as you can from the stock, then return the stock to the pan.

4 Meanwhile, rinse the pearl barley thoroughly in a sieve under cold running water, then cook it in a large pan of boiling water for about 10 minutes. Drain the barley in a sieve, rinse well again and drain thoroughly.

5 Add the pearl barley to the stock. Bring to the boil over a medium heat, then lower the heat and cook very gently for 15–20 minutes, or until the barley is just cooked and tender. Season the soup with 5ml/1 tsp salt and black pepper.

6 Add the prunes. Slice the remaining leeks and add them to the pan. Bring to the boil, then simmer for 10 minutes, or until the leeks are just cooked.

7 Slice the chicken fillets and add them to the soup with the remaining chicken meat, sliced or cut into neat pieces. Reheat if necessary, then ladle the soup into deep plates and sprinkle with chopped parsley.

INGREDIENTS

Serves Six
1 chicken, weighing about 2kg/4¼lb
900g/2lb leeks
1 bay leaf and a few each fresh parsley
  stalks and thyme sprigs
1 large carrot, thickly sliced
2.4 litres/4 pints/10 cups fresh chicken
  or beef stock
115g/4oz/generous ½ cup pearl barley
400g/14oz ready-to-eat prunes
salt and ground black pepper
chopped fresh parsley, to garnish

1 Cut the breast fillets off the chicken and set aside. Place the remaining chicken carcass in a large pan. Cut half the leeks into 5cm/2in lengths and add them to the pan.

2 Tie the bay leaf, parsley and thyme into a bouquet garni and add to the pan with the carrot and the stock. Bring to the boil, then reduce the heat and cover. Simmer gently for 1 hour. Skim off any scum when the water first boils and occasionally during simmering.

free from
- ✓ nuts
- ✓ dairy
- ✓ wheat
- ✓ seafood
- ✓ eggs
-    yeast
- ✓ citrus
- ✓ alcohol

NUTRITION NOTES

Per portion:	
Energy	341Kcal/1445kJ
Fat	3.9g
saturated fat	0.9g
Carbohydrate	45.4g
Fibre	7.6g
Calcium	131.7mg

chinese chicken and chilli soup

THE AROMATIC SPICES in this light and tasty soup may help to ease nasal congestion. Skinless chicken breast offers a good source of healthy low-fat protein.

INGREDIENTS

Serves six

150g/5oz boneless, skinless chicken breast portion, cut crossways into thin strips

2.5cm/1in piece fresh root ginger, finely chopped

5cm/2in piece lemon grass stalk, finely chopped

1 red chilli, seeded and thinly sliced

8 baby corn cobs, halved lengthwise

1 large carrot, scrubbed or peeled and cut into thin sticks

1 litre/1¾ pints/4 cups hot, fresh chicken stock

4 spring onions (scallions), thinly sliced

12 small shiitake mushrooms, sliced

115g/4oz/1 cup vermicelli rice noodles

30ml/2 tbsp tamari

salt

ground black pepper

2 Place the pot in an unheated oven. Set the temperature to 200°C/400°F/ Gas 6 and cook the soup for 30–40 minutes. Add the spring onions and mushrooms, cover and return to the oven for 10 minutes.

3 Soak the noodles following the packet instructions. Drain and divide among four bowls. Stir the tamari into the soup, then season and pour into the bowls. Serve immediately.

NUTRITION NOTES

Per portion:

Energy	112Kcal/470kJ
Fat	0.6g
saturated fat	0.1g
Carbohydrate	19.1g
Fibre	0.9g
Calcium	43.2mg

1 Place the chicken strips, fresh root ginger, lemon grass and red chilli in a Chinese sand pot. Add the halved baby corn and the carrot sticks. Pour over the hot chicken stock and cover the pot.

free from

✓ nuts
✓ dairy
✓ wheat
✓ seafood
✓ eggs
  yeast
✓ citrus
✓ alcohol

meat, poultry
and fish

The dishes in this chapter are inspiring – they each have their specific health-promoting properties. For a low-allergy meat, choose chicken or lamb. Try chicken, carrot and leek parcels to boost your immunity or roasted chicken with grapes and fresh root ginger to prevent respiratory infections. Braised shoulder of lamb with pearl barley is rich in valuable nutrients and lamb boulangère is ideal for asthma sufferers. Fish dishes include peppered salmon fillets baked with potatoes and thyme, a valuable source of essential fatty acids that help maintain healthy skin and baked sea bass with lemon grass and red onions, which contains spices that may help ease nasal congestion.

chicken, carrot and leek parcels

BAKING LOW-ALLERGEN chicken and vegetables in paper parcels is incredibly healthy. It helps to retain the valuable nutrients that are needed for good health.

INGREDIENTS

Serves four

4 chicken fillets or skinless, boneless
   breast portions
2 small leeks, sliced
2 carrots, grated
2 stoned black olives, chopped
1 garlic clove, crushed
salt and black pepper
black olives and fresh herb sprigs,
   to garnish

1 Preheat the oven to 200°C/400°F/ Gas 6. Season the chicken well. Cut out four sheets of lightly greased greaseproof (wax) paper about 23cm/9in square. Divide the leeks equally among them. Put a piece of chicken on top of each portion of leeks.

COOK'S TIP
Small, skinless turkey breast fillets also work well in this recipe.

2 Mix the grated carrots, chopped olives and crushed garlic together. Season lightly and place on top of the chicken portions, dividing them equally.

3 Carefully wrap up each parcel, making sure that the paper folds are sealed. Place the parcels on a baking sheet and bake for 20 minutes. Serve hot, in the paper, garnished with black olives and fresh herb sprigs.

free from

✓ nuts
✓ dairy
✓ wheat
✓ seafood
✓ eggs
✓ yeast
✓ citrus
✓ alcohol

NUTRITION NOTES

Per portion:
Energy	190Kcal/804kJ
Fat	2.8g
saturated fat	0.6g
Carbohydrate	6.6g
Fibre	2.9g
Calcium	42.2mg

chicken breasts with chilli salsa

THESE DELICIOUS marinated chicken breasts make a good allergy-free choice. The tomato salsa offers a good source of health-promoting vitamin C.

INGREDIENTS

Serves four

4 chicken breast portions, about 175g/
  6oz each, boned and skinned
30ml/2 tbsp fresh lemon juice
30ml/2 tbsp olive oil
10ml/2 tsp ground cumin
10ml/2 tsp dried oregano
15ml/1 tbsp coarse
  black pepper
salt

For the salsa

1 fresh hot green chilli
450g/1lb tomatoes, seeded
  and chopped
3 spring onions (scallions), chopped
15ml/1 tbsp chopped fresh parsley
30ml/2 tbsp chopped fresh
  coriander (cilantro)
30ml/2 tbsp fresh lemon juice
45ml/3 tbsp olive oil
5ml/1 tsp salt

1 With a meat mallet, pound the chicken between sheets of clear film until thin.

2 In a shallow dish, combine the lemon juice, oil, cumin, oregano and pepper. Add the chicken and turn to coat. Cover and leave to stand in a cool place for at least 2 hours, or place in the refrigerator and chill overnight.

3 To make the salsa, char the chilli skin either over a gas flame or under the grill (broiler). Leave to cool for 5 minutes. Wearing rubber gloves, carefully rub off the charred skin from the chillies. For a less hot flavour, discard the seeds.

4 Chop the chilli very finely and place in a bowl. Add the tomatoes, spring onions, parsley, coriander, lemon juice, olive oil and salt and mix well.

5 Remove the chicken from the marinade and then season lightly.

6 Heat a ridged grill pan. Add the chicken breasts and cook for about 3 minutes until browned on one side. Turn them over and cook for 3–4 minutes more. Serve with the chilli salsa.

NUTRITION NOTES

Per portion:

Energy	323Kcal/1352kJ
Fat	16.5g
saturated fat	2.5g
Carbohydrate	8.3g
Fibre	1.2g
Calcium	107.7mg

free from
✓ nuts
✓ dairy
✓ wheat
✓ seafood
✓ eggs
✓ yeast
  citrus
✓ alcohol

spinach and potato stuffed chicken

THE SPINACH STUFFING and tomato sauce both offer a good supply of vitamin C, which is recommended for its ability to boost immunity and combat histamine.

INGREDIENTS

Serves six

115g/4oz floury potatoes, diced
115g/4oz spinach leaves, finely chopped
1 egg, beaten
30ml/2 tbsp chopped fresh
   coriander (cilantro)
4 large chicken breasts
30ml/2 tbsp olive oil
mushrooms, to serve (optional)

For the sauce

400g/14oz can chopped tomatoes
1 garlic clove, crushed
150ml/¼ pint/⅔ cup fresh chicken stock
30ml/2 tbsp chopped fresh coriander
   (cilantro)
salt and ground black pepper

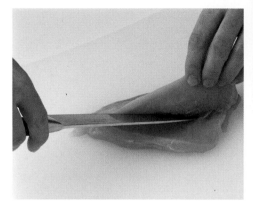

1 Preheat the oven to 180°C/350°F/ Gas 4. Boil the potatoes in a pan of boiling water for 15 minutes, or until tender. Drain them and roughly mash with a fork. Stir the spinach into the potato with the egg and coriander, then season to taste.

2 Cut almost all the way through the chicken breasts and open them out to form a pocket in each. Spoon the filling into the centre and fold the chicken back over again. Secure with cocktail sticks (toothpicks) and place in a roasting pan.

3 Sprinkle the chicken with the olive oil and cover. Bake for 25 minutes, then remove the foil and cook for 10 minutes, or until the chicken is brown and cooked.

4 While the chicken is cooking, make the sauce. Boil the tomatoes, garlic and stock rapidly for 10 minutes. Season and stir in the coriander. Serve with the chicken and mushrooms, if you like.

COOK'S TIP
Young spinach leaves have a sweet flavour and are ideal for this dish.

free from
✓ nuts
✓ dairy
✓ wheat
✓ seafood
  eggs
  yeast
✓ citrus
✓ alcohol

NUTRITION NOTES

Per portion:	
Energy	202Kcal/848kJ
Fat	6.2g
saturated fat	1.2g
Carbohydrate	5.7g
Fibre	1.4g
Calcium	60.9mg

slow-cooked chicken and potatoes

THIS FLAVOURFUL CHICKEN DISH contains plenty of onions, which are recommended for asthma. Sufferers are encouraged to try to eat an onion a day.

INGREDIENTS

Serves four
25g/1oz/2 tbsp butter, plus extra
 for greasing
15ml/1 tbsp vegetable oil
2 large bacon slices, chopped
4 large chicken joints, halved
1kg/2¼lb baking potatoes, cut into
 5mm/¼in slices
2 large onions, thinly sliced
15ml/1 tbsp chopped fresh thyme
600ml/1 pint/2½ cups fresh chicken stock
1 bay leaf
salt and ground black pepper

1 Heat the butter and oil in a large heavy frying pan, add the bacon and chicken and brown on all sides, stirring frequently.

2 Arrange half the potato slices in a large, lightly greased, flameproof baking dish.

3 Preheat the oven to 150°C/300°F/ Gas 2. Cover the potatoes with half the onions. Sprinkle with half the thyme, and season well. Using a slotted spoon, transfer the chicken and bacon to the baking dish. Reserve the fat in the pan.

4 Sprinkle the remaining thyme over the chicken, season, then cover with the remaining onion slices, followed by a layer of potato slices. Season again. Pour in the stock, add the bay leaf and brush the potatoes with the reserved fat from the pan.

COOK'S TIP
Instead of chicken joints, use eight chicken thighs or chicken drumsticks.

5 Cover tightly and bake for 2 hours, or until the chicken is tender. Preheat the grill (broiler). Take the cover off the baking dish and place it under the grill until the potato is just turning golden brown and crisp. Remove the bay leaf and serve hot.

NUTRITION NOTES

Per portion:	
Energy	714Kcal/2990kJ
Fat	36.8g
saturated fat	12.2g
Carbohydrate	50.8g
Fibre	4.5g
Calcium	82.4mg

free from
✓ nuts
  dairy
✓ wheat
✓ seafood
✓ eggs
✓ yeast
✓ citrus
✓ alcohol

roasted chicken with grapes and fresh root ginger

THE TASTY GRAPE STUFFING in this dish is a good choice for people avoiding wheat and nuts, which are often found in classic meat stuffings.

INGREDIENTS

Serves four

1–1.6kg/2¼–3½lb chicken
115–130g/4–4½oz fresh root ginger, grated
6–8 garlic cloves, roughly chopped
about 30ml/2 tbsp olive oil
2–3 large pinches of ground cinnamon
500g/1¼lb seeded red and green grapes
500g/1¼lb seedless green grapes
5–7 shallots, chopped
250ml/8fl oz/1 cup fresh chicken stock
salt and ground black pepper

1 Rub the chicken with half of the grated ginger, the chopped garlic, olive oil, cinnamon, salt and lots of black pepper. Leave to marinate in a cool place for about 1 hour.

2 Halve and seed the red and green seeded grapes and mix them with the seedless grapes.

COOK'S TIP

Always wash grapes thoroughly to remove dust, yeast and pesticides that are often present on grape skin.

3 Preheat the oven to 180°C/350°F/ Gas 4. Heat a heavy frying pan or flameproof casserole until hot.

4 Remove the chicken from the marinade, add to the pan or casserole and cook until browned on all sides. (There should be enough oil on the chicken to brown it but, if not, add a little extra.)

5 Put some of the shallots into the chicken cavity with the garlic and ginger from the marinade and as many of the red and green grapes that will fit inside. Roast in the oven in a roasting pan or casserole for 40–60 minutes, or until the chicken is tender and thoroughly cooked.

6 Remove the chicken from the pan and keep warm. Pour off any oil from the pan, and tip any sediment into a frying pan. Add the remaining shallots to the pan and cook, stirring occasionally, for 5 minutes.

7 Add half the remaining grapes, the remaining ginger, the stock and any chicken juices. Cook over a medium-high heat until the grapes have cooked down to a thick sauce. Season to taste.

8 Serve the chicken on a large, warmed serving dish, with the sauce and reserved grapes.

NUTRITION NOTES

Per portion:

Energy	492Kcal/2051kJ
Fat	20.6g
saturated fat	5.7g
Carbohydrate	44.6g
Fibre	0.5g
Calcium	70.5mg

braised shoulder of lamb

THIS WARMING, HEARTY WINTER STEW is rich in valuable nutrients and provides plenty of fibre.

INGREDIENTS

Serves four

45ml/3 tbsp olive oil
1 large onion, chopped
2 garlic cloves, chopped
2 celery sticks, sliced
a little plain (all-purpose) flour
675g/1½lb boned shoulder of lamb, cut into cubes
1 litre/1¾ pints/4 cups fresh lamb stock
115g/4oz/⅔ cup pearl barley
225g/8oz baby carrots
225g/8oz baby turnips
salt and ground black pepper
30ml/2 tbsp chopped fresh marjoram, to garnish

1 Heat 30ml/2 tbsp of the oil in a flameproof casserole. Cook the onion and garlic until softened, add the celery, then cook until the vegetables brown.

2 Season the flour and toss the lamb in it. Use a slotted spoon to remove the vegetables from the casserole.

3 Add and heat the remaining oil with the juices in the casserole. Brown the lamb in batches until golden. When all the meat is browned, return it to the casserole with the onion mixture.

4 Add 900ml/1½ pints/3¾ cups of the stock to the casserole. Add the pearl barley. Cover, then bring to the boil, reduce the heat and simmer for 1 hour, or until the pearl barley and lamb are tender.

5 Add the baby carrots and turnips to the casserole for the final 15 minutes of cooking. Stir the meat occasionally during cooking and add the remaining stock, if necessary. Season to taste, and serve piping hot, garnished with marjoram.

free from

✓ nuts
✓ dairy
  wheat
✓ seafood
✓ eggs
✓ yeast
✓ citrus
✓ alcohol

NUTRITION NOTES

Per portion:

Energy	642Kcal/2678kJ
Fat	40.4g
saturated fat	16.9g
Carbohydrate	36.8g
Fibre	4g
Calcium	129.2mg

lamb boulangère

NON-ALLERGENIC LAMB AND POTATOES are teamed with fragrant herbs in this mouthwatering dish.

INGREDIENTS

Serves six

50g/2oz/¼ cup butter, plus extra
  for greasing
4–6 garlic cloves
2 yellow onions, thinly sliced
12–18 small fresh thyme or
  rosemary sprigs
2 fresh bay leaves
1.8kg/4lb red potatoes, thinly sliced
450ml/¾ pint/scant 2 cups hot, fresh
  lamb or vegetable stock
2kg/4½lb leg of lamb
30ml/2 tbsp olive oil
salt and ground black pepper

1 Preheat the oven to 190°C/375°F/ Gas 5. Use a little butter to grease a large baking dish, about 6cm/2½in deep. Finely chop half the garlic and sprinkle a little over the prepared dish.

2 Fry the onions in 25g/1oz/2 tbsp of the butter for 5–8 minutes, or until softened. Roughly chop half the thyme or rosemary and crush the bay leaves.

3 Arrange a layer of potatoes in the dish, then season well and sprinkle with half the remaining chopped garlic, half the thyme or rosemary and bay leaves, and all of the onions. Add the remaining potatoes in an even layer and then scatter over the rest of the chopped garlic and herbs.

4 Pour in the stock plus a little hot water, if necessary, to bring the liquid to just below the level of the potatoes. Dot with the remaining butter, cover with foil and cook for 40 minutes. Increase the temperature to 200°C/400°F/Gas 6.

5 Meanwhile, cut the rest of the garlic into slivers. Make small slits all over the lamb with a narrow, sharp knife and insert slivers of garlic and sprigs of thyme or rosemary into the slits. Season the lamb well with salt and plenty of pepper.

6 Uncover the potatoes and scatter a few rosemary or thyme sprigs over them. Rest a roasting rack or ovenproof cooling rack over the dish and place the lamb on it. Rub the olive oil over the meat.

7 Return the lamb to the oven and cook, turning it once or twice, for 1½–1¾ hours, depending on how well done you prefer lamb. Leave it to rest for 20 minutes in a warm place, before carving.

NUTRITION NOTES

Per portion:

Energy	867Kcal/3627kJ
Fat	39.6g
saturated fat	18.5g
Carbohydrate	55.7g
Fibre	4.6g
Calcium	81.4mg

free from
✓ nuts
  dairy
✓ wheat
✓ seafood
✓ eggs
✓ yeast
✓ citrus
✓ alcohol

lamb shanks with beans and herbs

THIS LOW-ALLERGY DISH is perfect for those suffering from asthma and eczema. It contains anti-inflammatory onions, betacarotene and vitamin C for a healthy respiratory system, and B vitamins for healthy skin.

INGREDIENTS

Serves four

175g/6oz/1 cup dried cannellini beans, soaked overnight in cold water
150ml/¼ pint/⅔ cup water
45ml/3 tbsp olive oil
4 large lamb shanks, about 225g/8oz each
1 large onion, chopped
450g/1lb carrots, cut into thick chunks
2 celery sticks, cut into thick chunks
450g/1lb tomatoes, quartered
250ml/8fl oz/1 cup fresh vegetable stock
4 fresh rosemary sprigs
2 bay leaves
salt and ground black pepper

1 Soak a large clay pot in cold water for 20 minutes, drain. Drain and rinse the beans, place in a large pan of unsalted boiling water, boil rapidly for 10 minutes, then drain.

2 Place the water in the clay pot and add the drained beans.

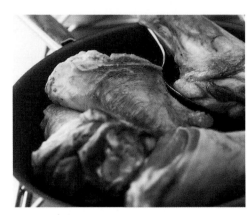

3 Heat 30ml/2 tbsp of the olive oil in a large frying pan, add the lamb and cook over a high heat, turning occasionally until brown on all sides. Remove the lamb with a slotted spoon and set aside.

4 Add the remaining oil to the pan, then add the onion and cook gently for 5 minutes until softened.

COOK'S TIP
If you don't have an unglazed clay pot, then simply use any large, shallow baking dish. Unglazed dishes must be soaked but, if the dish is glazed, there is no need to soak it before baking.

5 Add the carrots and celery to the pan and cook for 2–3 minutes. Stir in the tomatoes and stock and mix well. Transfer the vegetables to the pot and season well. Add the rosemary and bay leaves and stir.

6 Place the lamb shanks on top of the beans and vegetables. Cover the clay pot and place it in an unheated oven. Set the oven to 220°C/425°F/Gas 7 and cook for about 30 minutes, or until the liquid is bubbling.

7 Reduce the oven temperature to 160°C/325°F/Gas 3 and cook for about 1½ hours, or until the meat is tender. Check the seasoning and serve on warmed plates, placing each lamb shank on a bed of beans and vegetables.

free from
- ✓ nuts
- ✓ dairy
- ✓ wheat
- ✓ seafood
- ✓ eggs
- ✓ yeast
- ✓ citrus
- ✓ alcohol

NUTRITION NOTES

Per portion:	
Energy	606Kcal/2532kJ
Fat	31.3g
saturated fat	11.9g
Carbohydrate	38.2g
Fibre	12.1g
Calcium	159.7mg

peppered salmon fillets baked with potatoes and thyme

THIS SIMPLE FISH DISH offers a valuable supply of essential fatty acids, which can help maintain healthy skin.

INGREDIENTS

Serves four

675g/1½lb waxy potatoes, thinly sliced
1 onion, thinly sliced
10ml/2 tsp fresh thyme leaves
450ml/¾ pint/scant 2 cups fresh
    vegetable or fish stock
45ml/3 tbsp olive oil
4 skinless salmon fillets, about
    150g/5oz each
15ml/1 tbsp black peppercorns,
    roughly crushed
salt and ground black pepper
fresh thyme, to garnish
mangetouts (snow peas), to serve

1 Soak a fish clay pot in cold water for 20 minutes, then drain.

2 Layer the potato and onion slices in the clay pot, seasoning each layer and sprinkling with thyme. Pour over the vegetable or fish stock, sprinkle with half the oil, then cover and place in an unheated oven.

3 Set the oven to 190°C/375°F/Gas 5. Put the potatoes and onions in the unheated oven and cook for 40 minutes, then remove the lid and bake for a further 20 minutes, or until they are almost cooked through.

4 Meanwhile, brush the salmon fillets with the remaining olive oil and coat with the roughly crushed black peppercorns, pressing them in, if necessary, with the back of a spoon. Place the peppered salmon on top of the potatoes, cover and cook for 15 minutes, or until the salmon is opaque, removing the lid for the last 5 minutes. Garnish the salmon and potatoes with fresh thyme sprigs and serve with mangetouts.

free from
✓ nuts
✓ dairy
✓ wheat
  seafood
✓ eggs
✓ yeast
✓ citrus
✓ alcohol

NUTRITION NOTES

Per portion:	
Energy	499Kcal/2087kJ
Fat	25.4g
saturated fat	5.5g
Carbohydrate	34.6g
Fibre	2.6g
Calcium	88mg

roast cod with pancetta and white beans

LOW-ALLERGEN COD is preferable to fish with higher histamine levels such as mackerel.

INGREDIENTS

Serves four

200g/7oz/1 cup butter (lima) beans,
    soaked overnight in cold water to cover
2 leeks, thinly sliced
2 garlic cloves, chopped
8 fresh sage leaves
60ml/4 tbsp fruity olive oil
8 thin pancetta slices
4 thick cod steaks, skinned
12 cherry tomatoes
salt and ground black pepper

1 Drain the beans, tip into a pan and cover with cold water. Bring to the boil and skim off the foam on the surface.

2 Lower the heat, then stir in the leeks, garlic, 4 sage leaves and 30ml/2 tbsp of the olive oil. Simmer for 1–1½ hours until the beans are tender, adding more water if necessary. Drain, return to the pan, season, stir in 15ml/1 tbsp olive oil and keep warm.

3 Preheat the oven to 200°C/400°F/ Gas 6. Wrap two slices of pancetta around the edge of each cod steak, tying it on with fine kitchen string or securing it with a wooden cocktail stick (toothpick). Insert a sage leaf between the pancetta and the cod. Season the fish with salt and pepper.

4 Heat a frying pan, add 15ml/1 tbsp of the remaining olive oil and sear the cod steaks for 1 minute on each side. Transfer to an ovenproof dish and roast for 5 minutes.

5 Add the tomatoes and drizzle over the remaining olive oil. Roast for 5 minutes more until the cod steaks are cooked but still juicy. Serve with the butter beans and roasted tomatoes. Garnish with parsley.

NUTRITION NOTES

Per portion:

Energy	497Kcal/2086kJ
Fat	22.4g
saturated fat	5.5g
Carbohydrate	29.7g
Fibre	9.7g
Calcium	80.4mg

free from
✓ nuts
✓ dairy
✓ wheat
  seafood
✓ eggs
✓ yeast
✓ citrus
✓ alcohol

baked sea bass with lemon grass and red onions

THE SPICES IN THIS TASTY DISH may help to ease nasal congestion. Sea bass is a good source of low-fat protein.

INGREDIENTS

Serves two

1 sea bass, about 675g/1½lb, cleaned
   and scaled
30ml/2 tbsp olive oil
2 lemon grass stalks,
   finely sliced
1 red onion, finely shredded
1 chilli, seeded and finely chopped
5cm/2in piece fresh root ginger,
   finely shredded
45ml/3 tbsp chopped fresh
   coriander (cilantro)
rind and juice of 2 limes
30ml/2 tbsp tamari
salt and ground black pepper
steamed rice and sugar snap peas,
   to serve

free from
- ✓ nuts
- ✓ dairy
- ✓ wheat
- seafood
- ✓ eggs
- ✓ yeast
- citrus
- ✓ alcohol

1 Soak a fish clay pot in cold water for 20 minutes, then drain. Make four to five diagonal slashes on both sides of the fish. Repeat the slashes on one side in the opposite direction to give an attractive cross-hatched effect. Rub the sea bass inside and out with salt, pepper and 15ml/1 tbsp of the olive oil.

2 Mix together the lemon grass, onion, chilli, ginger, coriander and lime rind.

3 Place a little of the lemon grass and red onion mixture in the base of the clay pot, then lay the fish on top. Sprinkle the remaining mixture over the fish, then sprinkle over the lime juice, tamari and the remaining olive oil. Cover and place in an unheated oven.

4 Set the oven to 220°C/425°F/Gas 7 and place the spiced sea bass in the unheated oven. Cook for 30–40 minutes, or until the flesh flakes easily when tested with a sharp knife. Serve immediately with steamed rice and sugar snap peas.

NUTRITION NOTES

Per portion:
Energy	395Kcal/1652kJ
Fat	17.7g
saturated fat	2.7g
Carbohydrate	8.1g
Fibre	0.9g
Calcium	379.8mg

baked sardines with caper and tomato stuffing

FOR THOSE AVOIDING WHEAT, serve the stuffed sardines with rice or potatoes instead of crusty bread.

INGREDIENTS

Serves four

16 fresh sardines, cleaned
8–12 cherry tomatoes,
    on the vine, sliced
45ml/3 tbsp capers, chopped
½ small red onion, very finely chopped
60ml/4 tbsp olive oil
grated rind and juice 1 lemon
45ml/3 tbsp chopped fresh parsley
15ml/1 tbsp chopped fresh basil
basil sprigs and lemon wedges,
    to garnish
crusty bread, to serve

1 Remove the backbone from each sardine by placing it slit side down on a chopping board. Using your fingers, push firmly along the length of the backbone to loosen it from the flesh. Turn the sardine over and pull out the bone; cut the ends with a sharp knife to release it. Repeat with the remaining sardines.

2 Place the tomato slices inside each sardine; they may stick out slightly, depending on the size of the fish. Mix the capers and red onion together and place on top of the tomatoes.

3 Preheat the oven to 200°C/400°F/ Gas 6. Lay the sardines in a single layer in a large shallow baking dish.

4 Mix together the oil, lemon rind and juice and herbs.

COOK'S TIP
Removing the bones before cooking, as in step 1 of this recipe, makes the sardines easier to eat.

5 Drizzle the mixture over the sardines. Bake for 10 minutes until just cooked.

6 Garnish with basil and lemon wedges and serve with crusty bread.

NUTRITION NOTES

Per portion:

Energy	347Kcal/1444kJ
Fat	24.2g
saturated fat	4.1g
Carbohydrate	2.6g
Fibre	1g
Calcium	171.4mg

free from
✓ nuts
✓ dairy
  wheat
  seafood
✓ eggs
  yeast
  citrus
✓ alcohol

scallops with garlic and chilli

SCALLOPS ARE A GOOD SOURCE of the valuable mineral zinc, which is recommended for people who suffer from asthma, eczema and hayfever.

2 Cut the courgettes in half, then into four pieces. Heat the oil in a large frying pan. Add the courgettes to the pan and fry over a medium heat until soft. Remove from the pan. Add the chopped garlic and fry until golden. Stir in the hot chilli sauce.

3 Add the scallops to the sauce. Cook, stirring constantly, for 1–2 minutes only. So not overcook them or they will toughen. Stir in the lime juice, chopped coriander and the courgette pieces. Serve the scallops immediately on heated plates.

COOK'S TIP

Oil can withstand higher temperatures than butter, but butter gives added flavour. Using a mixture of oil and butter provides the perfect compromise.

INGREDIENTS

free from

✓ nuts
✓ dairy
✓ wheat
  seafood
✓ eggs
✓ yeast
  citrus
✓ alcohol

Serves four

20 scallops
2 courgettes (zucchini)
45ml/3 tbsp vegetable oil
4 garlic cloves, chopped
30ml/2 tbsp hot chilli sauce
juice of 1 lime
small bunch of fresh coriander (cilantro),
  finely chopped

1 If you have bought scallops in their shells, open them. Hold a scallop shell in the palm of your hand, with the flat side uppermost. Insert the blade of a knife close to the hinge that joins the shells and prise them apart. Run the blade of the knife across the inside of the flat shell to cut away the scallop. Only the white adductor muscle and the orange coral are eaten, so pull away and discard all other parts. Rinse the scallops under cold running water.

NUTRITION NOTES

Per portion:

Energy	204Kcal/849kJ
Fat	10g
saturated fat	1.4g
Carbohydrate	3.4g
Fibre	0.9g
Calcium	142.2mg

goan fish casserole

THIS WONDERFULLY FLAVOURED DISH of fish and prawns in a spicy, coconut sauce offers a supply of nutrients that are good for people who have asthma, eczema and hayfever.

INGREDIENTS

Serves four

7.5ml/1½ tsp ground turmeric
5ml/1 tsp salt
450g/1lb monkfish fillet, cut
  into eight pieces
15ml/1 tbsp lemon juice
5ml/1 tsp cumin seeds
5ml/1 tsp coriander seeds
5ml/1 tsp black peppercorns
1 garlic clove, chopped
5cm/2in piece fresh root ginger,
  finely chopped
25g/1oz tamarind paste
150ml/¼ pint/⅔ cup hot water
30ml/2 tbsp vegetable oil
2 onions, halved and sliced lengthways
400ml/14fl oz/1⅔ cups coconut milk
4 mild green chillies, seeded and sliced
16 large raw prawns (shrimp), peeled
30ml/2 tbsp chopped fresh coriander
  (cilantro) leaves, to garnish

1 Mix together the turmeric and salt. Place the monkfish in a dish and sprinkle over the lemon juice, then rub the turmeric and salt mixture over the fish fillets to coat them. Cover and chill until ready to cook.

2 Put the cumin and coriander seeds and black peppercorns in a blender and blend to a powder. Add the garlic and ginger and process for a few seconds more.

3 Preheat the oven to 200°C/400°F/ Gas 6. Mix the tamarind paste with the hot water and set aside.

4 Heat the oil in a frying pan, add the onions and cook for 5–6 minutes, until softened and golden. Transfer the onions to a shallow baking dish.

5 Add the fish fillets to the oil remaining in the frying pan, and fry briefly over a high heat, turning them to seal on all sides. Remove the fish from the pan and place on top of the onions. Add the ground spice mixture to the frying pan and cook over a medium heat, stirring constantly, for 1–2 minutes.

6 Stir in the tamarind liquid, coconut milk and chilli strips and bring to the boil.

7 Pour the sauce into the dish to coat the fish completely, then cover the dish and bake for 10 minutes. Add the prawns, pushing them into the liquid, then cover the dish again and return it to the oven for 5 minutes, or until the prawns turn pink. Do not overcook them. Check the seasoning, sprinkle with coriander leaves and serve.

NUTRITION NOTES

Per portion:

Energy	368Kcal/1538kJ
Fat	23.2g
saturated fat	14.8g
Carbohydrate	14.3g
Fibre	1g
Calcium	119.8mg

free from

✓ nuts
✓ dairy
✓ wheat
seafood
✓ eggs
✓ yeast
citrus
✓ alcohol

vegetarian
dishes

From stews and bakes to rice or barley risottos there are main courses here to tempt vegetarians and meat-eaters alike. Choose from classic recipes such as vegetable stew with roasted tomato and garlic sauce, packed with a range of health-giving nutrients, or peppers filled with spiced vegetables, which may help alleviate congestion. Or try something a little more unusual: roasted squash with rice stuffing, which is free from common allergens, or vegetables baked turkish style, full of vitamin C and betacarotene to ensure a healthy immune system.

peppers filled with spiced vegetables

THE GARLIC, ONION AND FRESH GINGER used in these spicy stuffed peppers may help to alleviate congestion, while the red peppers offer a useful supply of immune-boosting betacarotene.

INGREDIENTS

Serves three as a main course, six as first course

6 large red or yellow (bell) peppers
500g/1¼lb waxy potatoes, scrubbed
1 small onion, chopped
4–5 garlic cloves, chopped
5cm/2in piece fresh root ginger, chopped
1–2 green chillies, seeded and chopped
105ml/7 tbsp water
60ml/4 tbsp olive oil
1 aubergine (eggplant), cut into
    1cm/½in dice
10ml/2 tsp cumin seeds
5ml/1 tsp kalonji seeds
2.5ml/½ tsp ground turmeric
5ml/1 tsp ground coriander
5ml/1 tsp ground toasted cumin seeds
1–2 pinches of cayenne pepper
about 30ml/2 tbsp lemon juice
salt and ground black pepper
30ml/2 tbsp chopped fresh coriander
    (cilantro), to garnish

free from	
✓	nuts
✓	dairy
✓	wheat
✓	seafood
✓	eggs
✓	yeast
	citrus
✓	alcohol

1 Cut the tops off the red or yellow peppers, then remove and discard the seeds. Cut a thin slice off the base of the peppers, to make them stand upright.

2 Bring a large pan of lightly salted water to the boil. Add the peppers and cook for 5–6 minutes. Drain and leave the peppers upside down in a colander.

3 Cook the potatoes in boiling, salted water for 10–12 minutes, until just tender. Drain, cool and peel, then dice.

4 Purée the onion, garlic, ginger and chillies in a food processor with 60ml/4 tbsp of the water.

5 Heat 30ml/2 tbsp of the oil in a large frying pan and cook the aubergine stirring until browned. Remove and set aside. Add another 15ml/1 tbsp of the oil to the pan and cook the potatoes until lightly browned. Remove and set aside.

6 Add the cumin and kalonji seeds to the pan. Fry briefly, then add the turmeric, coriander and ground cumin. Cook for 15 seconds. Stir in the onion and garlic purée and fry for a few seconds. Return the potatoes and aubergines to the pan, season and add the cayenne.

7 Add the remaining water and 15ml/ 1 tbsp lemon juice and cook, stirring, until the liquid evaporates. Preheat the oven to 190°C/375°F/Gas 5.

8 Fill the peppers with the mixture and place on a greased baking tray. Brush with a little oil and bake for 30–35 minutes until cooked. Garnish with the chopped coriander and serve.

NUTRITION NOTES

Per portion:	
Energy	434Kcal/1814kJ
Fat	18.4g
saturated fat	2.1g
Carbohydrate	59.9g
Fibre	10.1g
Calcium	145.6mg

roasted squash with rice stuffing

THESE SIMPLE STUFFED VEGETABLES make a light and tasty vegetarian supper. They are free of the common allergens that can exacerbate the symptoms of asthma, eczema and hayfever.

INGREDIENTS

Serves four as a first course

4 whole gem squashes
225g/8oz cooked white long grain rice (about 90g/3½oz/½ cup raw weight)
75g/3oz sun-dried tomatoes in oil, drained and chopped
50g/2oz/½ cup pitted black olives, chopped
30ml/2 tbsp olive oil
15ml/1 tbsp chopped fresh basil leaves, plus basil sprigs to serve
green salad, to serve

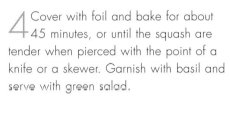

4 Cover with foil and bake for about 45 minutes, or until the squash are tender when pierced with the point of a knife or a skewer. Garnish with basil and serve with green salad.

NUTRITION NOTES

Per portion:	
Energy	252Kcal/1058kJ
Fat	10g
saturated fat	1.3g
Carbohydrate	38.5g
Fibre	5g
Calcium	116.6mg

3 Oil a shallow baking dish, just large enough to hold the squash side by side, with the remaining oil. Divide the rice mixture among the squash and place them in the baking dish.

1 Preheat the oven to 180°C/350°F/ Gas 4. Using a sharp knife, trim the base of each squash, then slice off the top of each and scoop out and discard the seeds.

2 Mix the rice, tomatoes, olives, half the oil and the chopped basil in a bowl.

free from
✓ nuts
✓ dairy
✓ wheat
✓ seafood
✓ eggs
✓ yeast
✓ citrus
✓ alcohol

vegetable paella

THIS VEGETARIAN VERSION of the traditional seafood-packed paella is great for anyone who needs to avoid fish and shellfish. Here it is crammed with health-promoting vegetables, including onions and garlic, which are reputed to aid and promote good respiratory function.

INGREDIENTS

Serves four

1 large aubergine (eggplant)
45ml/3 tbsp extra virgin olive oil
2 onions, quartered and sliced
2 garlic cloves, crushed
300g/11oz/1½ cups short grain
   Spanish or risotto rice
1.2–1.5 litres/2–2½ pints/5–6¼ cups
   fresh vegetable stock
1 red (bell) pepper, halved, seeded
   and sliced
200g/7oz fine green beans, halved
115g/4oz/2 cups chestnut mushrooms or
   button (white) mushrooms, halved
1 dried chilli, crushed
115g/4oz/1 cup frozen peas
salt and ground black pepper
fresh coriander (cilantro) leaves, to garnish

2 Heat 30ml/2 tbsp of the oil in a large frying pan, add the aubergine slices and quickly sauté them until slightly golden. Transfer to the sand pot or clay pot.

3 Add the remaining oil to the pan, add the onion and cook, stirring occasionally, for a 5–10 minutes until softened and golden brown. Add the garlic and rice and cook for 1–2 minutes, stirring, until the rice becomes transparent.

4 Pour in 900ml/1½ pints/3¾ cups of the stock into the sand pot or clay pot, then add the rice mixture.

1 Soak a Chinese sand pot or clay pot in cold water for 20 minutes, then drain. Cut the aubergine in half lengthwise, then cut it crosswise into thin slices.

VARIATION

Those with an allergy or intolerance to yeast should avoid eating mushrooms, use 115g/4oz carrots instead.

5 Add the peppers, halved green beans, mushrooms, crushed chilli and seasoning. Stir to mix, then cover the pot and place in an unheated oven.

6 Set the oven to 200°C/400°F/Gas 6 and cook for 1 hour, or until the rice is almost tender. After 40 minutes, remove the pot from the oven and add a little more stock to moisten the paella. Stir well, re-cover and return to the oven.

7 When the paella has cooked for 1 hour, add the peas and a little more stock and stir gently to mix, then return to the oven and cook for a further 10 minutes. Adjust the seasoning and sprinkle over the coriander. Lightly stir through and then serve.

free from
- ✓ nuts
- ✓ dairy
- ✓ wheat
- ✓ seafood
- ✓ eggs
- yeast
- ✓ citrus
- ✓ alcohol

NUTRITION NOTES

Per portion:

Energy	418Kcal/1745kJ
Fat	10.4g
saturated fat	1.5g
Carbohydrate	73.3g
Fibre	7.4g
Calcium	104.8mg

barley risotto with roasted squash and leeks

A HEARTY RISOTTO makes a good choice for those avoiding wheat. Barley contains magnesium, which is thought to be beneficial to sufferers of asthma, eczema and hayfever.

INGREDIENTS

Serves four

200g/7oz/1 cup pearl barley
1 butternut squash, peeled, seeded and
   cut into chunks
10ml/2 tsp chopped fresh thyme
60ml/4 tbsp olive oil
4 leeks, cut into fairly thick diagonal slices
2 garlic cloves, finely chopped
2 carrots, coarsely grated
120ml/4fl oz/½ cup fresh vegetable stock
30ml/2 tbsp chopped fresh flat leaf parsley
50g/2oz Pecorino cheese, grated or
   shaved (optional)
salt and ground black pepper

1 Rinse the barley. Cook it in simmering water, keeping the pan part-covered, for 35–45 minutes. Drain. Preheat the oven to 200°C/400°F/Gas 6.

free from
- ✓ nuts
- dairy
- ✓ wheat
- ✓ seafood
- ✓ eggs
- yeast
- ✓ citrus
- ✓ alcohol

2 Place the squash in a roasting pan with half the thyme. Season with pepper and toss with half the oil. Roast, stirring once, for 30–35 minutes until tender.

3 Heat the remaining oil in a large frying pan. Cook the leeks and garlic gently for 5 minutes.

4 Add the remaining thyme, then cook for 3 minutes. Stir in the carrots, cook for 2 minutes, then add the barley and most of the stock. Season well and part-cover the pan. Cook for 5 minutes more. Pour in the remaining stock if the mixture seems dry.

5 Stir in the parsley and half the Pecorino, if using, then stir in the squash. Add seasoning to taste and serve with the remaining Pecorino.

NUTRITION NOTES

Per portion:

Energy	396Kcal/1666kJ
Fat	13.1g
saturated fat	1.7g
Carbohydrate	64.7g
Fibre	7.6g
Calcium	165mg

rice and lentils with crisp caramelized onions

THE ONIONS IN THIS DISH offer anti-inflammatory properties for asthma sufferers, while lentils and rice are a good carbohydrate choice for those who suffer from wheat allergies.

INGREDIENTS

Serves six

400g/14oz/1¾ cups large brown or
   green lentils
30ml/2 tbsp olive oil
3–4 onions, 1 chopped and
   2–3 thinly sliced
5ml/1 tsp ground cumin
2.5ml/½ tsp ground cinnamon
3–5 cardamom pods
300g/11oz/1½ cups long grain
   rice, rinsed
250ml/8fl oz/1 cup fresh vegetable stock
salt and ground black pepper
natural (plain) yogurt, to serve (optional)

3 Heat the remaining oil in a frying pan, add the sliced onions and fry for 10 minutes, until brown and crisp. Sprinkle in the remaining cumin and cinnamon.

4 Add the fried chopped onion to the lentils with the cardamom, rice and stock.

5 Mix, then bring to the boil. Reduce the heat, cover and simmer until the rice is tender and the liquid has been absorbed. Season. To serve, pile the rice and lentil mixture on to a warmed serving dish, then top with the caramelized onions. Serve with natural yogurt, if you like.

NUTRITION NOTES

Per portion:

Energy	449Kcal/1903kJ
Fat	5.8g
saturated fat	0.6g
Carbohydrate	83.5g
Fibre	7.1g
Calcium	91.4mg

1 Put the lentils in a large pan with enough water to cover generously. Bring to the boil, then reduce the heat and simmer for about 30 minutes, or until the lentils are just tender. Once or twice during cooking, skim off any scum that forms on top.

2 Heat half the olive oil in a small pan, add the chopped onion and fry for 5 minutes, stirring frequently or until the onion is starting to turn golden brown. Stir in half the ground cumin and half the ground cinnamon.

free from
✓ nuts
   dairy
✓ wheat
✓ seafood
✓ eggs
✓ yeast
✓ citrus
✓ alcohol

vegetable stew with roasted tomato and garlic sauce

A TASTY STEW PACKED with fresh vegetables that offers a valuable supply of health-promoting nutrients. If you are on a yeast-free diet, simply omit the dried apricots.

INGREDIENTS

Serves six

45ml/3 tbsp olive oil
250g/9oz small pickling onions
   or shallots
1 large onion, chopped
2 garlic cloves, chopped
5ml/1 tsp cumin seeds
5ml/1 tsp ground coriander seeds
5ml/1 tsp paprika
5cm/2in piece cinnamon stick
2 fresh bay leaves
300–450ml/½–¾ pint/1¼–scant 2 cups
   fresh vegetable stock
good pinch of saffron strands
450g/1lb carrots, thickly sliced
2 green (bell) peppers, seeded and
   thickly sliced
115g/4oz ready-to-eat dried apricots
5ml/1 tsp ground toasted cumin seeds
450g/1lb squash, peeled, seeded and
   cut into chunks
pinch of sugar, to taste
salt and ground black pepper
45ml/3 tbsp fresh coriander (cilantro)
   leaves, to garnish

For the roasted tomato and garlic sauce

1kg/2¼lb tomatoes, halved
45ml/3 tbsp olive oil
1–2 fresh red chillies, seeded
   and chopped
2–3 garlic cloves, chopped
5ml/1 tsp fresh thyme leaves

free from
✓ nuts
✓ dairy
✓ wheat
✓ seafood
✓ eggs
 yeast
✓ citrus
✓ alcohol

1 Preheat the oven to 180°C/350°F/ Gas 4. First make the sauce. Place the tomatoes, cut sides uppermost, in a roasting tin. Season well, then drizzle with the olive oil. Roast for 30 minutes.

2 Scatter the chillies, garlic and thyme over the tomatoes, stir to mix and roast for another 30–45 minutes, or until the tomatoes are collapsed but still a little juicy. Leave the tomatoes to cool, then process in a food processor or blender to make a thick sauce. Sieve to remove the seeds.

3 Heat 30ml/2 tbsp of the olive oil in a large, wide pan or deep frying pan and cook the pickling onions or shallots until browned all over. Remove them from the pan and set aside. Add the chopped onion to the pan and cook over a low heat for 5–7 minutes until softened. Stir in the chopped garlic and cumin seeds and cook for a further 3–4 minutes.

4 Add the ground coriander seeds, paprika, cinnamon stick and bay leaves. Cook, stirring constantly, for another 2 minutes, then mix in the stock, saffron, carrots and green peppers. Season well, cover and simmer gently for 10 minutes.

5 Stir in the apricots, ground cumin, browned onions or shallots and squash. Stir in the tomato sauce. Cover and cook for 5 minutes more. Uncover the pan and cook, stirring occasionally, for 10–15 minutes, until the vegetables are cooked.

6 Add sugar to taste, adjust the seasoning, then discard the cinnamon stick. Serve scattered with the fresh coriander leaves.

NUTRITION NOTES

Per portion:

Energy	173Kcal/721kJ
Fat	6.8g
saturated fat	0.8g
Carbohydrate	25.2g
Fibre	5.9g
Calcium	120mg

vegetables baked turkish-style

THIS SPICY VEGETABLE STEW is packed with healthy non-allergenic vegetables, which are rich in nutrients such as vitamin C and betacarotene.

INGREDIENTS

Serves four

60ml/4 tbsp olive oil

1 large onion, chopped

2 aubergines (eggplant), cut into small cubes

4 courgettes (zucchini), cut into small chunks

1 green (bell) pepper, seeded and chopped

1 red or yellow (bell) pepper, seeded and chopped

115g/4oz/1 cup fresh or frozen peas

115g/4oz green beans

450g/1lb small new or salad potatoes, cubed

2.5ml/½ tsp ground cinnamon

2.5ml/½ tsp ground cumin

5ml/1 tsp paprika

4–5 tomatoes, skinned

400g/14oz can chopped tomatoes

30ml/2 tbsp chopped fresh flat leaf parsley

3–4 garlic cloves, crushed

350ml/12fl oz/1½ cups fresh vegetable stock

salt and ground black pepper

black olives and fresh parsley, to garnish

free from

✓ nuts
✓ dairy
✓ wheat
✓ seafood
✓ eggs
✓ yeast
✓ citrus
✓ alcohol

1 Preheat the oven to 190°C/375°F/ Gas 5. Heat 45ml/3 tbsp of the oil in a large frying pan, add the onion and fry until golden.

2 (left) Add the aubergine cubes and sauté for about 3 minutes, then add the courgette chunks, chopped green and red or yellow peppers, peas, green beans and cubed potatoes, together with the ground cinnamon, ground cumin, paprika and seasoning. Continue to cook for a further 3 minutes, stirring the mixture constantly. Transfer the vegetables to an ovenproof dish.

3 Halve the fresh skinned tomatoes, remove the seeds using a teaspoon and then roughly chop the tomato flesh. Mix the fresh tomato flesh with the canned tomatoes, chopped fresh parsley, crushed garlic and the remaining olive oil in a mixing bowl.

4 Pour the vegetable stock over the aubergine and pepper mixture and then spoon the prepared tomato mixture evenly over the top. Cover the dish with foil and bake for 30–45 minutes. Serve hot, garnished with olives and parsley.

NUTRITION NOTES

Per portion:	
Energy	336Kcal/1401kJ
Fat	14.3g
saturated fat	1.9g
Carbohydrate	42.5g
Fibre	10.9g
Calcium	144.3mg

spicy tomato and chickpea stew

TOMATOES OFFER a good supply of anti-inflammatory vitamin C, which can help asthma sufferers. Serve this healthy stew with flatbread or, for those with a wheat allergy, brown rice.

INGREDIENTS

Serves four

60ml/4 tbsp olive oil

1 large aubergine (eggplant), cut into bitesize chunks

2 onions, thinly sliced

3–5 garlic cloves, chopped

1–2 green (bell) peppers, thinly sliced

1–2 fresh hot chillies, chopped

4 fresh or canned tomatoes, diced

30–45ml/2–3 tbsp tomato purée (paste), if using fresh tomatoes

5ml/1 tsp ground turmeric

pinch of curry powder or ras el hanout

cayenne pepper, to taste

400g/14oz can chickpeas, drained and rinsed

30–45ml/2–3 tbsp chopped fresh coriander (cilantro) leaves

salt

flatbread or brown rice, to serve

1 Heat half the oil in a frying pan, add the aubergine chunks and fry until brown. When cooked, transfer the aubergine to a colander, standing over a bowl, and leave to drain.

2 Heat the remaining oil in the pan, add the onions, garlic, peppers and chillies and fry until softened. Add the diced tomatoes, tomato purée, if using, spices and salt, and cook, stirring, until the mixture is of a sauce consistency. Add a little water if necessary.

3 Add the drained and rinsed chickpeas to the sauce and cook for about 5 minutes, then add the browned aubergine, stir thoroughly to mix and cook for 5–10 minutes until the flavours are well combined. Add the chopped coriander leaves. Serve the stew hot or chill before serving.

VARIATION

This stew would be equally good with other vegetables. Try courgettes (zucchini) in place of some or all of the aubergine, or add chunks of squash, sweet potato or carrot.

NUTRITION NOTES

Per portion:	
Energy	243Kcal/1012kJ
Fat	13.9g
saturated fat	1.6g
Carbohydrate	23.2g
Fibre	7.2g
Calcium	76.1mg

free from

✓ nuts

✓ dairy

wheat

✓ seafood

✓ eggs

yeast

✓ citrus

✓ alcohol

mixed bean and aubergine tagine

BEANS ARE A GOOD SOURCE of B vitamins, which can help to maintain healthy skin, and onions and garlic are both recommended for respiratory problems. Garlic can also act as a natural decongestant, which can benefit hayfever sufferers.

INGREDIENTS

Serves four

115g/4oz/generous ½ cup dried red
   kidney beans, soaked overnight in cold
   water and drained
115g/4oz/generous ½ cup dried
   black-eyed beans (peas), soaked
   overnight in cold water and drained
600ml/1 pint/2½ cups water
2 bay leaves
2 celery sticks, each cut into four batons
75ml/5 tbsp olive oil
1 aubergine (eggplant), cut into chunks
1 onion, thinly sliced
3 garlic cloves, crushed
1–2 fresh red chillies, seeded and chopped
30ml/2 tbsp tomato purée (paste)
5ml/1 tsp paprika
2 large tomatoes, roughly chopped
300ml/½ pint/1¼ cups fresh stock
15ml/1 tbsp each chopped fresh mint,
   parsley and coriander (cilantro)
salt and ground black pepper
fresh herb sprigs, to garnish

2 Place the 600ml/1 pint/2½ cups of water in a soaked bean pot or a large tagine, add the bay leaves, celery and beans. Cover and place in an unheated oven. Set the oven to 190°C/375°F/ Gas 5. Cook for 1–1½ hours, or until the beans are tender. Drain.

3 Heat 60ml/4 tbsp of the oil in a large frying pan. Add the aubergine and cook, stirring for 4–5 minutes until evenly browned. Remove and set aside.

4 Add the remaining oil to the frying pan, then add the onion and cook, stirring, for 4–5 minutes until softened. Add the garlic and chillies and cook for a further 5 minutes, stirring frequently, until the onion is golden.

5 Reduce the oven temperature to 160°C/325°F/Gas 3. Add the tomato purée and paprika to the pan and cook, stirring, for 1–2 minutes. Add the chopped tomatoes, browned aubergine, drained kidney and black-eyed beans and stock. Stir well, then season to taste with salt and pepper.

6 Transfer the contents of the frying pan to a soaked clay tagine or a shallow baking dish. Place in the oven and cook for 1 hour, or until the vegetables are tender.

7 To serve, add the chopped mint, parsley and coriander to the tagine and lightly mix through the vegetables. Season to taste with salt and plenty of pepper. Garnish with fresh herb sprigs and serve.

1 Place the kidney beans in a large pan of unsalted boiling water. Bring back to the boil and boil rapidly for 10 minutes, then drain. Place the black-eyed beans in a separate large pan of boiling unsalted water and boil rapidly for 10 minutes, then drain.

NUTRITION NOTES

Per portion:	
Energy	334Kcal/1401kJ
Fat	15.5g
saturated fat	2.1g
Carbohydrate	35.5g
Fibre	12.6g
Calcium	139.6mg

salads and
side dishes

It's so easy to stick with the old favourites when it comes to main course or side salads and accompanying vegetable dishes, but try just one of these alternatives and you'll soon be converted to serving vegetables with a twist. Try salads such as beetroot with fresh mint, a wonderfully colourful dish with immune-boosting betacarotene or beef and grilled sweet potato salad with shallot and herb dressing that has anti-viral properties. Accompanying vegetable dishes include spinach with raisins and pine nuts (a good source of vitamin C) and oven-roasted red onions with natural anti-inflammatory properties.

beetroot with fresh mint

THIS REFRESHING SALAD is a tasty way to serve beetroot. Avoid the pickled variety, as it is loaded with histamines and may aggravate allergies.

INGREDIENTS

Serves four

4 large or 6–8 large cooked
  beetroot (beets)
5–10ml/1–2 tsp sugar
juice of ½ lemon
30ml/2 tbsp extra virgin olive oil
1 bunch fresh mint, leaves stripped and
  thinly sliced

COOK'S TIP

If you are going to buy ready-cooked beetroot for this salad, ensure that it is not the pickled variety. If you prefer to cook it yourself, simmer the unskinned beetroot for about 1½ hours.

1 Slice the beetroot or cut into even-size dice with a sharp knife. Put the beetroot in a bowl. Add the sugar, lemon juice, olive oil and a pinch of salt and toss together to combine.

2 Add half the thinly sliced fresh mint to the salad and toss lightly until well combined. Place the salad in the refrigerator and chill for about 1 hour. Serve garnished with the remaining mint.

NUTRITION NOTES

Per portion:

Energy	79Kcal/327kJ
Fat	5.6g
saturated fat	0.8g
Carbohydrate	6.3g
Fibre	1g
Calcium	20.1mg

free from

✓	nuts
✓	dairy
✓	wheat
✓	seafood
✓	eggs
✓	yeast
	citrus
✓	alcohol

carrot salad

THIS TASTY SALAD is rich in health-promoting nutrients including betacarotene and vitamin C. The generous quantities of garlic can act as a decongestant and provides anti-viral properties.

INGREDIENTS

Serves four

3–4 carrots, thinly sliced
5ml/1 tsp sugar
3–4 garlic cloves, chopped
1.5ml/¼ tsp ground cumin,
    or to taste
juice of ½ lemon
30–45ml/2–3 tbsp extra virgin
    olive oil
30ml/2 tbsp chopped fresh coriander
    (cilantro) leaves or a mixture of
    coriander and flat leaf parsley
salt and ground black pepper

1 Cook the carrots by either steaming or boiling in lightly salted water until they are just tender but not soft. Drain, leave for a few moments to dry, then put in a bowl.

2 Add the sugar, garlic, cumin, lemon juice and olive oil to the carrots and toss together. Add the herbs and season. Serve warm or chill before serving.

NUTRITION NOTES	
Per portion:	
Energy	97Kcal/401kJ
Fat	5.9g
saturated fat	0.8g
Carbohydrate	10.3g
Fibre	2.6g
Calcium	35.7mg

free from
✓ nuts
✓ dairy
✓ wheat
✓ seafood
✓ eggs
✓ yeast
    citrus
✓ alcohol

bean salad with tuna and red onion

THE ESSENTIAL FATTY ACIDS found in tuna fish and B vitamins found in beans may help to improve the skin of eczema sufferers.

2 Place all the dressing ingredients apart from the lemon juice in a jug (pitcher) and whisk until mixed. Season to taste with salt, pepper and lemon juice, if you like.

3 Blanch the French beans in boiling water for 3–4 minutes. Drain, refresh under cold water and drain again.

4 Place both types of beans in a bowl. Add half the dressing and toss to mix. Stir in the onion and half the parsley, then season to taste with salt and pepper. Flake the tuna into large chunks and lightly toss it into the beans with the tomatoes.

5 Arrange the salad on four plates. Drizzle the remaining dressing over and scatter the remaining parsley on top.

INGREDIENTS

Serves four

250g/9oz/1⅓ cups dried haricot or cannellini beans, soaked overnight in cold water
1 bay leaf
200–250g/7–9oz fine French beans, trimmed
1 large red onion, very thinly sliced
45ml/3 tbsp chopped fresh flat leaf parsley
200–250g/7–9oz good-quality canned tuna in olive oil, drained
200g/7oz cherry tomatoes, halved
salt and ground black pepper

For the dressing

90ml/6 tbsp extra virgin olive oil
5ml/1 tsp tarragon mustard
1 garlic clove, finely chopped
5ml/1 tsp grated lemon rind
a little lemon juice

1 Drain the beans and place them in a large pan with fresh water. Add the bay leaf, then bring to the boil. Boil rapidly for 10 minutes, then reduce the heat and boil steadily for 1–1½ hours until tender. The cooking time depends on the age of the beans. Drain well. Discard the bay leaf.

free from

✓	nuts
✓	dairy
✓	wheat
	seafood
✓	eggs
	yeast
	citrus
	alcohol

NUTRITION NOTES

Per portion:

Energy	445Kcal/1864kJ
Fat	21.9g
saturated fat	3.1g
Carbohydrate	37.8g
Fibre	13.2g
Calcium	168.8mg

lentil and spinach salad

A HEALTHY SALAD packed with nutrients that will help to keep the body in peak condition, boost the immune system and promote good skin health.

INGREDIENTS

Serves six

225g/8oz/1 cup Puy lentils
1 fresh bay leaf
1 celery stick
fresh thyme sprig
30ml/2 tbsp olive oil
1 onion or 3–4 shallots, finely chopped
10ml/2 tsp crushed toasted cumin seeds
400g/14oz young spinach
salt and ground black pepper
30–45ml/2–3 tbsp chopped fresh parsley
toasted French bread, to serve (optional)

For the dressing

75ml/5 tbsp extra virgin olive oil
5ml/1 tsp Dijon mustard
1 small garlic clove, finely chopped
15ml/1 tbsp lemon juice, plus 2.5ml/
½ tsp finely grated lemon rind

1 Rinse the lentils and place them in a large saucepan. Add plenty of water to cover. Tie the bay leaf, celery and thyme into a bundle and add to the pan, then bring to the boil. Reduce the heat so that the water boils steadily. Cook the lentils for 30–45 minutes until just tender. Do not add salt at this stage, as it toughens the lentils.

2 Meanwhile, to make the dressing, mix the oil, mustard, garlic and lemon juice and rind, and season well.

3 Thoroughly drain the lentils and tip them into a bowl. Add most of the dressing and toss well, then set the lentils aside, stirring occasionally.

4 Heat the oil in a deep frying pan and cook the onion or shallots over a low heat for about 4–5 minutes until they are beginning to soften. Add the cumin and cook for 1 minute. Add the spinach and season to taste, cover and cook for 2 minutes. Stir, then cook again briefly until wilted.

5 Stir the lightly cooked spinach into the lentils and then leave the salad to cool, then chill until ready to serve. Bring back to room temperature if necessary. Stir in the remaining dressing and chopped parsley.

6 Adjust the seasoning, adding plenty of black pepper, then tip the salad on to a serving dish or into a large salad bowl and serve with toasted French bread, if you like.

NUTRITION NOTES	
Per portion:	
Energy	177Kcal/746kJ
Fat	5.3g
saturated fat	0.6g
Carbohydrate	21.9g
Fibre	5.3g
Calcium	173.6mg

free from

✓ nuts
✓ dairy
  wheat
✓ seafood
✓ eggs
  yeast
  citrus
  alcohol

spicy white bean salad

TENDER WHITE BEANS, a good source of B vitamins, are delicious in this spicy sauce with the bite of fresh, crunchy green pepper. The dish is perfect for preparing ahead of time.

INGREDIENTS

Serves four

750g/1⅔lb tomatoes, diced
1 onion, finely chopped
½–1 mild fresh chilli, finely chopped
1 green (bell) pepper, seeded and
    chopped
pinch of sugar
4 garlic cloves, chopped
400g/14oz can cannellini beans, drained
45–60ml/3–4 tbsp olive oil
grated rind and juice of 1 lemon
15ml/1 tbsp cider vinegar or
    wine vinegar
salt and ground black pepper
chopped fresh parsley, to garnish

2 Add the olive oil, grated lemon rind, lemon juice and vinegar to the salad and toss lightly to combine. Chill before serving, garnished with chopped parsley.

1 Put the tomatoes, onion, chilli, green pepper, sugar, garlic, cannellini beans, salt and plenty of ground black pepper in a bowl and toss together until well combined.

NUTRITION NOTES

Per portion:
Energy	195Kcal/1810kJ
Fat	9.6g
saturated fat	1.3g
Carbohydrate	21.5g
Fibre	6.2g
Calcium	63.8mg

free from
✓ nuts
✓ dairy
✓ wheat
✓ seafood
✓ eggs
  yeast
  citrus
  alcohol

beef and grilled sweet potato salad

A SOPHISTICATED SALAD that makes a delicious low-allergy lunch or supper. Sweet potato contains immune-boosting betacarotene and shallots may act as a decongestant.

INGREDIENTS

Serves six

800g/1¾lb fillet steak (beef tenderloin)
5ml/1 tsp black peppercorns, coarsely crushed
10ml/2 tsp chopped fresh thyme
45ml/3 tbsp olive oil
450g/1lb orange-fleshed sweet potato, peeled
salt and ground black pepper

For the dressing

1 garlic clove, chopped
15g/½oz flat leaf parsley
30ml/2 tbsp chopped fresh coriander (cilantro)
½–1 fresh green chilli, seeded and chopped
10ml/2 tsp Dijon mustard
45ml/3 tbsp extra virgin olive oil
2 shallots, finely chopped

1 Roll the beef fillet in the coarsely crushed peppercorns and thyme, then set aside to marinate for a few hours.

2 Preheat the oven to 200°C/400°F/ Gas 6. Heat half the olive oil in a heavy frying pan. Add the beef and brown it all over, turning frequently, to seal it.

3 Place on a baking tray and cook in the oven for 10–15 minutes. Remove the beef from the oven, and cover with foil, then leave to rest for 10–15 minutes.

4 Meanwhile, preheat the grill. Cut the sweet potatoes into 1cm/½in slices. Brush with the remaining olive oil, season to taste with salt and pepper, and grill for about 5–6 minutes on each side, until tender and browned. Cut the sweet potato slices into strips and place them in a bowl. Cut the beef into strips and toss with the sweet potato. Set the bowl aside.

5 To make the dressing, process the garlic, parsley, coriander, chilli and mustard in a food processor or blender until chopped. With the motor still running, gradually pour in the oil to make a smooth dressing. Season, then stir in the shallots.

6 Toss the dressing into the sweet potatoes and beef and leave to stand in a cool place for up to 2 hours before serving.

VARIATION

Skinless, boneless chicken breasts would make a lower-fat alternative to beef in this salad – ensure that it is cooked right through.

NUTRITION NOTES

Per portion:	
Energy	350Kcal/1457kJ
Fat	19.6g
saturated fat	5g
Carbohydrate	14.8g
Fibre	1.7g
Calcium	41.5mg

free from

✓ nuts
✓ dairy
✓ wheat
✓ seafood
✓ eggs
  yeast
✓ citrus
  alcohol

spinach with raisins and pine nuts

AN ENERGIZING SIDE DISH that aids the elimination of toxins and enhances immunity, helping the body fight off infection. Those with a nut allergy should simply omit the pine nuts.

INGREDIENTS

Serves four

60ml/4 tbsp raisins
1kg/2¼lb fresh spinach leaves, washed
45ml/3 tbsp olive oil
6–8 spring onions (scallions), thinly sliced
   or 1–2 small yellow or white onions,
   finely chopped
60ml/4 tbsp pine nuts (optional)
salt and ground black pepper

1 Put the raisins in a small bowl and pour over boiling water to cover. Leave to stand for about 10 minutes, then drain.

2 Steam the spinach over a medium-high heat, with only the water that clings to it after washing, for 1–2 minutes until the leaves are bright green and wilted. Drain well leave to cool. When the spinach has cooled, chop roughly with a sharp knife.

3 Heat the oil in a frying pan over a medium-low heat, then lower the heat a little and add the sliced spring onions or onions. Fry for about 5 minutes, stirring occasionally, or until soft, then add the spinach, raisins and pine nuts, if using.

4 Raise the heat a little and then cook the spinach mixture for 2–3 minutes to warm through. Season with salt and plenty of pepper to taste and serve hot or warm.

free from

nuts
✓ dairy
✓ wheat
✓ seafood
✓ eggs
yeast
✓ citrus
✓ alcohol

NUTRITION NOTES

Per portion:

Energy	195Kcal/810kJ
Fat	10.4g
saturated fat	1.6g
Carbohydrate	18.4g
Fibre	5.8g
Calcium	440.2mg

baked winter squash in tomato sauce

THIS HEALTHY ANTI-ASTHMA SIDE DISH contains immune-boosting betacarotene, health-promoting and histamine-fighting vitamin C, and anti-inflammatory onions.

INGREDIENTS

Serves four

45–75ml/3–5 tbsp olive oil
1kg/2¼lb pumpkin or orange winter
   squash, peeled and sliced
1 onion, chopped
1–2 garlic cloves, chopped
2 x 400g/14oz cans chopped tomatoes
pinch of sugar
2–3 sprigs of fresh rosemary, stems
   removed and leaves chopped
salt and ground black pepper

1 Preheat the oven to 160°C/325°F/ Gas 3. Heat 45ml/3 tbsp of the oil in a frying pan and fry the pumpkin or orange squash slices in batches until golden brown on all sides. Remove the pumpkin or orange squash slices from the pan as they are cooked and keep warm.

2 Add the onion to the pan, with more oil if necessary, and fry for about 5 minutes, stirring, until softened.

3 Add the garlic to the pan and cook for 1 minute, stirring all the time, then add the tomatoes and sugar and cook over a medium-high heat, stirring occasionally, until the mixture is of a thick sauce consistency. Stir in the chopped rosemary leaves and season with salt and and plenty of pepper to taste.

4 Layer the fried pumpkin or squash slices and the tomato sauce in a shallow ovenproof dish, ending with a layer of tomato sauce.

5 Transfer the dish to the oven and bake for about 35 minutes, or until the top layer of sauce is lightly glazed and the pumpkin or squash is tender and just beginning to turn a light golden brown. Serve immediately.

NUTRITION NOTES

Per portion:	
Energy	143Kcal/595kJ
Fat	8.9g
saturated fat	1.2g
Carbohydrate	12.4g
Fibre	4.2g
Calcium	78.8,g

free from
✓ nuts
✓ dairy
✓ wheat
✓ seafood
✓ eggs
✓ yeast
✓ citrus
✓ alcohol

oven-roasted red onions

SWEET RED ONIONS are the perfect side dish for those striving to combat the symptoms of asthma. Onions have natural anti-inflammatory properties, which can help to calm an irritated respiratory system.

3 Rub the onions with half the olive oil, salt and pepper and the juniper berries. Place the onions in the baker, inserting the rosemary in among the onions. Pour the remaining olive oil over.

4 Cover and place in an unheated oven. Set the oven to 200°C/400°F/Gas 6 and cook for 40 minutes. Remove the lid and cook for a further 10 minutes until the onions are tender and the skins slightly crisp.

COOK'S TIP

To help hold back the tears during preparation, chill the onions first for about 30 minutes and then remove the root end last. The root contains the largest concentration of the sulphuric compounds that make the eyes water.

INGREDIENTS

Serves four

4 large or 8 small red onions
45ml/3 tbsp olive oil
6 juniper berries, crushed
8 small sprigs of fresh rosemary
salt and ground black pepper

1 Soak a clay onion baker in cold water for 15 minutes, then drain. If the base of the baker is glazed, only the lid will need to be soaked.

VARIATION

If you like, try using just fresh thyme in place of the juniper and rosemary.

2 Trim the roots from the onions and remove the skins, if you like. Cut the onions from the tip to the root, cutting the large onions into quarters and the small onions in half.

NUTRITION NOTES

Per portion:

Energy	141Kcal/583kJ
Fat	8.7g
saturated fat	1.2g
Carbohydrate	14.5g
Fibre	2.5g
Calcium	49.8mg

braised red cabbage with beetroot

CABBAGE AND, TO A LESSER EXTENT, BEETROOT, are excellent sources of vitamin C, which can help to promote the immune system and eliminate histamines that are produced during an allergic reaction.

INGREDIENTS

Serves six

675g/1½lb red cabbage
30ml/2 tbsp olive oil
1 Spanish onion, thinly sliced into rings
2 tart eating apples, peeled, cored and sliced
300ml/½ pint/1¼ cups fresh vegetable stock
375g/13oz raw beetroot (beet), peeled and coarsely grated
salt and ground black pepper

1 Soak a large clay pot or bean pot in cold water for 20 minutes, then drain. Finely shred the red cabbage and place in the soaked clay or bean pot.

2 Heat the olive oil in a large frying pan, add the thinly sliced Spanish onion and cook gently for about 5 minutes, stirring occasionally, until the onion is soft and transparent.

3 Add the apple slices to the pan and pour in the vegetable stock, then transfer the mixture to the clay or bean pot. Season with salt and plenty of pepper and stir well to combine the sliced apple, onion and cabbage.

4 Cover the clay or bean pot and place in an unheated oven. Set the oven temperature to 190°C/375°F/Gas 5 and cook for about 1 hour. Stir in the beetroot, then re-cover the pot and cook for 20–30 minutes, or until tender.

NUTRITION NOTES

Per portion:

Energy	111Kcal/463kJ
Fat	4.2g
saturated fat	0.5g
Carbohydrate	16.3g
Fibre	5.1g
Calcium	97.4mg

COOK'S TIP

When buying cabbage, choose one that is firm and heavy for its size. The leaves should look healthy – avoid any with curling leaves or blemishes. These guidelines apply to any type of cabbage – red, green or white.

free from

✓ nuts
✓ dairy
✓ wheat
✓ seafood
✓ eggs
✓ yeast
✓ citrus
✓ alcohol

potatoes baked with fennel and onions

VEGETABLES FLAVOURED WITH aromatic spices make a perfect accompaniment to grilled or roasted meat.

INGREDIENTS

Serves six

500g/1¼lb small waxy potatoes, cut into chunks or wedges
good pinch of saffron threads
1 head of garlic, separated into cloves
12 small red or yellow onions, peeled
3 fennel bulbs, cut into wedges, feathery tops reserved
4–6 fresh bay leaves
6–9 fresh thyme sprigs
175ml/6fl oz/¾ cup fresh vegetable stock
5ml/1 tsp fennel seeds, lightly crushed
2.5ml/½ tsp paprika
45ml/3 tbsp olive oil
salt and ground black pepper

1 Boil the potatoes in salted water for 8–10 minutes. Drain. Preheat the oven to 190°C/375°F/Gas 5. Soak the saffron in 30ml/2 tbsp warm water for 10 minutes.

2 Peel and finely chop 2 of the garlic cloves and set them aside. Place the potatoes, onions, unpeeled garlic cloves, fennel wedges, bay leaves and thyme sprigs in a roasting dish.

COOK'S TIP
Don't worry about the amount of garlic in this dish – it becomes very mellow after cooking.

3 Mix together the stock, saffron and its soaking liquid, then pour over the vegetables. Stir in the fennel seeds, paprika, chopped garlic and oil, and season with salt and pepper.

4 Cook in the oven for 1–1¼ hours, stirring occasionally, until the vegetables are tender. Chop the reserved feathery fennel tops and sprinkle over the vegetables and serve.

NUTRITION NOTES

Per portion:	
Energy	167Kcal/699kJ
Fat	6.2g
saturated fat	0.8g
Carbohydrate	25g
Fibre	4.1g
Calcium	63.4mg

free from
✓ nuts
✓ dairy
✓ wheat
✓ seafood
✓ eggs
✓ yeast
✓ citrus
✓ alcohol

rice with dill and broad beans

THIS FIBRE-RICH SIDE DISH makes a good accompaniment to any low-allergy main dish.

INGREDIENTS

Serves four

275g/10oz/1½ cups basmati or long
   grain rice, soaked in cold water
   and drained
750ml/1¼ pints/3 cups water
45ml/3 tbsp olive oil
175g/6oz/1½ cups frozen baby broad
   (fava) beans, thawed and peeled
90ml/6 tbsp finely chopped fresh dill,
   plus fresh dill sprigs to garnish
5ml/1 tsp ground cinnamon
5ml/1 tsp ground cumin
2–3 saffron threads, soaked in 15ml/
   1 tbsp boiling water

1 Tip the soaked and drained rice into a large pan with the water. Add a little salt. Bring to the boil, then simmer very gently for 5 minutes. Drain, rinse in warm water and drain again

2 Pour 15ml/1 tbsp of the oil into the rinsed-out pan. Spoon enough rice into the pan to cover the base. Add one-quarter of the beans and a little dill.

3 Spread over another layer of rice, then a layer of beans and dill. Repeat the layers until all the beans and dill have been used, ending with a layer of rice. Cook over a gentle heat for 8 minutes, without stirring, until nearly tender.

4 Pour the remaining oil evenly over the rice, then sprinkle the ground cinnamon and cumin over the top. Cover the pan with a clean dishtowel or cloth and a tight-fitting lid, lifting the corners of the towel or cloth back over the lid. Cook over a low heat for 25–30 minutes.

5 Spoon about 45ml/3 tbsp of the cooked rice into the bowl of saffron water and then mix the rice and liquid together. Spoon the remaining rice mixture on to a large serving plate and spoon the saffron rice on one side to garnish. Serve immediately, decorated with fresh sprigs of dill.

NUTRITION NOTES	
Per portion:	
Energy	368Kcal/1531kJ
Fat	12.4g
saturated fat	11.6g
Carbohydrate	59.5g
Fibre	3.4g
Calcium	98.1mg

free from
✓ nuts
✓ dairy
✓ wheat
✓ seafood
✓ eggs
✓ yeast
✓ citrus
✓ alcohol

desserts

Eating to beat an allergy doesn't mean you have to miss out on dessert. If you fancy something a little indulgent then choose rich and creamy coconut ice cream – ideal if you have an allergy to dairy products – or deliciously aromatic figs and pears in honey, which is rich in vitamin C. If you prefer a refreshing, fruity dessert then go for gooseberry and elderflower sorbet with a subtle floral hint – it is the ideal choice for asthma and eczema sufferers – or try simple to prepare melon salad with sweet ginger syrup, a light fruit salad with ginger that has decongestive properties.

tropical scented red and orange fruit salad

| A COLOURFUL FRESH FRUIT SALAD rich in vitamin C, which can be beneficial for sufferers of asthma, eczema and hayfever because of its anti-inflammatory properties.

INGREDIENTS

Serves four

350–400g/12–14oz/3–3½ cups
   strawberries, hulled and halved
3 oranges, peeled and segmented
3 blood oranges, peeled and segmented
1–2 passion fruit
120ml/4fl oz/½ cup freshly squeezed
   orange juice
sugar to taste

free from

✓	nuts
✓	dairy
✓	wheat
✓	seafood
✓	eggs
✓	yeast
	citrus
✓	alcohol

VARIATION

Other fruit that can be added include pear, kiwi fruit and banana.

1 Put the strawberries and oranges into a serving bowl. Halve the passion fruit and spoon the flesh into the fruit.

2 Pour the orange juice over the fruit and add sugar to taste. Toss gently and then chill until ready to serve.

NUTRITION NOTES

Per portion:	
Energy	127Kcal/532kJ
Fat	0.4g
saturated fat	0g
Carbohydrate	29.5g
Fibre	4.8g
Calcium	114.4mg

melon salad
with sweet ginger syrup

THIS LIGHT AND REFRESHING FRUIT SALAD is a good source of vitamin C and betacarotene. Ginger is reputed to have decongestive properties.

INGREDIENTS

Serves four

¼ watermelon
½ honeydew melon
½ Charentais melon
60ml/4 tbsp syrup from a jar of preserved
  stem ginger

COOK'S TIPS

- For an even prettier effect, scoop the melon flesh into balls with the large end of a melon baller.
- Make sure the melons are ripe – they should have a strong scent.

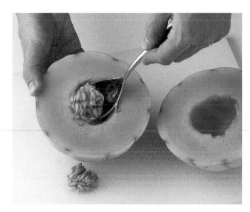

1 Remove the seeds from the melons, cut them into wedges, then slice off the rind.

2 Cut all the flesh into chunks and mix in a bowl. Stir in the ginger syrup, cover and chill until ready to serve.

NUTRITION NOTES

Per portion:

Energy	111Kcal/469kJ
Fat	0.4g
saturated fat	0g
Carbohydrate	27.4g
Fibre	0.8g
Calcium	23.8mg

free from

✓ nuts
✓ dairy
✓ wheat
✓ seafood
✓ eggs
✓ yeast
✓ citrus
✓ alcohol

figs and pears in honey

SIMPLY COOKED FRUIT makes a delicious and refreshing dessert. Pears make an excellent choice as very few people have an allergic response to them.

2 Place the lemon rind, honey, cinnamon stick, cardamom pod and the water in a pan and boil, uncovered, for about 10 minutes until reduced by about half.

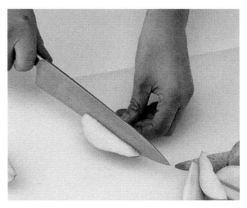

3 Cut the pears into eighths, discarding the core. Leave the peel on or discard as preferred. Place in the syrup, add the figs and simmer for about 5 minutes until the fruit is tender.

4 Transfer the fruit to a serving bowl. Continue cooking the liquid until syrupy, then discard the cinnamon stick and pour over the figs and pears.

VARIATION
The combination of pears and figs is delightful, but in autumn and winter you could make this dessert with just pears.

NUTRITION NOTES

Per portion:

Energy	150Kcal/629kJ
Fat	0.5g
saturated fat	0g
Carbohydrate	36.5g
Fibre	3.1g
Calcium	81.5mg

INGREDIENTS

Serves four

1 lemon
90ml/6 tbsp clear honey
1 cinnamon stick
1 cardamom pod
350ml/12fl oz/1½ cups water
2 pears
8 fresh figs, halved

free from
✓ nuts
✓ dairy
✓ wheat
✓ seafood
✓ eggs
✓ yeast
  citrus
✓ alcohol

COOK'S TIP
Choose a flavourful honey for this salad – look out for one of the flower- or herb-scented varieties.

1 Pare the rind from the lemon using a zester or vegetable peeler and cut it into very thin strips usig a small sharp knife.

spiced red fruit compote

A DELICIOUS DESSERT that is perfect in summer when fresh berries are in season. It is packed with vitamin C, which is essential for good health.

INGREDIENTS

Serves four

4 ripe red plums, halved
225g/8oz/2 cups strawberries, halved
  or quartered
225g/8oz/2 cups fresh or
  frozen raspberries
15ml/1 tbsp light brown sugar
1 cinnamon stick
3 pieces star anise
6 cloves

4 Cover the pan and let the fruit infuse over a very low heat for about 5 minutes. Remove the whole spices from the compote before serving.

COOK'S TIP

In winter, you can use frozen fruit for this dessert. It won't need extra water, as there are usually plenty of ice crystals clinging to the berries.

NUTRITION NOTES

Per portion:

Energy	62Kcal/262kJ
Fat	0.3g
saturated fat	0g
Carbohydrate	14.3g
Fibre	2.9g
Calcium	31.8mg

1 Place the fruit in a heavy pan with the sugar and 30ml/2 tbsp cold water.

2 Add the cinnamon stick, star anise and cloves to the pan.

3 Heat the fruit gently, without boiling, until the sugar dissolves and the fruit juices run.

free from

✓ nuts
✓ dairy
✓ wheat
✓ seafood
✓ eggs
✓ yeast
✓ citrus
✓ alcohol

summer fruit tofu cheesecake

THIS CREAMY CHEESECAKE is perfect for people with a dairy allergy as its made with tofu rather than cheese.

2 Tip the mixture into a 23cm/9in round flan tin (pie pan) and press down firmly. Leave to set.

3 To make the filling, place the tofu and yogurt in a food processor and process them until smooth. Soak the gelatine in the apple juice, then heat to dissolve. Stir into the tofu mixture.

4 Spread the tofu mixture over the chilled base, smoothing it evenly. Chill for an hour or two until the filling has set.

5 Carefully remove the flan tin and place the cheesecake on a serving plate.

6 Arrange the fruits on top of the cheesecake. Melt the redcurrant jelly with the hot water. Let it cool, and then spoon or brush over the fruit to serve.

INGREDIENTS

Serves six

425g/15oz tofu
300g/11oz sheep's milk yogurt
25ml/1½ tbsp/1½ sachets powdered
  gelatine
90ml/6 tbsp apple juice
175g/6oz/1¾ cups soft fruit, such as
  raspberries, strawberries and blueberries
30ml/2 tbsp redcurrant jelly
30ml/2 tbsp hot water

For the base

50g/2oz/4 tbsp dairy-free, low-fat spread
  or margarine
30ml/2 tbsp apple juice
115g/4oz/6 cups bran flakes

free from

✓ nuts
✓ dairy
  wheat
✓ seafood
✓ eggs
  yeast
✓ citrus
✓ alcohol

1 To make the base, place the low-fat spread or margarine and apple juice in a pan and heat them gently until the spread or margarine has melted. Crush the cereal and stir it into the juice mixture.

NUTRITION NOTES

Per portion:

Energy	181Kcal/761kJ
Fat	7.1g
saturated fat	1.9g
Carbohydrate	21.1g
Fibre	3.1g
Calcium	308.9mg

grilled pineapple with papaya sauce

| BROMELAIN, AN ENZYME FOUND in pineapple, has
anti-inflammatory properties and is recommended for asthmatics.

2 Line a baking sheet with foil, rolling up the sides to make a rim. Grease the foil with melted butter. Preheat the grill (broiler). Arrange the pineapple slices on the lined baking sheet. Brush with butter, then top with the ginger matchsticks, sugar and cinnamon. Drizzle over the stem ginger syrup. Grill (broil) for 5–7 minutes, or until the slices are golden and lightly charred on top.

3 Meanwhile, make the sauce. Cut a few slices from the papaya and set aside, then purée the rest with the apple juice in a food processor or blender.

4 Sieve the purée, then stir in any cooking juices from the pineapple. Serve the pineapple drizzled with the sauce and decorated with mint.

INGREDIENTS

Serves six

1 sweet pineapple
melted butter, for greasing
    and brushing
2 pieces drained stem ginger in syrup,
    cut into fine matchsticks, plus 30ml/
    2 tbsp of the syrup from the jar
30ml/2 tbsp demerara sugar
pinch of ground cinnamon
fresh mint sprigs, to decorate

For the sauce

1 ripe papaya, peeled and seeded
175ml/6fl oz/¾ cup apple juice

1 Peel the pineapple and cut spiral slices off the outside to remove the eyes. Cut it crossways into six 2.5cm/1in thick slices.

COOK'S TIP
Try the papaya sauce with grilled chicken.

NUTRITION NOTES

Per portion:

Energy	142Kcal/594kJ
Fat	1.8g
saturated fat	0.9g
Carbohydrate	32.6g
Fibre	3g
Calcium	51.7mg

free from
✓ nuts
  dairy
✓ wheat
✓ seafood
✓ eggs
✓ yeast
✓ citrus
✓ alcohol

gooseberry and elderflower sorbet

THIS LOW-FAT, DAIRY-FREE SORBET is an excellent choice for those who are looking to avoid ice cream and dairy-based sorbets.

INGREDIENTS

Serves six

130g/4½oz/⅔ cup granulated sugar
175ml/6fl oz/¾ cup water
10 elderflower heads
500g/1¼lb/4 cups gooseberries
200ml/7fl oz/scant 1 cup apple juice
elderflowers, to decorate

1 Put 30ml/2 tbsp of the sugar in a pan with 30ml/2 tbsp of the water. Set aside. Mix the remaining sugar and water in a separate, heavy saucepan. Heat gently, stirring occasionally, until the sugar has dissolved. Bring to a boil and boil for 1 minute, without stirring, to make a syrup.

2 Remove the pan from heat and add the elderflower heads, pressing them into the syrup with a wooden spoon. Leave to infuse for about 1 hour.

3 Strain the elderflower syrup through a sieve placed over a bowl. Set the syrup aside. Add the gooseberries to the pan containing the reserved sugar and water. Cover and cook very gently for about 5 minutes, until the gooseberries have softened.

4 Transfer to a food processor and add the apple juice. Process until smooth, then press through a sieve into a bowl. Let cool. Stir in the elderflower syrup and chill until very cold.

5 If making by hand, pour the mixture into a shallow container and freeze until thick, preferably overnight. If using an ice cream maker, churn the mixture until it holds its shape. Transfer to a freezerproof container and freeze for several hours or overnight. Scoop the sorbet carefully into the glasses, decorate with elderflowers and serve.

free from

✓ nuts
✓ dairy
✓ wheat
✓ seafood
✓ eggs
✓ yeast
✓ citrus
✓ alcohol

NUTRITION NOTES

Per portion:

Energy	114Kcal/485kJ
Fat	0.4g
saturated fat	0g
Carbohydrate	28.6g
Fibre	2g
Calcium	31.2mg

raspberry sorbet

THIS MOUTHWATERING DESSERT is low in fat and rich in vitamin C, which can help to eliminate histamines, boost the immune system and reduce inflammation.

5 After this time, beat it again. If using an ice cream maker, churn the mixture until it is thick but too soft to scoop. Scrape into a freezerproof container.

6 Crush the remaining raspberries between your fingers and add them to the partially frozen ice cream. Mix lightly, then return the ice cream to the freezer for a further 2–3 hours until firm. Scoop the ice cream into dishes and serve with the extra raspberries.

INGREDIENTS

Serves six

150g/5oz/¾ cup granulated sugar
150ml/5fl oz/⅔ cup water
500g/1¼lb/3 cups raspberries, plus extra to serve
450g/1lb/2 cups virtually fat-free fromage frais

1 Put the sugar and water in a pan and bring to the boil, stirring until the sugar has dissolved. Leave to cool.

2 Put 425g/15oz/2½ cups of the raspberries in a food processor or blender. Process into a purée, then press through a sieve placed over a large bowl to remove the seeds. Stir the sugar syrup into the raspberry purée and chill the mixture until it is very cold.

3 Add the fromage frais to the purée and whisk until smooth.

4 If making by hand, pour the mixture into a plastic or other freezerproof container and freeze for 4 hours, beating once with a fork, electric beater or in a food processor to break up the ice crystals.

COOK'S TIP

If you intend to make this in an ice cream maker, check your handbook before you begin churning as this recipe makes 800g/1¾lb/3¼ cups of mixture. If this is too much for your machine, make it in two batches or by hand.

NUTRITION NOTES

Per portion:	
Energy	163Kcal/693kJ
Fat	0.4g
saturated fat	0.1g
Carbohydrate	35.2g
Fibre	2.1g
Calcium	91.4mg

free from

✓ nuts
dairy
✓ wheat
✓ seafood
✓ eggs
✓ yeast
✓ citrus
✓ alcohol

coconut ice cream

RICH AND CREAMY COCONUT MILK is the perfect alternative for anyone avoiding cow's milk or cream.

2 Grate the limes finely, taking care to avoid the bitter pith. Squeeze them and pour the juice and rind into the pan of syrup. Add the coconut milk to the lime syrup in the pan.

3 If making by hand, pour the mixture into a plastic or other freezerproof container and freeze for 5–6 hours until firm, beating twice with a fork, electric beater or in a food processor to break up the crystals.

4 If using an ice cream maker, churn the mixture until firm enough to scoop.

5 Scoop the ice cream into wide glasses or small dishes and decorate with the toasted coconut shavings.

INGREDIENTS

Serves four

150ml/¼ pint/⅔ cup water
90g/3½oz/½ cup granulated sugar
2 limes
400ml/14fl oz can coconut milk
toasted coconut shavings, to decorate
  (see Cook's Tip)

free from
✓ nuts
✓ dairy
✓ wheat
✓ seafood
✓ eggs
✓ yeast
  citrus
✓ alcohol

COOK'S TIP
Use the flesh from a coconut to make a pretty decoration. Rinse the flesh with cold water and cut off thin slices using a vegetable peeler. Toast the slices under a medium grill until the coconut has curled and turned golden.

1 Put the water in a small pan. Add the sugar and bring to the boil, stirring constantly, until the sugar has all dissolved. Remove the pan from heat and leave the syrup to cool, then chill well.

NUTRITION NOTES

Per portion:	
Energy	280Kcal/1178kJ
Fat	19.2g
saturated fat	16.4g
Carbohydrate	26.8g
Fibre	0.6g
Calcium	43.5mg

damson ice

TRY THIS WONDERFULLY SIMPLE dessert for the perfect end to any meal. Enjoy it when damsons are in season.

INGREDIENTS

Serves six

500g/1¼lb/2¼ cups ripe damsons, washed
450ml/¾ pint/scant 2 cups water
130g/4½oz/⅔ cup granulated sugar

1 Put the damsons into a pan and add 150ml/¼ pint/⅔ cup of the water. Cover and simmer for 10 minutes or until the damsons are tender

2 Pour the remaining water into a second pan. Add the sugar and bring to the boil, stirring until the sugar has dissolved. Pour the syrup into a bowl, leave to cool, then chill.

3 Break up the cooked damsons in the pan with a wooden spoon and scoop out any stones (pits). Pour the fruit and juices into a large sieve set over a bowl. Press the fruit through the sieve and discard the skins and any remaining stones from the sieve.

4 If making by hand, pour the damson purée into a shallow plastic container. Stir in the syrup and freeze for 6 hours, beating once or twice to break up the ice crystals. If using an ice cream maker, mix the purée with the syrup and churn until firm enough to scoop.

5 Spoon the ice cream into tall glasses or dishes and serve immediately.

VARIATIONS

Apricot ice can be made in the same way. Flavour the water ice with cinnamon by adding a broken cinnamon stick to the pan when poaching the fruit.

NUTRITION NOTES

Per portion:
Energy	114Kcal/473kJ
Fat	0g
saturated fat	0g
Carbohydrate	29.9g
Fibre	1.3g
Calcium	29.1mg

free from
✓ nuts
✓ dairy
✓ wheat
✓ seafood
✓ eggs
✓ yeast
✓ citrus
✓ alcohol

further information

USEFUL ADDRESSES

AUSTRALIA

ASCIA (Australasian Society of Clinical Immunology and Allergy)
ASCIA is the peak professional body of Clinical Allergists and Immunologists in Australia and New Zealand.
PO Box 450
Balgowlah
NSW Australia 2093
Email: education@allergy.org.au
Website: www.allergy.org.au

Asthma Australia
State/Territory Asthma Foundations
Free Call: 1800 645 130
Website: www.asthmaaustralia.org.au

Food Anaphylactic Children Training Support (FACTS)
Tel: 61 29913 7793
Website: www.allergyfacts.org.au

Institute of Respiratory Medicine
University of Sydney
Tel: 61 2 9515 8710
Website: www.irm.usyd.edu.au

CANADA

Alberta Lung Association
P.O. Box 4500
Station South
Edmonton
AB T6E 6K2
Tel: 780 407 6819
Toll Free: 1 800 931 9111
   or 1 888 566 5864
Health Ed Line: 1 800 661 5864
Fax: 780-407-6829
Email: info@ab.lung.ca

Allergy Home Care Products
P.O. Box 2471
Silver Spring
MD 20915
Tel: 800 327 4382
E-mail: ahcp@aol.com
Website: www.ahcp.com

Asthma Society of Canada
130 Bridgeland Avenue, Suite 425
Toronto
Ontario, M6A 1Z4
Toll Free: 1 800 787 3880
Tel: 416 787 4050
Fax: 416 787 5807
Website: www.asthma.ca

The Food Allergy & Anaphylaxis Network
10400 Eaton Place, Suite 107
Fairfax, VA 22030-2208
Tel: 800 929 4040
Fax: 703 691 2713
E-mail: faan@foodallergy.org

The National Asthma and Allergy Network
10875 Main Street, Suite 210
Fairfax
VA 22030
Tel: 703 385 4031

Ontario Lung Association
573 King Street East, Suite 201
Toronto
Ontario M5A 4L3
Toll Free: 1 800 972-2636
Tel: 416 864 9911
e-mail: olalung@on.lung.ca

NEW ZEALAND

Asthma and Respiratory Foundation of New Zealand
National Office
P. O. Box 1459
Wellington
Tel: 04-499 4592
Email: arf@asthmanz.co.nz
Website: www.asthmanz.co.nz

Asthma New Zealand
Asthma Society Inc Auckland
581 Mt Eden Rd
Mt Eden
Tel: 09 623 0236
Email: aas@asthma-nz.org.nz

Allergy New Zealand
Box 56–117
Dominion Rd
Auckland
Helpline: 09 303 2024
Toll Free: 0 800 34 0800
Tel: 09 623 3912
Fax: 09 623 0091
Email: mail@allergy.org.nz
Website: www/help@allergy.org.nz

SOUTH AFRICA

Allergy Society Of South
  Africa (ALLSA)
P.O. BOX 88
Observatory, 7735
Capetown
Tel: 27 21 479019
Fax: 27 21 4480846
E-mail: allsa@gem.co.sa

UNITED KINGDOM

The British Allergy Foundation
Deepdene House
30 Bellegrove Road
Welling
Kent DA16 3PY
Helpline: 020 8303 8583
Tel: 02083038525
E-mail: allergybaf@compuserve.com
Website: www.allergyfoundation.com

The National Asthma Campaign
Providence House
Providence Place
London N1 0NT
Helpline: 0845 701 0203
Tel: 020 7226 2260
Fax: 020 7704 0740
Website: www.asthma.org.uk

The National Asthma Campaign
  Scotland
2a North Charlotte Street
Edinburgh EH2 4HR
Tel: 0131 226 2544
Fax: 0131 226 2401

National Eczema Society
Hill House
Highgate Hill
London N19 5NA
Helpline: 0870 241 3604
Tel: 020 7281 3553
Fax : 020 7281 6395

NATIONAL SOCIETY FOR CLEAN AIR
  & ENVIRONMENTAL PROTECTION
Address: 163 North Street, Brighton,
  BN1 1RG
Telephone: 01273 326313
Fax: 01273 892503
E-mail: admin@nsca.org.uk
Website: www.greenchannel.com/nsca

UNITED STATES

Allergy and Asthma
Mothers of Asthmatics, Inc.
2751 Prosperity Ave., Suite 150
Fairfax, Virginia 22031
Tel: 703-641-9595
Fax: 703-573-7794
E-mail: aanma@aol.com

Allergy Control Products
Specializing in anti-allergen bedding HEPA
air purifiers and vacuum cleaners.
96 Danbury Road
Ridgefield, CT 06877
Tel: 203 438 9580
Website: www.achooallergy.com

American Lung Association
  of California
424 Pendleton Way
Oakland, CA 94631
Tel: 510 638 5864
Fax: 510 638 8984
E-mail: contact@california lung.org
Website: www.californialung.org

Asthma and Allergy Foundation
  of America
1125 15th Street N.W., Suite 502
Washington, DC 20005
Tel: 202 466 7643
Fax: 800 878 4403
Website: www.aafa.org

The National Asthma Education
  Program
National Heart, Lung and Blood Institute
NHLBI Information Centre
P.O. Box 30105
Bethesda
MD 20824-0105
Tel: 301 951 3260
Email: NHLBInfo@rover.nhlbi.nih.gov

index

150 desserts:
pastries, bakes, cakes, tarts and pies

150 desserts:
pastries, bakes, cakes, tarts and pies

From carrot cake to apple and orange pie, and from chocolate cheesecake to raspberry and lemon tartlets – an array of deliciously tempting ideas for all dessert occasions

Edited by Ann Kay

southwater

This edition is published by Southwater, an imprint of Anness Publishing Ltd, Hermes House, 88–89 Blackfriars Road, London SE1 8HA; tel. 020 7401 2077; fax 020 7633 9499

www.southwaterbooks.com; www.annesspublishing.com

If you like the images in this book and would like to investigate using them for publishing, promotions or advertising, please visit our website www.practicalpictures.com for more information.

UK agent: The Manning Partnership Ltd;
tel. 01225 478444; fax 01225 478440; sales@manning-partnership.co.uk

UK distributor: Grantham Book Services Ltd;
tel. 01476 541080; fax 01476 541061; orders@gbs.tbs-ltd.co.uk

North American agent/distributor: National Book Network;
tel. 301 459 3366; fax 301 429 5746; www.nbnbooks.com

Australian agent/distributor: Pan Macmillan Australia;
tel. 1300 135 113; fax 1300 135 103; customer.service@macmillan.com.au

New Zealand agent/distributor: David Bateman Ltd;
tel. (09) 415 7664; fax (09) 415 8892

Publisher: Joanna Lorenz
Editorial Director: Helen Sudell
Editors: Ann Kay and Elizabeth Woodland
Copy-editor: Julia Canning
Design: Diane Pullen and Design Principals
Cover Design: Adelle Morris
Production Controller: Claire Rae

© Anness Publishing Ltd 2007

Previously published as part of a larger volume, *500 Desserts*

Main front cover image shows Tangy Raspberry & Lemon Tartlets – for recipe, see page 61

Ethical Trading Policy

At Anness Publishing we believe that business should be conducted in an ethical and ecologically sustainable way, with respect for the environment and a proper regard to the replacement of the natural resources we employ.
As a publisher, we use a lot of wood pulp to make high-quality paper for printing, and that wood commonly comes from spruce trees. We are therefore currently growing more than 500,000 trees in two Scottish forest plantations near Aberdeen – Berrymoss (130 hectares/320 acres) and West Touxhill (125 hectares/305 acres). The forests we manage contain twice the number of trees employed each year in paper-making for our books.
Because of this ongoing ecological investment programme, you, as our customer, can have the pleasure and reassurance of knowing that a tree is being cultivated on your behalf to naturally replace the materials used to make the book you are holding.
Our forestry programme is run in accordance with the UK Woodland Assurance Scheme (UKWAS) and will be certified by the internationally recognized Forest Stewardship Council (FSC). The FSC is a non-government organization dedicated to promoting responsible management of the world's forests. Certification ensures forests are managed in an environmentally sustainable and socially responsible basis. For further information about this scheme, go to www.annesspublishing.com/trees

Notes

Bracketed terms are intended for American readers.
For all recipes, quantities are given in both metric and imperial measures and, where appropriate, in standard cups and spoons. Follow one set of measures, but not a mixture, because they are not interchangeable.
Standard spoon and cup measures are level.
1 tsp = 5ml, 1 tbsp = 15ml, 1 cup = 250ml/8fl oz.
Australian standard tablespoons are 20ml. Australian readers should use 3 tsp in place of 1 tbsp for measuring small quantities.
American pints are 16fl oz/2 cups. American readers should use 20fl oz/2.5 cups in place of 1 pint when measuring liquids.
Electric oven temperatures in this book are for conventional ovens. When using a fan oven, the temperature will probably need to be reduced by about 10–20°C/20–40°F. Since ovens vary, you should check with your manufacturer's instruction book for guidance.
The nutritional analysis given for each recipe is calculated per portion (i.e. serving or item), unless otherwise stated. If the recipe gives a range, such as Serves 4–6, then the nutritional analysis will be for the smaller portion size, i.e. 6 servings. Measurements for sodium do not include salt added to taste. Medium (US large) eggs are used unless otherwise stated.

Important: pregnant women, the elderly, the ill and very young children should avoid recipes using raw or lightly cooked eggs.

Contents

Introduction

Desserts are always popular, whether they are sumptuous creations or the simplest of dishes. Indeed, a well-chosen dessert is guaranteed to round off a meal on a high note and can turn even the most ordinary meal into a memorable occasion. As a finale, a mouthwatering fruit tart, a spicy peach crumble or a luxurious chocolate cheesecake will delight guests and give you, the cook, great satisfaction.

Whether you are planning an elaborate dinner party or an everyday family meal, the key to success is to make sure that the dessert you select balances perfectly with the main course. If you are serving a filling or rich main course you will need to choose a delicate or fruity option to follow, while you can afford to indulge in a rich, creamy dessert if you opt for a light main dish. With the fantastic selection of recipes featured in this book, you will never be at a loss for ideas to create a perfectly balanced menu.

The other factors that might affect your choice of dessert, such as seasonal availability and the amount of time you have for preparation, are also catered for in this collection. Many of the desserts can be made a day or two in advance, while others can be started early in the day and finished off just before you eat, ready to serve whenever you need them. When it comes to successful entertaining, the more preparation you can do ahead, the better, as this

will give you more time to relax and enjoy the meal with your guests instead of being in the kitchen. However, there's also a wide choice of quick-to-make recipes that can be rustled up in a matter of minutes. In addition, whatever the season, you'll find a recipe to suit the time of year, and with the wide variety of tropical ingredients now available in the stores, there's a range of exciting dishes that will add an exotic flavour to your meals.

As a back-up to the recipes in this book, the introductory pages provide helpful information on preparing and baking pastry for pies and tarts, plus an invaluable guide to preparing fruit, from making perfect orange segments to creating delicate decorations. There are also ideas for easy dessert sauces to help you whip up instant desserts, plus clever presentation methods that will help you to achieve professional finishing touches. All the recipes in this book have clear, step-by-step instructions, so that even dishes that are commonly regarded as tricky, such as truffles

and roulades, are easy to make and will look and taste delicious. The important thing is to read the whole recipe through before you start, so that you understand all the steps involved and can plan the preparation properly. A large number of recipes have helpful Cook's Tips and Variations boxes, offering advice on specific aspects of a dish or interesting alternatives to get your imagination going or to help out when you don't necessarily have all the specified ingredients to hand.

The recipe chapters feature over 150 tempting dishes, grouped under helpful categories such as Cakes and Bakes, Perfect Pies, Tempting Tarts and Posh Pastries and Accompaniments. Within each chapter, you will find a selection of popular classics and more unusual recipes that are destined to become new family favourites. Many of the recipes feature a colour photograph, showing the finished dessert so you can see what you are aiming to achieve.

Have fun leafing through these pages at any time of year and for any occasion. For summer days you can't go wrong with a lovely Raspberry Tart or a Maple and Walnut Meringue Gâteau, while Hot Plum Batter Pudding or a classic Apple and Cranberry Lattice Pie are warming choices for winter. For entertaining, try a Marbled Swiss Roll, or individual Fruit Tartlets made with a divine chocolate pastry are sure to impress. International classics range from Greek Honey and Lemon Cake to Boston Banoffee Pie, and baked delights from a White Chocolate Cheesecake to Peach and Blueberry Pie. Whether you are a novice or an experienced chef, are in a hurry, on a budget, preparing a mid-week family meal or catering for a lavish or important event, this ultimate dessert collection will provide all the answers, and indulge every taste.

Working with Pastry

Making your own pastry may seem daunting at first, but if you follow a few basic rules and stick to the right quantities, you will soon find the technique easy. The key is not to hurry and to keep your hands cool when handling the dough. The crisp, light results are always worth the effort and the popularity of your home-made tarts and pies will be truly satisfying.

SHORTCRUST PASTRY

With shortcrust pastry and its variations, once the dough has been formed into a ball, it is usually chilled for about 20 minutes to make handling easier. After the pastry has been rolled out and used to line a tin (pan), it should be chilled again to minimize shrinkage during baking. A filled tart or pie needs only about 30 minutes otherwise the pastry will turn soggy. An empty shell, prior to blind baking, can be chilled for longer.

Heating the Oven

Whatever type of pastry you are baking, always allow time to preheat the oven; it will take about 15 minutes to reach the required temperature (fan ovens may heat more quickly). If you are baking blind or cooking a double-crust pie, it's a good idea to put a heavy baking sheet in the oven to heat up. The hot baking sheet will give the base of the pie an initial blast of heat to help keep the base crisp. It will also make it easier to slide the dish in and out of the oven.

Baking Shortcrust Pastry

Shortcrust pastries are usually baked at 200°C/400°F/Gas 6, but the temperature is often reduced part-way through baking to allow the filling to cook sufficiently. As a general rule, bake pastry in the middle of the oven, or just above the middle, unless the recipe tells you otherwise. Take care with pastries that contain added sugar; they should be removed from the oven as soon as they are golden, because they can burn quickly at this stage.

Baking Rules

When following a recipe, baking times may vary slightly depending on your oven and how chilled the pie was before cooking. Always check the pie at least 5 minutes before the end of the suggested cooking time. Don't keep opening the oven door though, or the temperature will drop and the pastry will not be as crisp. Avoid cooking the pastry with other foods that release a lot of steam as this also prevents a crisp result.

Baking Blind

This process is used for a number of reasons. It is used to partly cook an empty pastry case so that it does not become soggy when the filling is added and the final baking is done. It is also used to completely bake a pastry case when the filling cooks in a relatively short time and you need to ensure that the pastry is fully cooked through. The process is also required when the pastry case is to contain a precooked mixture or an uncooked filling. Lining the pastry case with baking parchment or foil and filling it with baking beans stops the pastry from rising up during cooking.

1 Cut out a round of baking parchment or foil about 7.5cm/3in larger than the flan tin (tart pan). Prick the base of the pastry all over with a fork.

2 Lay the baking parchment or foil in the pastry case and press it smoothly over the base and up the side.

3 Put either the commercially made ceramic baking beans, or dried beans or peas, in the case, spreading them out evenly to cover the base. Whichever kind you choose, they can be used over and over again.

4 To partially bake the pastry, bake in an oven preheated to 200°C/400°F/Gas 6 for 15 minutes, or until the pastry is set and the rim is dry and golden. Remove and lift out the paper and beans. Return the case to the oven for a further 5 minutes. The pastry case can now be filled and the baking completed.

5 For fully baked pastry, bake the case at 200°C/400°F/Gas 6 for 15 minutes, then remove the paper and beans and return to the oven. Bake for a further 5–10 minutes, or until golden brown. Cool completely before filling.

6 To bake tartlets, bake blind in the same way as flans, but allow only 6–8 minutes for partial baking, and 12–15 minutes for fully baked pastry.

Cook's Tip

Fully baked pastry cases, both large and small, may be baked up to two days ahead if carefully stored in airtight containers. Interleave them with greaseproof (waxed) paper, or use baking parchment, if you are keeping several, and always make sure that they are cooled before storing.

Cook's Tips

• *When moving rolled-out pastry dough to line a tin (pan) or dish or top a pie, roll the dough loosely around the rolling pin, lift up, then carefully unroll it on top of the container. Press gently in place.*

• *If you find any small holes in a cooked pastry case, repair them by brushing with a little beaten egg, then return the case to the oven for 2–3 minutes to seal. Any larger holes or tears that appear during baking should be repaired by pressing a little raw pastry in the gap, brushing with beaten egg, and then returning to the oven.*

• *If the pastry starts to bubble up during baking, remove from the oven, prick again with a fork to allow the trapped air to escape and return to the oven. If it has bubbled up when you take it out after cooking, don't try to press it flat, or you will crack the pastry. Make a very small slit in the case with a knife and leave it to shrink back on its own.*

• *If the pastry becomes fully browned before the filling has cooked through completely, then you should protect it by covering with foil. Cover single or double-crust pies completely, but make a hole in the top of the foil to allow the steam to escape. When baking open flans, cover the pastry edge only – by using strips of foil.*

PUFF PASTRY

The baking method for puff, rough puff and flaky pastry has much in common with that used for shortcrust. Chilling the pastry before baking is essential, and shaped puff pastries should be chilled for at least an hour to prevent the pastry becoming mis-shapen during baking. Take great care when brushing the pastry with egg glaze; any that runs down the sides of the pastry will make the layers stick together and prevent the pastry from rising well and evenly.

Oven Temperature

This type of pastry must be cooked in a preheated hot oven, so that the air trapped within the layers expands and lifts up the pastry. If the oven is too cool, the butter will melt before the dough has a chance to cook, and the pastry will not rise well. The oven temperature is usually 230°C/450°F/Gas 8, but small pastries are sometimes cooked at 220°C/425°F/Gas 7. Reduce the temperature after about 15 minutes, to give the filling time to cook through.

Releasing Steam

When baking puff pastry pies, up to three slits or holes (depending how moist the filling is) should be made in the pastry top to allow the steam from the filling to escape. Don't make too many steam holes though, or too much air will be lost and the pastry won't rise well. After baking, cover steam holes with cooked pastry decorations.

Unlike shortcrust pastries, a steamy atmosphere helps the puff pastry to rise. Put a dish of hot water on the lowest shelf when preheating the oven. Remove it for the last few minutes of cooking. If the pastry starts to sink after cooking, it hasn't cooked sufficiently and should be returned to the oven for a little longer.

FILO PASTRY

Unlike shortcrust and puff pastries, filo pastry does not require chilling before baking. The most important point to remember is that filo must never dry out, or it will become brittle and hard to fold and shape. Keep the sheets you are not working with covered with a damp dish towel. It may also crumble if it is too cold so, before using, remove the unopened packet from the refrigerator and allow to stand for 1 hour.

Filo must always be lightly brushed with melted butter before baking to give it a shiny glaze; unsalted (sweet) butter is ideal because it has a lower water content than ordinary butter, or oil can also be used. Choose a mild-flavoured oil when making sweet pastries as you do not want the flavour of the oil to overpower delicate tastes. Be careful not to overdo the melted fat; it should be brushed as thinly and evenly as possible to create light crisp layers. Never brush filo with egg or milk as this would make it soggy.

Oven Temperature

The usual temperature for baking filo pastry is 200°C/400°F/Gas 6, although it can be cooked at a slightly lower temperature without its crisp texture being affected. Filo pastry colours very quickly, so always check frequently towards the end of the cooking time. If the pastry has browned sufficiently before the filling is cooked, cover it loosely with foil, then remove again for the last few minutes to make sure the top of the pie is dry and crisp.

Leftover Filo Pastry

Wrap any unused filo in clear film (plastic wrap) and return it to the refrigerator. It will keep for seven to ten days. It is possible to re-freeze filo, but don't do this more than once.

Preparing Fruit

Fresh fruit provides the perfect base for all manner of delicious and healthy desserts. To make the most of the different types of fruit, there are certain preparation techniques that will always be useful, whether you are making a fresh fruit salad or creating a more elaborate dessert. For professional results, just follow the step instructions below.

BUYING FRUIT

Obviously, the best time to buy fruit is when it is fully ripe and at its peak. The exceptions are fruits such as bananas and pears, which ripen quickly and can therefore be bought in an under-ripe condition and allowed to ripen fully at home. You are most likely to find top-quality fruits in markets and shops that have a quick turnover of fresh produce, preferably with a daily delivery. Although most fruits are now available almost all the year round, they are nearly always best and cheapest when in season in the country of origin. Only buy as much fruit as you need at one time so that it remains fresh and appetizing.

PREPARING FRUIT

For some fruits, the only preparation needed is washing or wiping with a damp cloth; others must be peeled, cored, stoned (pitted) or seeded. Wash fruit only just before using. If necessary, cut away any bruised or damaged parts.

Peeling Firm Fruit

Some firm fruits, such as eating apples and pears, can be served raw without peeling. For cooking, peeling is often necessary. Pare off the skin as thinly as possible to avoid losing the valuable nutrients under the skin.

1 To peel fruit, first wash it and then pat it dry by using kitchen paper. Use a small, sharp paring knife or a vegetable peeler to pare off the skin in long, thin vertical strips all round the fruit, making sure that you cut into the fruit as thinly as possible. Pears in particular are best peeled by this method.

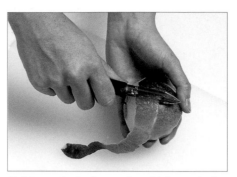

2 Alternatively, for apples, thinly peel all round the fruit in a spiral.

Coring Firm Fruit

1 To core whole apples and pears, place the sharp edge of a corer over the stem end of the fruit.

2 Press the corer down firmly into the fruit, and then twist it slightly; the core, complete with all of the pips (seeds), should come away in the centre of the corer. Now push out the corer from the handle end to remove the complete core cleanly.

Cook's Tips
Storage methods depend on the type of fruit, but there are some basic guidelines:
• Do not wash fruit before storing, but only when ready to use.
• Store fruit at the bottom of the refrigerator or in the salad crisper.
• Do not refrigerate unripe fruit; keep it at room temperature or in a cool, dark place, depending on the variety.
• Fragile fruits such as summer berries are easily squashed during storage, so spread them out in a single layer on a tray lined with kitchen paper.

Segmenting Firm Fruit

1 Halve the fruit lengthways, then cut into quarters or segments.

2 Now cut out the central core and pips using a small, sharp knife, taking care not to cut yourself as you work the knife towards you.

Cook's Tip
Some fruits, such as apples, pears and bananas, quickly oxidize and turn brown when exposed to the air. To prevent discoloration, brush cut fruits with lemon juice. Alternatively, acidulate a bowl of cold water by stirring in the juice of half a lemon. Drop the cut fruits into the bowl immediately after preparing.

Peeling Citrus Fruit

It is very important to remove all of the bitter white pith that lies just beneath the rind of citrus fruits.

1 To peel firm-skinned fruits, hold the fruit over a bowl to catch the juice and use a sharp knife to cut off the rind.

2 Alternatively, cut a slice off the top and bottom of the fruit, place on a board and, cutting downwards, slice off the rind in strips.

3 For loose-skinned fruit, such as tangerines, pierce the skin with your forefinger at the stalk end and peel off the rind. Pull off all the white shreds adhering to the fruit.

Segmenting Citrus Fruit

1 Using a small serrated knife, cut down between the membranes enclosing the segments; ease out the flesh.

Grating Citrus Fruit

1 For finely grated rind, grate the fruit against the fine face of a grater. Remove only the coloured rind; if you grate too deeply into the peel, you will be in danger of including the bitter white pith.

2 For thinly pared strips of rind, use a cannelle knife (zester) or vegetable peeler, then cut into shreds if necessary.

Decorating with Citrus Fruit

1 To make thick julienne strips of rind, cut lengthways, using a cannelle knife.

2 To make twists, slice the fruits thinly, cut to the centre, then twist the ends in opposite directions to make an S-shape.

Peeling Soft Fruit

Fruits such as peaches, nectarines and apricots can be peeled with a sharp paring knife, but this may waste some of the delicious flesh. It is better to loosen the skins by dipping them briefly in boiling water.

1 To remove the skins quickly and cleanly from peaches, nectarines and apricots, start by making a tiny nick in the skin, using the point of a sharp knife. This is done in order to help the skins spring off the flesh when the fruits are immersed in water. Take care when you are handling the soft fruit as the flesh can be easily damaged by clutching the fruit too firmly.

2 Cover with boiling water and leave for 15–30 seconds, depending on the ripeness of the fruit. Remove the fruit with a slotted spoon and peel off the skin, which should come away easily.

Removing Stones (Pits) and Seeds

1 Cut all round the fruit through the seam. Twist the halves in opposite directions, then lever out the stone (pit).

2 To pit cherries, simply place a cherry in a cherry stoner and then push the bar firmly into the fruit. The pit will be neatly ejected.

3 To remove the seeds from grapes, first cut the grapes in half, and then pick out the tiny pips using the tip of a small sharp knife.

4 To remove either papaya or melon seeds, you should first cut the fruit in half using a sharp knife, and then neatly scoop out all of the seeds with a spoon.

Dessert Sauces

Fresh custards and flavoured sweet white sauces are classic dessert sauces, but quick and easy dessert toppings can be made almost instantly from ready-made ingredients. These are ideal to serve over scoops of ice cream or with crêpes to create no-fuss desserts. Simple sauces can also be used imaginatively to create special finishing touches to desserts.

USING VANILLA PODS (BEANS)

Vanilla pods are often used in sweet dessert sauces – most commonly to flavour milk, cream or sugar.

Vanilla Infusions

1 To infuse (steep) vanilla flavour into milk or cream for a sauce, put the milk or cream in a pan, add the whole vanilla pod and heat gently over a low heat until almost boiling. Remove from the heat, cover and leave to stand for 10 minutes. Remove the pod, rinse and dry; it may be re-used several times.

2 To get maximum flavour, use a sharp knife to slit the pod lengthways, then open it out. Use the tip of the knife to scrape out the sticky black seeds inside: add to the hot sauce.

Vanilla Sugar

Many dessert sauces benefit from the delicate flavour of vanilla-flavoured sugar. This is available ready-made from shops but it is easy to make your own version.

1 To make vanilla sugar, simply bury a vanilla pod in a jar of white sugar. Cover tightly for a few weeks until the sugar takes on the vanilla flavour. Shake the jar occasionally.

SPEEDY SAUCES FOR TOPPING ICE CREAM

Store-cupboard (pantry) ingredients can often be transformed into irresistible sauces to spoon on top of ice cream.

Marshmallow Melt

1 Melt 90g/3½oz marshmallows with 30ml/2 tbsp milk or cream in a small pan. Add a little grated nutmeg and stir until smooth. Serve immediately.

Black Forest Sauce

1 Drain a can of black cherries, reserving the juice. Blend a little of the juice with a little arrowroot or cornflour (cornstarch).

2 Add the cornflour mixture to the rest of the juice in a pan. Stir until boiling and lightly thickened, then add the cherries and a dash of kirsch and heat through.

Raspberry Coulis

1 Purée some thawed frozen raspberries, with icing (confectioners') sugar to taste, then press through a sieve (strainer).

2 Blend a little cornflour (cornstarch) with some orange juice, and stir into the purée; cook for 2 minutes until thick. Cool.

Chocolate-Toffee Sauce

1 Chop a Mars bar and heat very gently in a pan, stirring until just melted. Spoon over scoops of vanilla ice cream and sprinkle with chopped nuts.

Marmalade Whisky Sauce

1 Heat 60ml/4 tbsp chunky marmalade in a pan with 30ml/2 tbsp whisky, until just melted. Allow to bubble for a few seconds then spoon over ice cream.

Nutty Butterscotch Sauce

1 Melt 75g/3oz/6 tbsp butter and 175g/6oz/¾ cup soft dark brown sugar in a heavy pan, then bring to the boil and boil for 2 minutes. Cool the mixture for 5 minutes.

2 Heat 175ml/6fl oz/¾ cup evaporated (unsweetened condensed) milk to just below boiling point, then gradually stir into the sugar mixture. Cook over a low heat for 2 minutes, stirring frequently.

3 Spread 50g/2oz/½ cup hazelnuts on a baking sheet and toast under a hot grill (broiler). Turn them on to a clean dish towel and rub off the skins. Chop the nuts roughly and stir into the sauce.

PRESENTATION IDEAS

When you've made a delicious sauce for a special dessert, why not make more of it by using it for decoration on the plate, too? Try one of the following simple ideas to make your sauce into a talking point. Individual slices of desserts, cakes or tarts, or a stuffed baked peach, look especially good served with sauce presented in this way.

Marbling

Use this technique when you have two contrasting sauces of a similar thickness, such as a fruit purée with cream or thin fresh custard.

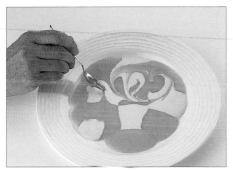

1 Spoon alternate spoonfuls of the two sauces on to a serving plate or shallow dish. Using a spoon, stir the sauces lightly together, gently swirling to create a marbled effect.

Yin-Yang Sauces

This oriental pattern is ideal for two contrasting colours of purée or coulis, such as a raspberry and a mango fruit coulis. It is important to make sure that the flavours of the sauce complement one another.

1 Spoon a sauce on one side of a serving plate or shallow bowl. Add the second sauce to the other side, then gently push the two sauces together with the spoon, swirling one around the other, to make a yin-yang shape.

Drizzling

1 Pour a smooth sauce or coulis into a container or tube with a fine pouring lip.

2 Drizzle the sauce in droplets or fine wavy lines on to the plate around the area where the dessert will sit.

Piping Outlines

1 Spoon a small amount of fruit coulis or chocolate sauce into a piping (pastry) bag fitted with a plain writing nozzle.

2 Carefully pipe the outline of a simple shape on to a serving plate, then spoon in the same sauce to fill the space within the outline.

Feathering Hearts

1 Flood the plate with a smooth sauce such as chocolate sauce or fruit purée. Add small droplets of pouring cream into it at intervals.

2 Draw the tip of a small knife through the droplets of cream, to drag each drop into a heart.

QUICK SAUCES FOR CRÊPES

Give crêpes and pancakes a lift with these three easy ideas.

Rich Butterscotch Sauce

1 Heat 75g/3oz/6 tbsp butter, 175g/6oz/¾ cup soft light brown sugar and 30ml/2 tbsp golden (light corn) syrup in a pan over a low heat until melted.

2 Remove from the heat and add 75ml/5 tbsp double (heavy) cream, stirring constantly, until smooth.

Orange Caramel Sauce

1 Melt 25g/1oz/2 tbsp unsalted (sweet) butter in a heavy pan. Stir in 50g/2oz/¼ cup caster (superfine) sugar and cook until golden brown.

2 Add the juice of 2 oranges and ½ lemon; stir until the caramel has dissolved.

Summer Berry Sauce

1 Melt 25g/1oz/2 tbsp butter in a frying pan. Add 50g/2oz/¼ cup caster (superfine) sugar and cook until golden.

2 Add the juice of 2 oranges and the rind of ½ orange and cook until syrupy. Add 350g/12oz/3 cups mixed summer berries and warm through.

3 Add 45ml/3 tbsp orange-flavoured liqueur and set alight. Serve immediately.

Tuscan Citrus Sponge

This tangy cake comes from the little Tuscan town of Pitigliano. It is a light whisked sponge made with matzo and potato flours rather than traditional wheat flour.

Serves 6–8

12 eggs, separated
300g/11oz/1½ cups caster (superfine) sugar
120ml/4fl oz/½ cup fresh orange juice

grated rind of 1 orange
grated rind of 1 lemon
50g/2oz/½ cup potato flour, sifted
90g/3½oz/¾ cup fine matzo meal or matzo meal flour, sifted
icing (confectioners') sugar, for dusting
orange juice and segments of orange, to serve

1 Preheat the oven to 160°C/325°F/Gas 3. Whisk the egg yolks until pale and frothy, then whisk in the sugar, orange juice, orange rind and lemon rind.

2 Fold the sifted flours or flour and meal into the egg and sugar mixture. In a clean bowl, whisk the egg whites until stiff, then fold into the egg yolk mixture.

3 Pour the cake mixture into a deep, ungreased 25cm/10in cake tin (pan) and bake for about 1 hour, or until a cocktail stick (toothpick), inserted in the centre, comes out clean. Leave to cool in the tin.

4 When cold, turn out the cake and invert on to a serving plate. Dust with a little icing sugar and serve in wedges with orange segments, moistened with a little fresh orange juice.

Cook's Tips
• When testing to see if the cake is cooked, if you don't have a cocktail stick (toothpick) to hand, use a strand of raw dried spaghetti instead – it will work just as well.
• If you cannot find matzo meal, try fine polenta instead.

Greek Yogurt & Fig Cake

Baked fresh figs, thickly sliced, make a delectable base for a featherlight sponge. Figs that are a bit on the firm side work best for this particular recipe. Serve with yogurt as a finale to a Greek-style meal.

Serves 6–8

6 firm fresh figs, thickly sliced
45ml/3 tbsp clear honey, plus extra for glazing cooked figs
200g/7oz/scant 1 cup butter, softened, plus extra for greasing

175g/6oz/¾ cup caster (superfine) sugar
grated rind of 1 lemon
grated rind of 1 orange
4 eggs, separated
225g/8oz/2 cups plain (all-purpose) flour
5ml/1 tsp baking powder
5ml/1 tsp bicarbonate of soda (baking soda)
250ml/8fl oz/1 cup Greek (US strained plain) yogurt

1 Preheat the oven to 180°C/350°F/Gas 4. Grease a 23cm/9in cake tin (pan) and line the base with baking parchment. Arrange the figs over the base of the tin and drizzle over the honey.

2 In a large mixing bowl, cream the butter and caster sugar with the lemon and orange rinds until the mixture is pale and fluffy, then gradually beat in the egg yolks.

3 Sift the dry ingredients together. Add a little to the creamed mixture, beat well, then beat in a spoonful of Greek yogurt. Repeat this process until all the dry ingredients and Greek yogurt have been incorporated.

4 Whisk the egg whites in a grease-free bowl until they form stiff peaks. Stir half the whites into the cake mixture to soften it slightly, then fold in the rest. Pour the mixture over the figs in the tin, then bake for 1¼ hours or until golden and a skewer inserted in the centre of the cake comes out clean.

5 Turn the cake out on to a wire rack, peel off the lining paper and leave to cool. Drizzle the figs with extra honey before serving warm or cold.

Tuscan Sponge Energy 328Kcal/1381kJ; Protein 11.1g; Carbohydrate 53.7g, of which sugars 40.5g; Fat 8.8g, of which saturates 2.3g; Cholesterol 285mg; Calcium 66mg; Fibre 0.4g; Sodium 109mg.
Yogurt & Fig Cake Energy 473Kcal/1981kJ; Protein 8.2g; Carbohydrate 59.4g, of which sugars 38g; Fat 24.2g, of which saturates 14g; Cholesterol 149mg; Calcium 167mg; Fibre 2g; Sodium 225mg.

Angel Food Cake

This beautifully light cake is wonderful served with fresh fruit.

Serves 12–14

115g/4oz/1 cup self-raising (self-rising) flour, sifted
285g/10½oz/1½ cups caster (superfine) sugar

300ml/½ pint/1¼ cups egg whites (about 10–11 eggs)
6.5ml/1¼ tsp cream of tartar
1.5ml/¼ tsp salt
5ml/1 tsp vanilla extract
1.5ml/¼ tsp almond extract
icing (confectioners') sugar, for dusting

1 Preheat the oven to 160°C/325°F/Gas 3. Sift the flour before measuring, then sift it four times with 90g/3½oz/½ cup of the sugar. Transfer to a bowl.

2 Beat the egg whites with an electric whisk until foamy. Sift the cream of tartar and salt over and continue to beat until the whites hold soft peaks when the beaters are lifted.

3 Add the remaining sugar in three batches, beating well after each addition. Stir in the vanilla and almond extracts. Add the flour mixture, ½ cup at a time, folding in gently with a large metal spoon after each addition.

4 Transfer to an ungreased 25cm/10in straight-sided ring mould and bake for about 1 hour until delicately browned on top.

5 Turn the ring mould upside down on to a cake rack and leave to cool for 1 hour. If the cake does not turn out, run a spatula around the edge to loosen it. Invert on to a serving plate.

6 When cool, lay a star-shaped template on top of the cake, sift with icing sugar, then lift off.

Cook's Tip
Sifting the flour over and over again lets plenty of air into the mixture and is the key to the cake's lightness.

Sponge Cake with Fruit & Cream

Called Génoise, this French cake is used as the base for both simple and elaborate creations. You could simply dust it with icing sugar, or layer it with fresh fruits to serve as a seasonal dessert.

Serves 6

butter, for greasing
115g/4oz/1 cup plain (all-purpose) flour
pinch of salt
4 eggs, at room temperature

115g/4oz/generous ½ cup caster (superfine) sugar
2.5ml/½ tsp vanilla extract
50g/2oz/4 tbsp butter, melted or clarified and cooled

For the filling
450g/1lb fresh strawberries or raspberries
30–60ml/2–4 tbsp caster (superfine) sugar
475ml/16fl oz/2 cups whipping cream
5ml/1 tsp vanilla extract

1 Preheat the oven to 180°C/350°F/Gas 4. Lightly butter a 23cm/9in springform or deep cake tin (pan). Line the base with baking parchment), and dust lightly with flour. Sift the flour and salt together twice.

2 Half-fill a medium pan with hot water and set over a low heat (do not allow the water to boil). Put the eggs in a heatproof bowl that just fits into the pan without touching the water. Using an electric whisk, beat the eggs at medium-high speed, gradually adding the sugar, for 8–10 minutes until the mixture is very thick and pale and leaves a ribbon trail when the beaters are lifted. Remove the bowl from the pan, add the vanilla extract and continue beating until the mixture is cool.

3 Fold in the flour mixture in three batches, using a balloon whisk or metal spoon. Before the third addition of flour, stir a large spoonful of the mixture into the melted or clarified butter to lighten it, then fold the butter into the remaining mixture with the last addition of flour. Work quickly, but gently, so the mixture does not deflate. Pour into the prepared tin, smoothing the top so the sides are slightly higher than the centre.

4 Bake in the oven for about 25–30 minutes until the top of the cake springs back when touched and the edge begins to shrink away from the sides of the tin. Cool the cake in its tin on a wire rack for 5–10 minutes, then turn the cake out on to the rack to cool completely. Peel off the lining paper.

5 Make the filling. Slice the strawberries, place in a bowl, sprinkle with 15–30ml/1–2 tbsp of the sugar and set aside. Beat the cream with 15–30ml/1–2 tbsp of the sugar and the vanilla extract until it holds soft peaks.

6 To assemble the cake (up to 4 hours before serving), split the cake horizontally, using a serrated knife. Place the top, cut side up, on a serving plate. Spread with a third of the cream and cover with an even layer of sliced strawberries.

7 Place the bottom half of the cake, cut side down, on top of the filling and press lightly. Spread the remaining cream over the top and sides of the cake. Chill until ready to serve. Serve the remaining strawberries with the cake.

Angel Food Cake Energy 117Kcal/500kJ; Protein 3.1g; Carbohydrate 27.7g, of which sugars 21.4g; Fat 0.1g, of which saturates 0g; Cholesterol 0mg; Calcium 24mg; Fibre 0.3g; Sodium 49mg.
Sponge Cake Energy 592Kcal/2466kJ; Protein 8.8g; Carbohydrate 45.8g, of which sugars 31.2g; Fat 42.9g, of which saturates 25.5g; Cholesterol 228mg; Calcium 125mg; Fibre 2.5g; Sodium 121mg.

Carrot Cake with Maple Butter Frosting

A good, quick dessert cake for a family supper.

Serves 12
450g/1lb carrots, peeled
175g/6oz/1½ cups plain
  (all-purpose) flour
10ml/2 tsp baking powder
2.5ml/½ tsp bicarbonate of soda
  (baking soda)
5ml/1 tsp salt
10ml/2 tsp ground cinnamon
4 eggs
10ml/2 tsp vanilla extract
225g/8oz/1 cup muscovado
  (molasses) sugar

90g/3½oz/½ cup granulated
  sugar
300ml/½ pint/1¼ cups sunflower
  oil, plus extra for greasing
115g/4oz/1 cup walnuts, finely
  chopped
65g/2½oz/½ cup raisins
walnut halves, for decorating
  (optional)

For the frosting
75g/3oz/6 tbsp unsalted (sweet)
  butter, at room temperature
350g/12oz/3 cups icing
  (confectioners') sugar
50ml/2fl oz/¼ cup maple syrup

1 Preheat the oven to 180°C/350°F/Gas 4. Line a 28 × 20cm/ 11 × 8in rectangular cake tin (pan) with baking parchment and grease. Grate the carrots and set aside.

2 Sift the flour, baking powder, bicarbonate of soda, salt and cinnamon into a bowl. Set aside.

3 With an electric whisk, beat the eggs until blended. Add the vanilla, sugars and oil; beat to incorporate. Fold in the flour mixture in three batches. Fold in the carrots, walnuts and raisins.

4 Pour into the prepared tin and bake for 40–45 minutes until springy to the touch. Stand for 10 minutes, then turn out.

5 Make the frosting. Cream the butter with half the sugar until soft. Add the syrup, then beat in the remaining sugar. Spread the frosting over the top of the cake. Using a metal spatula, make decorative ridges in the frosting. Cut into squares. Decorate with walnut halves, if you like.

Black & White Pound Cake

A great dish for feeding a crowd, served with fresh custard or pouring cream.

Serves 16
115g/4oz plain (semisweet)
  chocolate, broken into squares
350g/12oz/3 cups plain
  (all-purpose) flour, plus extra
  for dusting

5ml/1 tsp baking powder
450g/1lb/2 cups butter, at room
  temperature, plus extra
  for greasing
650g/1lb 7oz/3⅓ cups sugar
15ml/1 tbsp vanilla extract
10 eggs, at room temperature
icing (confectioners') sugar,
  for dusting

1 Preheat the oven to 180°C/350°F/Gas 4. Line the base of a 25cm/10in straight-sided ring mould with baking parchment and grease. Dust with flour spread evenly with a brush.

2 Melt the chocolate in a heatproof bowl set over a pan of hot water. Stir occasionally. Set aside.

3 In a bowl, sift together the flour and baking powder. In another bowl, cream the butter, sugar and vanilla extract with an electric whisk until light and fluffy. Add the eggs, two at a time, then gradually incorporate the flour mixture on low speed.

4 Spoon half of the batter into the prepared pan. Stir the chocolate into the remaining batter, then spoon into the pan. Using a metal spatula, swirl the two batters together to create a marbled effect.

5 Bake for about 1¾ hours until a metal skewer inserted into the centre comes out clean. Cover with foil halfway through baking. Allow to stand for 15 minutes, then turn out and transfer to a cooling rack. To serve, dust with icing sugar.

> **Cook's Tip**
> This delicious cake is also known as Marbled Cake because of its distinctive appearance.

Carrot Cake Energy 595Kcal/2495kJ; Protein 5.5g; Carbohydrate 79.6g, of which sugars 68.2g; Fat 30.5g, of which saturates 6.4g; Cholesterol 77mg; Calcium 82mg; Fibre 1.8g; Sodium 90mg.
Pound Cake Energy 527Kcal/2205kJ; Protein 6.7g; Carbohydrate 64.2g, of which sugars 47.5g; Fat 28.9g, of which saturates 16.9g; Cholesterol 179mg; Calcium 77mg; Fibre 0.9g; Sodium 218mg.

Lemon Coconut Layer Cake

The flavours of lemon and coconut complement each other beautifully in this light dessert cake.

Serves 8–10
115g/4oz/1 cup plain
 (all-purpose) flour
pinch of salt
8 eggs
350g/12oz/1¾ cups granulated
 sugar
15ml/1 tbsp grated orange rind
grated rind of 2 lemons
juice of 1 lemon

40g/1½oz/½ cup desiccated (dry
 unsweetened) coconut
30ml/2 tbsp cornflour (cornstarch)
75g/3oz/6 tbsp butter

For the frosting
115g/4oz/½ cup unsalted (sweet)
 butter, at room temperature
115g/4oz/1 cup icing
 (confectioners') sugar
grated rind of 1 lemon
90–120ml/6–8 tbsp freshly
 squeezed lemon juice
400g/14oz desiccated (dry
 unsweetened) coconut

1 Preheat the oven to 180°C/350°F/Gas 4. Line three 20cm/8in cake tins (pans) with baking parchment and grease. In a bowl, sift together the flour and salt and set aside.

2 Place six of the eggs in a large heatproof bowl set over hot water. With an electric whisk, beat until frothy. Gradually beat in 150g/5oz/¾ cup of the granulated sugar until the mixture doubles in volume and is thick enough to leave a ribbon trail when the beaters are lifted, this takes about 10 minutes.

3 Remove the bowl from the hot water. Fold in the orange rind, half the grated lemon rind and 15ml/1 tbsp of the lemon juice until blended. Fold in the coconut.

4 Sift over the flour mixture in three batches, folding in thoroughly after each addition. Divide the mixture between the prepared tins.

5 Bake for 25–30 minutes until the cakes pull away from the sides of the tin. Allow to stand for 3–5 minutes, then turn out on to a wire rack to cool.

6 In a bowl, blend the cornflour with a little cold water. Whisk in the remaining eggs until just blended. Set aside.

7 In a pan, combine the remaining lemon rind and juice, the remaining sugar, the butter and 250ml/8fl oz/1 cup of water.

8 Bring the mixture to the boil over a medium heat. Whisk in the eggs and cornflour, and return to the boil. Whisk constantly for about 5 minutes, until thick. Remove from the heat. Cover with baking parchment to stop a skin forming and set aside.

9 Make the frosting. Cream the butter and icing sugar until smooth. Stir in the lemon rind and enough lemon juice to give a thick, spreading consistency.

10 Sandwich the three cake layers together with the cooled lemon custard mixture. Spread the frosting over the top and sides of the cake. Cover the cake with the coconut, pressing it gently into the frosting to keep in place.

Marmalade Cake

Orange marmalade and cinnamon give this moist cake a deliciously warm flavour. Served as a dessert, with thick yogurt or even fresh custard, it is sure to go down well with the whole family.

Serves 8
200g/7oz/1¾ cups plain
 (all-purpose) flour
5ml/1 tsp baking powder
6.25ml/1¼ tsp ground cinnamon

90g/3½oz/scant ½ cup butter or
 margarine, plus extra
 for greasing
50g/2oz/¼ cup soft light
 brown sugar
60ml/4 tbsp chunky orange
 marmalade
1 egg, beaten
about 45ml/3 tbsp milk
50g/2oz/½ cup icing
 (confectioners') sugar
about 15ml/1 tbsp warm water
thinly pared and shredded orange
 and lemon rind, to decorate

1 Preheat the oven to 160°C/325°F/Gas 3. Butter a 900ml/1½ pint/3¾ cup loaf tin (pan), then line the base with baking parchment and grease.

2 Sift the flour, baking powder and cinnamon into a mixing bowl, then rub in the butter with your fingertips until the mixture resembles fine breadcrumbs. Stir in the sugar.

3 Mix together the marmalade, egg and most of the milk, then stir into the bowl to make a soft dropping (pourable) consistency, adding a little more milk if necessary.

4 Transfer the mixture to the prepared tin and bake for about 1¼ hours until firm to the touch. Leave the cake to cool for 5 minutes, then turn on to a wire rack.

5 Carefully peel off the lining paper and leave the cake on the rack to cool completely.

6 When the cake is cold, make the icing. Sift the icing sugar into a bowl and mix in the water a little at a time to make a thick glaze. Drizzle the icing over the top of the cake and decorate with the orange and lemon rind.

Layer Cake Energy 698Kcal/2912kJ; Protein 8.9g; Carbohydrate 63g, of which sugars 51.8g; Fat 47.5g, of which saturates 34.7g; Cholesterol 193mg; Calcium 78mg; Fibre 6.4g; Sodium 188mg.
Marmalade Cake Energy 250Kcal/1050kJ; Protein 3.5g; Carbohydrate 38g, of which sugars 19g; Fat 10.4g, of which saturates 6.2g; Cholesterol 48mg; Calcium 56mg; Fibre 0.8g; Sodium 86mg.

Almond & Raspberry Swiss Roll

An airy whisked sponge cake is rolled up with a mouthwatering fresh cream and raspberry filling to make a stunning dessert.

Serves 8

oil, for greasing
4 eggs, separated
115g/4oz/generous ½ cup caster (superfine) sugar
25g/1oz/¼ cup ground almonds
40g/1½oz/⅓ cup plain (all-purpose) flour, sifted
caster (superfine) sugar, for sprinkling
250ml/8fl oz/1 cup double (heavy) cream
275g/10oz/1½ cups fresh raspberries
16 flaked (sliced) almonds, toasted, to decorate

1 Preheat the oven to 190°C/375°F/Gas 5. Grease a 33 × 23cm/13 × 9in Swiss roll tin (jelly roll pan) and line with baking parchment, cut to fit.

2 In a large bowl, beat the egg yolks with half the caster sugar until light and foamy. Lightly fold in the almonds and flour. Whisk the egg whites until they form stiff peaks. Gradually whisk in the remaining sugar to form a stiff meringue. Stir half the meringue mixture into the egg yolk mixture, then fold in the rest.

3 Pour the mixture into the prepared tin, level the surface and bake for 10 minutes or until risen and spongy to the touch.

4 Sprinkle a sheet of baking parchment with caster sugar. Turn out the cake on to this. Leave to cool with the tin still in place.

5 Lift the tin off the cooled cake and peel off the lining. Whip the cream until it holds its shape. Fold in 250g/9oz/1¼ cups of the raspberries, and spread the cream and raspberry mixture over the cooled cake, leaving a narrow border around the edge.

6 Carefully roll up the cake from a short end, using the paper as a guide. Sprinkle the roll liberally with caster sugar.

7 To serve, slice the roll and top each portion with the remaining raspberries and the toasted almonds.

Lemon Curd Roulade

This featherlight roulade, filled with tangy lemon curd, is a delicious dessert.

Serves 8

4 eggs, separated
115g/4oz/generous ½ cup caster (superfine) sugar
finely grated rind of 2 lemons
5ml/1 tsp vanilla extract
25g/1oz/¼ cup ground almonds
40g/1½oz/⅓ cup plain (all-purpose) flour, sifted
45g/1¾oz/3 tbsp icing (confectioners') sugar, for dusting

For the lemon curd cream

300ml/½ pint/1¼ cups double (heavy) cream
60ml/4 tbsp lemon curd

1 Preheat the oven to 190°C/375°F/Gas 5. Grease a 33 × 23cm/13 × 9in Swiss roll tin (jelly roll pan) and line with baking parchment, cut to fit.

2 In a large bowl, beat the egg yolks with half the caster sugar until light and foamy. Beat in the lemon rind and vanilla extract, then lightly fold in the ground almonds and flour.

3 Whisk the egg whites in a grease-free bowl until they form stiff peaks. Gradually whisk in the remaining caster sugar to form a stiff meringue. Stir half the meringue mixture into the egg yolk mixture, then fold in the rest.

4 Pour into the prepared tin, level the surface with a metal spatula and bake for 10 minutes or until risen and spongy to the touch. Cover loosely with a sheet of baking parchment and a damp dish towel. Leave to cool in the tin. Make the lemon curd cream. Whip the cream, then lightly fold in the lemon curd.

5 Sift the icing sugar liberally over a piece of baking parchment, then turn the sponge out on to it. Peel off the lining paper and spread the lemon curd cream over the surface of the sponge, leaving a border around the edge.

6 Using the baking parchment underneath as a guide, roll up the sponge from one of the long sides. Place on a serving platter, with the seam underneath, and cut into slices to serve.

Swiss Roll Energy 293Kcal/1222kJ; Protein 5.3g; Carbohydrate 21.2g, of which sugars 17.3g; Fat 21.5g, of which saturates 11.4g; Cholesterol 138mg; Calcium 60mg; Fibre 1.3g; Sodium 44mg.
Roulade Energy 337Kcal/1401kJ; Protein 5g; Carbohydrate 24.5g, of which sugars 18.9g; Fat 25.1g, of which saturates 13.6g; Cholesterol 148mg; Calcium 55mg; Fibre 0.4g; Sodium 50mg.

Bizcocho Borracho

The name of this moist Spanish dessert translates as "drunken cake" – very appropriate as it is steeped in a delicious, brandy-soaked syrup. The cake can be layered with cream, but this version is made in a mould, then turned out. Pipe with whipped cream if you like.

Serves 6–8

butter, for greasing
90g/3½oz/¾ cup plain
   (all-purpose) flour
6 large (US extra large) eggs
90g/3½oz/½ cup caster
   (superfine) sugar
finely grated rind of 1 lemon
90ml/6 tbsp toasted flaked
   (sliced) almonds
250ml/8fl oz/1 cup whipping
   cream, to serve

For the syrup

115g/4oz/generous ½ cup caster
   (superfine) sugar
15ml/1 tbsp water
120ml/4fl oz/½ cup boiling water
105ml/7 tbsp Spanish brandy

1 Starting 1–2 days ahead, preheat the oven to 200°C/400°F/Gas 6. Butter a shallow tin (pan), about 28 × 18cm/11 × 7in. Line the tin with baking parchment and butter well.

2 Sift the flour a couple of times into a bowl. Separate the eggs, putting the whites in a large, grease-free bowl. Put the yolks in a food processor with the sugar and lemon rind and beat until light. Whisk the whites to soft peaks, then work a little white into the yolk mixture.

3 Drizzle two spoonfuls of the yolk mixture across the whites, sift some flour over the top and cut in gently with a large spoon. Continue folding together in this way until all the egg yolk mixture and flour have been incorporated.

4 Turn the mixture into the prepared tin and and level the surface. Bake for 12 minutes. Leave the cake to set for 5 minutes, then turn out on to a wire rack. Peel off the paper and leave to cool completely.

5 Make the syrup. Place 50g/2oz/¼ cup of the sugar in a small pan with the water. Heat until it caramelizes, shaking the pan a little if one side starts to brown too fast. As soon as the syrup colours, dip the base of the pan into a bowl of cold water. Add the remaining sugar and pour in the boiling water. Bring back to a simmer, stirring until the sugar has dissolved. Pour into a measuring jug (cup) and add the brandy.

6 Put the cake back in the tin and drizzle half the syrup over. Cut the cake into scallops with a spoon and layer half in the bottom of a 700ml/1½ pint/3 cup mould or cake tin (pan). Sprinkle 30ml/2 tbsp almonds over the top, and push them into the cracks. Top with the remaining cake and 30ml/2 tbsp nuts.

7 Pour the remaining syrup over the cake, cover with foil and weight down the top. Chill until ready to serve.

8 To serve, whip the cream. Run a knife round the mould and turn the cake out on to a long dish. Sprinkle with the remaining almonds and serve with the cream.

Marbled Swiss Roll

A sensational combination of chocolate sponge and rich walnut buttercream.

Serves 6–8

90g/3½oz/¾ cup plain
   (all-purpose) flour
15ml/1 tbsp cocoa powder
   (unsweetened)
25g/1oz plain (semisweet)
   chocolate, grated
25g/1oz white chocolate, grated
3 eggs
115g/4oz/generous ½ cup caster
   (superfine) sugar
30ml/2 tbsp boiling water

For the filling

75g/3oz/6 tbsp unsalted (sweet)
   butter or margarine, softened
175g/6oz/1½ cups icing
   (confectioners') sugar
15ml/1 tbsp cocoa powder
   (unsweetened)
2.5ml/½ tsp vanilla extract
45ml/3 tbsp chopped walnuts

1 Preheat the oven to 200°C/400°F/Gas 6. Grease a 30 × 20cm/12 × 8in Swiss roll tin (jelly roll pan) and line with baking parchment. Sift half the flour with the cocoa into bowl. Stir in the grated plain chocolate. Sift the remaining flour into another bowl; stir in the grated white chocolate.

2 Whisk the eggs and sugar in a heatproof bowl, set over a pan of hot water, until it holds its shape when the whisk is lifted.

3 Remove from the heat and turn half the mixture into a separate bowl. Fold the white chocolate mixture into one half, then fold the plain chocolate mixture into the other. Stir 15ml/1 tbsp boiling water into each half to soften the mixtures.

4 Place alternate spoonfuls of mixture in the tin and swirl lightly together for a marbled effect. Bake for 12–15 minutes, or until firm. Turn out on to a sheet of baking parchment and cover with a damp, clean dish towel. Cool.

5 Make the filling. Beat the butter, icing sugar, cocoa and vanilla together in a bowl until smooth, then mix in the walnuts. Uncover the sponge, peel off the lining and spread the surface with the filling. Roll up carefully from a long side, using the paper underneath as a guide, then place on a serving plate.

Bizcocho Borracho Energy 294Kcal/1235kJ; Protein 8.3g; Carbohydrate 36.3g, of which sugars 27.4g; Fat 10.6g, of which saturates 1.7g; Cholesterol 143mg; Calcium 78mg; Fibre 1.2g; Sodium 56mg.
Marbled Swiss Roll Energy 361Kcal/1518kJ; Protein 5.6g; Carbohydrate 51.1g, of which sugars 42g; Fat 16.4g, of which saturates 7.4g; Cholesterol 92mg; Calcium 67mg; Fibre 1.1g; Sodium 125mg.

Apricot & Pear Filo Roulade

A truly delicious mix of dried and fresh fruit and almonds, all wrapped up in light-as-a-feather filo pastry, makes a really great dessert. This dish is also amazingly quick to prepare and cook. Use your imagination and vary the fruits you use, depending on what is in season or what you have readily to hand.

Serves 4–6

115g/4oz/½ cup ready-to-eat
   dried apricots, chopped
30ml/2 tbsp apricot jam
5ml/1 tsp freshly squeezed
   lemon juice
50g/2oz/¼ cup soft brown sugar
2 medium pears, peeled, cored
   and chopped
50g/2oz/½ cup ground almonds
30ml/2 tbsp slivered almonds
25g/1oz/2 tbsp butter
8 sheets filo pastry
icing (confectioners') sugar, to dust

1 Put the dried apricots, apricot jam, lemon juice, brown sugar and prepared pears into a pan and heat gently, stirring all the time, for 5–7 minutes.

2 Remove the pan with the fruit mixture from the heat and cool. Mix in the ground and slivered almonds. Preheat the oven to 200°C/400°F/Gas 6. Melt the butter in a pan.

3 Lightly grease a baking sheet. Layer the filo pastry on the baking sheet, brushing each separate layer carefully with the melted butter.

4 Spoon the fruit-and-nut filling down the pastry, placing the filling just to one side of the centre and within 2.5cm/1in of each end.

5 Lift the other side of the pastry up by sliding a metal spatula underneath. Fold this pastry over the filling, tucking the edge under. Seal the ends neatly and brush all over with melted butter again.

6 Bake for 15–20 minutes, until golden. Dust with icing sugar and serve immediately.

Pear & Polenta Cake

Polenta gives the light sponge topping and sliced pears a nutty corn flavour that complements the fruit perfectly. Serve as a dessert with custard or cream.

Makes 10 slices

butter or margarine, for greasing
175g/6oz/¾ cup golden caster
   (superfine) sugar

4 ripe pears
juice of ½ lemon
30ml/2 tbsp clear honey
3 eggs
seeds from 1 vanilla pod (bean)
120ml/4fl oz/½ cup sunflower oil
115g/4oz/1 cup self-raising
   (self-rising) flour
50g/2oz/⅓ cup instant polenta

1 Preheat the oven to 180°C/350°F/Gas 4. Generously grease and line a 21cm/8½in round cake tin (pan). Sprinkle 30ml/2 tbsp of the golden caster sugar over the base of the prepared tin.

2 Peel and core the pears. Cut them into chunky slices and toss in the lemon juice. Arrange them on the base of the prepared cake tin. Drizzle the honey over the pears and set aside.

3 Mix together the eggs, seeds from the vanilla pod and the remaining golden caster sugar in a bowl.

4 Beat the egg mixture until thick and creamy, then gradually beat in the oil. Sift together the flour and polenta and fold into the egg mixture.

5 Pour the mixture carefully into the tin over the pears. Bake for about 50 minutes or until a skewer inserted into the centre comes out clean. Cool in the tin for 10 minutes, then turn the cake out on to a plate, peel off the lining paper, invert and slice.

> **Cook's Tip**
> Use the tip of a small, sharp knife to scrape out the vanilla seeds. If you do not have a vanilla pod, use 5ml/1 tsp pure vanilla extract instead.

Apricot & Pear Energy 212Kcal/890kJ; Protein 3.7g; Carbohydrate 31.3g, of which sugars 24.7g; Fat 8.8g, of which saturates 2.6g; Cholesterol 9mg; Calcium 59mg; Fibre 3.3g; Sodium 34mg.
Pear & Polenta Energy 256kcal/1077kJ; Protein 3.7g; Carbohydrate 38.5g, of which sugars 26.7g; Fat 10.5g, of which saturates 1.5g; Cholesterol 57mg; Calcium 65mg; Fibre 1.8g; Sodium 66mg.

Dutch Apple Cake

The apple topping makes this cake really moist. It is just as good hot as it is cold.

Makes 8–10 slices
250g/9oz/2¼ cups self raising
   (self-rising) flour
10ml/2 tsp baking powder
5ml/1 tsp ground cinnamon
130g/4½oz/generous ½ cup
   caster (superfine) sugar

50g/2oz/¼ cup butter, melted
2 eggs, beaten
150ml/¼ pint/⅔ cup milk

For the topping
2 eating apples
15g/½oz/1 tbsp butter, melted
60ml/4 tbsp demerara
   (raw) sugar
1.5ml/¼ tsp ground cinnamon

1 Preheat the oven to 200°C/400°F/Gas 6. Grease and line a 20cm/8in round cake tin (pan). Sift the flour, baking powder and cinnamon into a large mixing bowl. Stir in the caster sugar. In a separate bowl, whisk the melted butter, eggs and milk together, then stir the mixture into the dry ingredients.

2 Pour the cake mixture into the prepared tin, smooth the surface, then make a shallow hollow in a ring around the edge of the mixture.

3 Make the topping. Peel and core the apples, slice them into wedges and slice the wedges thinly. Arrange the slices around the edge of the cake mixture, in the hollowed ring. Brush with the melted butter, then scatter the demerara sugar and ground cinnamon over the top.

4 Bake for 45–50 minutes or until the cake has risen well, is golden and a skewer inserted into the centre comes out clean.

5 Serve immediately, or remove from the tin, peel off the lining paper and cool on a wire rack before serving cold with cream.

Variation
Add a few seedless raisins to the sliced apples if you like.

Sachertorte

This glorious gâteau was created in Vienna in 1832 by Franz Sacher, a royal chef.

Serves 10–12
225g/8oz dark (bittersweet)
   chocolate, broken into squares
150g/5oz/10 tbsp unsalted (sweet)
   butter, softened
115g/4oz/generous ½ cup caster
   (superfine) sugar
8 eggs, separated
115g/4oz/1 cup plain
   (all-purpose) flour

For the glaze
225g/8oz/generous ¾ cup
   apricot jam
15ml/1 tbsp lemon juice

For the icing
225g/8oz plain dark chocolate,
   broken into squares
200g/7oz/1 cup caster
   (superfine) sugar
15ml/1 tbsp golden (light corn) syrup
250ml/8fl oz/1 cup double
   (heavy) cream
5ml/1 tsp vanilla extract

1 Preheat the oven to 180°C/350°F/Gas 4. Grease a 23cm/9in round springform cake tin (pan) and line with baking parchment. Melt the chocolate in a heatproof bowl.

2 Cream the butter and sugar in a bowl until pale and fluffy. Add the egg yolks, one at a time, beating after each addition. Beat in the melted chocolate. Sift the flour over the mixture. Fold in evenly.

3 Whisk the egg whites until stiff, then stir a quarter into the chocolate mixture to lighten it. Fold in the remaining whites. Turn the mixture into the cake tin and smooth level. Bake for 50–55 minutes, or until firm. Turn out on to a wire rack to cool.

4 Heat the apricot jam with the lemon juice in a small pan until melted, then sieve. Slice the cake horizontally into two equal layers. Brush the cut surfaces and sides of each layer with the apricot glaze, then sandwich together, with the jam covered surfaces against each other. Place on a wire rack.

5 Mix the icing ingredients in a heavy pan. Heat gently, stirring until thick. Simmer for 3–4 minutes, without stirring, until the mixture registers 95°C/200°F on a sugar thermometer. Pour quickly over the cake and spread evenly. Leave to set.

Dutch Apple Cake Energy 225Kcal/951kJ; Protein 3.7g; Carbohydrate 40g, of which sugars 21.4g; Fat 6.8g, of which saturates 3.8g; Cholesterol 52mg; Calcium 105mg; Fibre 1g; Sodium 145mg.
Sachertorte Energy 625Kcal/2618kJ; Protein 7.6g; Carbohydrate 73.1g, of which sugars 65.5g; Fat 35.8g, of which saturates 20.8g; Cholesterol 184mg; Calcium 73mg; Fibre 1.2g; Sodium 143mg.

Strawberry Roulade

A roulade packed with summer fruit is the perfect choice for a family supper.

Serves 6
oil, for greasing
4 egg whites
115g/4oz/generous ½ cup golden caster (superfine) sugar
75g/3oz/⅔ cup plain (all-purpose) flour, sifted
30ml/2 tbsp orange juice
caster (superfine) sugar, for sprinkling
115g/4oz/1 cup strawberries, chopped
150g/5oz/⅔ cup low-fat fromage frais or cream cheese
strawberries, to decorate

1 Preheat the oven to 200°C/400°F/Gas 6. Grease a 33 × 23cm/13 × 9in Swiss roll tin (jelly roll pan) and line with baking parchment, cut to fit.

2 Place the egg whites in a grease-free bowl and whisk to form soft peaks. Gradually whisk in the sugar. Fold in half of the sifted flour, then fold in the rest of the flour with the orange juice.

3 Spoon the mixture into the prepared tin, spreading evenly. Bake for 15–18 minutes, or until the sponge is golden brown and firm to the touch.

4 Meanwhile, spread out a sheet of baking parchment and sprinkle with caster sugar. Turn out the cake on to this and peel off the lining paper. Roll up the sponge loosely from one short side, with the paper inside. Leave to cool.

5 Unroll and remove the paper. Stir the strawberries into the fromage frais and spread over the sponge. Roll up and serve decorated with strawberries.

Cook's Tip
Cooling the cake rolled up in paper makes it easier to roll up again once spread with the filling.

Chocolate Mousse Strawberry Layer Cake

To ring the changes, try replacing the strawberries with raspberries or blackberries, and use a complementary liqueur.

Serves 10
oil, for greasing
115g/4oz good-quality white chocolate, chopped
120ml/4fl oz/½ cup whipping or double (heavy) cream
120ml/4fl oz/½ cup milk
15ml/1 tbsp rum essence or vanilla extract
115g/4oz/½ cup unsalted (sweet) butter, softened
175g/6oz/¾ cup granulated sugar
3 eggs

275g/10oz/2½ cups plain (all-purpose) flour, plus extra for dusting
5ml/1 tsp baking powder
pinch of salt
675g/1½lb fresh strawberries, sliced, plus extra for decoration
750ml/1¼ pints/3 cups whipping cream
30ml/2 tbsp rum or strawberry-flavour liqueur

For the mousse
250g/9oz good-quality white chocolate, chopped
350ml/12fl oz/1½ cups whipping or double (heavy) cream
30ml/2 tbsp rum or strawberry-flavoured liqueur

1 Preheat the oven to 180°C/350°F/Gas 4. Grease and flour two 23cm/9in cake tins (pans). Line the base of the tins with baking parchment. Melt the chocolate and cream in a double boiler over a low heat, stirring until smooth. Stir in the milk and rum essence or vanilla extract; set aside to cool.

2 In a large bowl, beat the butter and sugar together with an electric whisk until light and creamy. Add the eggs one at a time, beating well after each addition.

3 In a small bowl, stir together the flour, baking powder and salt. Alternately add the flour and melted chocolate to the egg mixture, just until blended. Pour evenly into the tins.

4 Bake for 20–25 minutes until a metal skewer inserted into the centre comes out clean. Cool in the tins on a wire rack for 10 minutes. Turn the cakes out on to the rack, peel off the lining and leave to cool completely.

5 Make the mousse. Melt the chocolate and cream in a medium pan over low heat, stirring frequently, until smooth. Stir in the rum or strawberry-flavoured liqueur and pour into a bowl. Chill until just set. Using a wire whisk, whip the mixture lightly until it has a "mousse" consistency.

6 Using a large knife, carefully slice both cake layers in half horizontally. Sandwich the four layers together with the mousse and strawberries.

7 To decorate the cake, whip the cream with the rum or liqueur to form firm peaks. Spread half the flavoured cream over the top and sides of the cake. Spoon the remaining cream into a piping (pastry) bag with a star nozzle and pipe scrolls on top. Decorate with strawberries and serve.

Strawberry Roulade Energy 164Kcal/695kJ; Protein 4.7g; Carbohydrate 34.8g, of which sugars 25.1g; Fat 1.6g, of which saturates 0.9g; Cholesterol 5mg; Calcium 54mg; Fibre 0.6g; Sodium 53mg.
Layer Cake Energy 964Kcal/4008kJ; Protein 10.9g; Carbohydrate 69g, of which sugars 48g; Fat 72.1g, of which saturates 44.1g; Cholesterol 210mg; Calcium 253mg; Fibre 1.6g; Sodium 174mg.

Chocolate Layer Cake

Round off a meal in style with this heavenly cake.

Serves 10–12

cocoa powder (unsweetened), for dusting
225g/8oz can cooked whole beetroot (beets), drained and juice reserved
115g/4oz/½ cup unsalted (sweet) butter, softened
500g/1¼lb/2½ cups light brown sugar, firmly packed
3 eggs
15ml/1 tbsp vanilla extract

75g/3oz plain (semisweet) chocolate, melted
250g/9oz/2¼ cups plain (all-purpose) flour
10ml/2 tsp baking powder
2.5ml/½ tsp salt
120ml/4fl oz/½ cup buttermilk
chocolate curls (optional)

For the chocolate ganache
475ml/16fl oz/2 cups whipping or double (heavy) cream
500g/1¼lb good-quality chocolate, chopped
15ml/1 tbsp vanilla extract

1 Preheat the oven to 180°C/350°F/Gas 4. Grease two 23cm/9in cake tins (pans); dust the base and sides with cocoa. Grate the beetroot and add to the beet juice. Using an electric whisk, beat the butter, sugar, eggs and vanilla for 3–5 minutes until pale and fluffy. Reduce the speed and beat in the chocolate.

2 In a bowl, sift the flour, baking powder and salt. With the mixer on low speed, alternately beat in the flour mixture in fourths and buttermilk in thirds. Add the beetroot and juice and beat for 1 minute. Divide between the tins and bake for 30–35 minutes. Cool for 10 minutes, then unmould. Cool completely.

3 Make the ganache. Heat the cream in a heavy pan over medium heat, stirring occasionally, until it just begins to boil. Remove from the heat and add the chocolate, stirring constantly until smooth. Stir in the vanilla. Strain into a bowl and chill for about 1 hour, stirring every 10 minutes, until spreadable.

4 Place one cake on a plate and spread with one-third of the ganache. Add the other cake, upside down, and spread the remaining ganache over the top and sides. Top with chocolate curls. Allow the ganache to set for 30 minutes, then chill.

Lemon Ricotta Cake

This delicious lemon dessert originated in Sardinia.

Serves 6–8

75g/3oz/6 tbsp butter, plus extra for greasing
175g/6oz/¾ cup granulated sugar
75g/3oz/generous ⅓ cup ricotta cheese

3 eggs, separated
175g/6oz/1½ cups plain (all-purpose) flour, plus extra for dusting
grated rind of 1 lemon
45ml/3 tbsp fresh lemon juice
7.5ml/1½ tsp baking powder
icing (confectioners') sugar, for dusting

1 Grease a 23cm/9in round cake or springform tin (pan). Line the bottom with baking parchment. Grease the paper with butter, then lightly dust with flour. Set aside. Preheat the oven to 180°C/350°F/Gas 4.

2 Cream the butter and sugar together until smooth. Beat in the ricotta cheese.

3 Beat in the egg yolks, one at a time. Add 30ml/2 tbsp of the flour, together with the lemon rind and juice. Sift the baking powder into the remaining flour and beat into the batter just until it is well blended.

4 In a grease-free bowl, beat the egg whites until they form stiff peaks. Fold them carefully into the batter.

5 Turn the mixture into the prepared tin. Bake for 45 minutes, or until a cake tester inserted in the centre of the cake comes out clean. Allow the cake to cool for 10 minutes before turning it out on to a rack to cool. Dust the cake generously with icing sugar before serving.

Cook's Tip
Serve this cake with single (light) cream and a bowl of summer fruit to make a delectable dessert.

Layer Cake Energy 733Kcal/3073kJ; Protein 7.7g; Carbohydrate 93.5g, of which sugars 77.1g; Fat 39.1g, of which saturates 23.6g; Cholesterol 113mg; Calcium 116mg; Fibre 2.2g; Sodium 116mg.
Ricotta Cake Energy 275Kcal/1156kJ; Protein 5.4g; Carbohydrate 40.2g, of which sugars 23.5g; Fat 11.4g, of which saturates 6.4g; Cholesterol 95mg; Calcium 55mg; Fibre 0.7g; Sodium 85mg.

Easy Blueberry Cake

Ready-made cake mixes make life extremely easy and are available in most supermarkets. Simply top with blueberries or an equivalent favourite fruit, as detailed here, to serve up as a simple, yet totally scrumptious, dessert.

Serves 6–8

oil, for greasing
225g/8oz packet sponge
    cake mix
I egg, if needed
I 15g/4oz/I cup blueberries

I Preheat the oven to 190°C/375°F/Gas 5. Grease a 20cm/8in cake tin (pan). Make up the sponge cake mix according to the instructions on the packet, using the egg if required. Spoon the mixture into the prepared cake tin (pan).

2 Bake the cake according to the instructions provided on the packet. Ten minutes before the end of the cooking time, sprinkle the blueberries over the top of the cake and then return the cake to the oven to finish cooking. (You must work quickly when adding the blueberries – the cake should be out of the oven for as short a time as possible, otherwise it may sink in the middle.)

3 Leave the cake to cool in the tin for 2–3 minutes, then carefully remove from the tin and transfer to a wire rack. Leave to cool completely before serving.

Cook's Tip
This cake is especially delicious served with either vanilla or blueberry ice cream.

Variation
The blueberry topping can be replaced with other fresh fruit, such as raspberries or blackberries.

Simple Chocolate Cake

An easy-to-make chocolate cake that is transformed into a terrific dessert when served with cream or mixed summer fruit.

Serves 6–8

I 15g/4oz plain (semisweet)
    chocolate, broken into squares
45ml/3 tbsp milk
150g/5oz/⅔ cup unsalted (sweet)
    butter or margarine, softened,
    plus extra for greasing
150g/5oz/¾ cup light muscovado
    (brown) sugar
3 eggs

200g/7oz/1¾ cups self-raising
    (self-rising) flour
15ml/1 tbsp cocoa powder
    (unsweetened)
icing (confectioners') sugar and
    cocoa powder, for dusting

For the buttercream

75g/3oz/6 tbsp unsalted (sweet)
    butter or margarine, softened
175g/6oz/1½ cups icing
    (confectioners') sugar
15ml/1 tbsp cocoa powder
    (unsweetened)
2.5ml/½ tsp vanilla extract

I Preheat the oven to 180°C/350°F/Gas 4. Grease two 18cm/7in round sandwich cake tins (layer pans) and line the base of each with baking parchment. Melt the chocolate with the milk in a heatproof bowl set over a pan of simmering water.

2 Cream the butter or margarine with the sugar in a mixing bowl until pale and fluffy. Add the eggs one at a time, beating well after each addition. Stir in the chocolate mixture.

3 Sift the flour and cocoa over the mixture and fold in with a metal spoon until evenly mixed. Turn into the prepared tins, level the surfaces and bake for 35–40 minutes or until well risen and firm. Turn out on to wire racks and leave to cool.

4 Make the buttercream. Beat the butter or margarine, icing sugar, cocoa powder and vanilla extract together in a bowl until the mixture is smooth.

5 Spread buttercream over one of the cakes, then top with the second layer. Dust with a mixture of icing sugar and cocoa just before serving.

Blueberry Cake Energy 223Kcal/930kJ; Protein 3.1g; Carbohydrate 25.3g, of which sugars 15g; Fat 12.8g, of which saturates 2.7g; Cholesterol 52mg; Calcium 38mg; Fibre 0.9g; Sodium 153mg.
Chocolate Cake Energy 567Kcal/2377kJ; Protein 6.6g; Carbohydrate 71.4g, of which sugars 52.2g; Fat 30.4g, of which saturates 18.2g; Cholesterol 133mg; Calcium 141mg; Fibre 1.6g; Sodium 328mg.

Chocolate Orange Marquise

Here is a cake for people who are passionate about chocolate. The rich, dense flavour is accentuated by fresh orange to make it a truly delectable treat.

Serves 6–8

200g/7oz/1 cup caster (superfine)
    sugar
60ml/4 tbsp freshly squeezed
    orange juice
350g/12oz dark (bittersweet)
    chocolate, broken into squares
225g/8oz/1 cup unsalted (sweet)
    butter, diced, plus extra for
    greasing
5 eggs
finely grated rind of 1 orange
45g/1¾oz/3 tbsp plain
    (all-purpose) flour
icing (confectioners') sugar and
    finely pared strips of orange
    rind, to decorate

1 Preheat the oven to 180°C/350°F/Gas 4. Grease a 23cm/9in shallow cake tin (pan) with a depth of 6cm/2½in. Line the base of the tin with baking parchment.

2 Place 90g/3½oz/½ cup of the sugar in a pan. Add the orange juice and stir over a low heat until dissolved.

3 Remove from the heat and stir in the chocolate until melted, then add the butter, piece by piece, until melted.

4 Whisk the eggs with the remaining sugar in a large bowl, until the mixture is pale and very thick. Add the orange rind, then lightly fold the chocolate mixture into the egg mixture. Sift the flour over the top and fold in.

5 Pour the mixture into the prepared tin. Place in a roasting pan, then pour hot water into the roasting pan to reach about halfway up the sides of the cake tin.

6 Bake for 1 hour, or until the cake is firm to the touch. Remove the tin from the roasting pan and cool for 20 minutes. Turn out the cake on to a baking sheet, place a serving plate upside down on top, then carefully turn the plate and baking sheet over together. Dust with a little icing sugar; decorate with strips of orange rind and serve slightly warm or chilled.

Chocolate & Cherry Polenta Cake

Polenta and almonds add an unusual nutty texture to this tasty dessert. It is delicious served on its own, but also tastes good served with thin cream or yogurt.

Serves 8

50g/2oz/⅓ cup quick-cook
    polenta
about 120ml/4fl oz/½ cup
    boiling water
oil, for greasing
200g/7oz plain (semisweet)
    chocolate, broken into squares
5 eggs, separated
175g/6oz/¾ cup caster
    (superfine) sugar
115g/4oz/1 cup ground almonds
50g/2oz/½ cup plain
    (all-purpose) flour
finely grated rind of 1 orange
115g/4oz/½ cup glacé (candied)
    cherries, halved
icing (confectioners') sugar, for
    dusting

1 Place the polenta in a heatproof bowl and pour over just enough of the boiling water to cover. Stir well, then cover the bowl and leave to stand for about 30 minutes, until the polenta has absorbed all the excess moisture.

2 Preheat the oven to 190°C/375°F/Gas 5. Grease a deep 22cm/8½in round cake tin (pan) and line the base with baking parchment. Melt the chocolate in a heatproof bowl set over a pan of hot water.

3 Whisk the egg yolks with the sugar in a bowl until thick and pale. Beat in the chocolate, then fold in the polenta, ground almonds, flour and orange rind.

4 Whisk the egg whites in a clean bowl until stiff. Stir 15ml/ 1 tbsp of the whites into the chocolate mixture, then fold in the rest. Finally, fold in the cherries.

5 Scrape the mixture into the prepared tin and bake for 45–55 minutes or until well risen and firm to the touch. Turn the cake out on to a wire rack and leave to cool. Dust with icing sugar just before serving.

Marquise Energy 553Kcal/2309kJ; Protein 3.1g; Carbohydrate 59.1g, of which sugars 54.4g; Fat 35.5g, of which saturates 22g; Cholesterol 63mg; Calcium 41mg; Fibre 1.3g; Sodium 176mg.
Polenta Cake Energy 420Kcal/1764kJ; Protein 9.6g; Carbohydrate 56.4g, of which sugars 45.5g; Fat 18.8g, of which saturates 5.8g; Cholesterol 120mg; Calcium 89mg; Fibre 2.2g; Sodium 53mg.

Eve's Pudding

The tempting apples beneath the sponge topping are the reason for the pudding's name.

Serves 4–6

115g/4oz/½ cup butter
115g/4oz/generous ½ cup caster (superfine) sugar
2 eggs, beaten
grated rind and juice of 1 lemon
90g/3½oz/¾ cup self-raising (self-rising) flour
40g/1½oz/⅓ cup ground almonds
115g/4oz/scant ½ cup soft brown sugar
675g/1½lb cooking apples, cored and thinly sliced
25g/1oz/¼ cup flaked (sliced) almonds
bought fresh custard or single (light) cream, to serve

1 Beat together the butter and caster sugar in a large mixing bowl until the mixture is very light and fluffy.

2 Gradually beat the eggs into the butter mixture, beating well after each addition, then fold in the lemon rind, flour and ground almonds.

3 Mix the brown sugar with the apples and lemon juice in a bowl, then turn into an ovenproof dish. Spoon the sponge mixture on top of the apples, levelling the surface, then sprinkle with the almonds.

4 Bake for 40–45 minutes, until golden. Serve immediately with fresh custard or cream.

Variations
• To ring the changes, replace half the apples with fresh blackberries. Halved apricots and sliced peaches can also be used instead of the apples as they go well with the topping.
• To vary the sponge topping, leave out the ground and flaked almonds and use demerara (raw) sugar instead of the caster sugar, then serve sprinkled with icing (confectioners') sugar.

Chocolate Cinnamon Cake with Banana Sauce

This mouthwatering cake, bursting with lovely flavours, is brilliantly complemented by the tasty banana sauce.

Serves 6

25g/1oz plain (semisweet) chocolate, chopped into small pieces
115g/4oz/½ cup unsalted (sweet) butter, at room temperature
15ml/1 tbsp instant coffee powder
5 eggs, separated
225g/8oz/1 cup granulated sugar
115g/4oz/1 cup plain (all-purpose) flour
10ml/2 tsp ground cinnamon

For the sauce
4 ripe bananas
45ml/3 tbsp soft light brown sugar
15ml/1 tbsp fresh lemon juice
175ml/6fl oz/¾ cup whipping cream
15ml/1 tbsp rum (optional)

1 Preheat the oven to 180°C/350°F/Gas 4. Grease a 20cm/8in round cake tin (pan).

2 Place the chocolate and butter in the top of a double boiler or in a heatproof bowl set over a pan of simmering water. Stir until the chocolate and butter have melted. Remove from the heat and stir in the coffee. Set aside.

3 Beat the egg yolks with the granulated sugar until thick and lemon-coloured. Add the chocolate mixture and beat on low speed until just blended.

4 Stir the flour and cinnamon together in a bowl. In another bowl, beat the egg whites until they hold stiff peaks.

5 Fold a dollop of whites into the chocolate mixture to lighten it. Fold in the remaining whites in three batches, alternating with the sifted flour mixture.

6 Pour the mixture into the prepared tin. Bake for 40–50 minutes or until a skewer inserted in the centre comes out clean. Remove from the oven and turn the cake out on to a wire rack. Preheat the grill (broiler).

7 Make the sauce. Slice the bananas into a shallow, flameproof dish. Stir in the brown sugar and lemon juice. Place under the grill for 8 minutes, stirring occasionally, until caramelized.

8 Mash the banana mixture until almost smooth. Tip into a bowl and stir in the cream and rum, if using. Slice the cake and serve with the sauce.

Cook's Tip
Take care when folding the egg white and flour into the chocolate mixture – do not be tempted to stir, otherwise you will break down the air bubbles in the mixture and the cake will not rise well.

Eve's Pudding Energy 473Kcal/1988kJ; Protein 6.4g; Carbohydrate 62.3g, of which sugars 50.8g; Fat 24g, of which saturates 11g; Cholesterol 104mg; Calcium 116mg; Fibre 3.1g; Sodium 200mg.
Choc. Cake Energy 642Kcal/2691kJ; Protein 8.9g; Carbohydrate 80.9g, of which sugars 64.8g; Fat 33.8g, of which saturates 19.4g; Cholesterol 230mg; Calcium 100mg; Fibre 1.4g; Sodium 186mg.

Hot Chocolate Cake

This is wonderfully wicked served as a dessert with a white chocolate sauce. The basic cake freezes well – thaw, then warm in the microwave before serving.

Makes 10–12 slices
200g/7oz/1¾ cups self-raising wholemeal (self-rising whole-wheat) flour
25g/1oz/¼ cup cocoa powder (unsweetened)
pinch of salt
175g/6oz/¾ cup soft margarine
175g/6oz/¾ cup soft light brown sugar
few drops vanilla extract
4 eggs
75g/3oz white chocolate, roughly chopped
chocolate leaves and curls, to decorate

For the chocolate sauce
75g/3oz white chocolate
150ml/¼ pint/⅔ cup single (light) cream
30–45ml/2–3 tbsp milk

1 Preheat the oven to 160°C/325°F/Gas 3. Sift the flour, cocoa and salt into a bowl, adding in the whole wheat flakes from the sieve (strainer).

2 Cream the margarine, sugar and vanilla extract together until light and fluffy, then gently beat in one egg.

3 Gradually stir in the remaining eggs, one at a time, alternately folding in some of the flour mixture, until the eggs and flour have been used up and the mixture is blended in.

4 Stir in the white chocolate and spoon into a 675–900g/1½–2lb loaf tin (pan) or an 18cm/7in greased cake tin (pan). Bake for 30–40 minutes, or until just firm to the touch and shrinking away from the sides of the tin.

5 Meanwhile, make the sauce. Heat the white chocolate and cream very gently in a pan until the chocolate is melted. Add the milk and stir until cool.

6 Serve the cake sliced, in a pool of sauce and decorated with chocolate leaves and curls.

Magic Chocolate Mud Cake

Guaranteed to be a big hit, this scrumptious dessert can be put together in no time at all.

Serves 4
50g/2oz/¼ cup butter, plus extra for greasing
90g/3½oz/¾ cup self-raising (self-rising) flour
5ml/1 tsp ground cinnamon
75ml/5 tbsp cocoa powder (unsweetened)
200g/7oz/1 cup light muscovado (brown) or demerara (raw) sugar
475ml/16fl oz/2 cups milk
crème fraîche, Greek (US strained plain) yogurt or vanilla ice cream, to serve

1 Preheat the oven to 180°C/350°F/Gas 4. Grease a 1.5 litre/2½ pint/6¼ cup ovenproof dish with butter. Place the dish on a baking sheet and set aside.

2 Sift the flour and ground cinnamon into a bowl. Sift in 15ml/1 tbsp of the cocoa and mix well.

3 Place the butter in a pan. Add 115g/4oz/½ cup of the sugar and 150ml/¼ pint/⅔ cup of the milk. Heat gently without boiling, stirring from time to time, until the butter has melted and all the sugar has dissolved. Remove the pan from the heat.

4 Stir in the flour mixture, mixing evenly. Pour the mixture into the prepared dish and level the surface.

5 Mix the remaining sugar and cocoa in a bowl, then sprinkle over the pudding mixture. Pour the remaining milk evenly over the pudding.

6 Bake for 45–50 minutes or until the sponge has risen to the top and is firm to the touch. Serve hot, with the crème fraîche, yogurt or ice cream.

> **Cook's Tip**
> A delicious sauce "magically" appears beneath the sponge.

Hot Choc. Cake Energy 343Kcal/1432kJ; Protein 5.4g; Carbohydrate 35.7g, of which sugars 23.1g; Fat 20.8g, of which saturates 7.1g; Cholesterol 71mg; Calcium 124mg; Fibre 0.8g; Sodium 221mg.
Mud Cake Energy 480Kcal/2025kJ; Protein 10g; Carbohydrate 77.6g, of which sugars 58.3g; Fat 16.7g, of which saturates 10.2g; Cholesterol 34mg; Calcium 227mg; Fibre 3g; Sodium 309mg.

Iced Chocolate Nut Gâteau

A divine dessert of rich chocolate ice cream encased in brandy-soaked sponge.

Serves 6–8
75g/3oz/³⁄₄ cup shelled hazelnuts
about 32 sponge fingers
150ml/¹⁄₄ pint/²⁄₃ cup cold strong
   black coffee
30ml/2 tbsp brandy
475ml/16fl oz/2 cups double
   (heavy) cream
75g/3oz/²⁄₃ cup icing
   (confectioners') sugar, sifted
150g/5oz plain (semisweet)
   chocolate, chopped into small
   pieces
icing (confectioners') sugar and
   cocoa powder (unsweetened),
   for dusting

1 Preheat the oven to 200°C/400°F/Gas 6. Spread out the hazelnuts on a baking sheet and toast them in the oven for 5 minutes until golden. Turn the nuts on to a clean dish towel and rub off the skins while still warm. Cool, then chop finely.

2 Line a 1.2 litre/2 pint/5 cup loaf tin (pan) with clear film (plastic wrap) and cut the sponge fingers to fit the base and sides. Reserve the remaining fingers. Mix the coffee with the brandy in a shallow dish. Dip the sponge fingers briefly into the coffee mixture and return to the tin, sugar side down, to fit.

3 Whip the cream with the icing sugar until it holds soft peaks. Fold half the chopped chocolate into the cream with the hazelnuts. Use a gentle figure-of-eight action to distribute the chocolate and nuts evenly.

4 Melt the remaining chocolate in a bowl set over a pan of barely simmering water. Cool, then fold into the cream mixture. Spoon into the tin.

5 Moisten the remaining fingers in the coffee mixture – take care not to soak the fingers, otherwise they will collapse. Lay the moistened fingers over the filling. Wrap and freeze until firm.

6 To serve, remove from the freezer 30 minutes before serving to allow the ice cream to soften slightly. Turn out on to a serving plate and dust with icing sugar and cocoa powder.

Chocolate Fudge Gâteau

A glorious dessert that is sure to delight everyone.

Serves 8–10
275g/10oz/2¹⁄₂ cups self-raising
   wholemeal (self-rising whole-
   wheat) flour
50g/2oz/¹⁄₂ cup cocoa powder
   (unsweetened)
45ml/3 tbsp baking powder
225g/8oz/1 cup caster
   (superfine) sugar
few drops of vanilla extract
135ml/9 tbsp sunflower oil
350ml/12fl oz/1¹⁄₂ cups water
sifted cocoa powder
   (unsweetened), for sprinkling
25g/1oz/¹⁄₄ cup chopped nuts

For the chocolate fudge
50g/2oz/¹⁄₄ cup soya
   margarine
45ml/3 tbsp water
250g/9oz/2 cups icing
   (confectioners') sugar
30ml/2 tbsp cocoa powder
   (unsweetened)
15–30ml/1–2 tbsp hot water

1 Preheat the oven to 160°C/325°F/Gas 3. Grease a deep 20cm/8in round cake tin (pan), line with baking parchment and grease the paper lightly with a little sunflower oil.

2 Sift the flour, cocoa and baking powder into a mixing bowl. Add the sugar and vanilla extract, then gradually beat in the oil. Gradually add the water, beating constantly to produce a thick batter. Pour into the prepared tin and level the surface.

3 Bake the cake for about 45 minutes or until a fine metal skewer inserted in the centre comes out clean. Leave in the tin for about 5 minutes, before turning out on to a wire rack. Peel off the lining and cool. Cut in half to make two equal layers.

4 Make the chocolate fudge. Place the margarine and water in a pan and heat gently until the margarine has melted. Remove from the heat and sift in the icing sugar and cocoa powder, beating until shiny, adding more hot water if needed. Pour into a bowl and cool until firm enough to spread and pipe.

5 Sandwich the cake layers together with two-thirds of the chocolate fudge. Pipe the remaining chocolate fudge over the cake. Sprinkle with cocoa powder and decorate with the nuts.

Iced Choc. Nut Energy 573Kcal/2380kJ; Protein 5.8g; Carbohydrate 36.8g, of which sugars 30.8g; Fat 44.9g, of which saturates 23.9g; Cholesterol 140mg; Calcium 73mg; Fibre 1.3g; Sodium 37mg.
Choc. Fudge Energy 446Kcal/1878kJ; Protein 4.5g; Carbohydrate 71.5g, of which sugars 50.1g; Fat 17.8g, of which saturates 3.2g; Cholesterol 0mg; Calcium 134mg; Fibre 1.9g; Sodium 218mg.

Devil's Food Cake with Orange Frosting

The classic combination of chocolate and orange makes this dessert irresistible.

Serves 8–10
50g/2oz/½ cup cocoa powder
  (unsweetened)
175ml/6fl oz/¾ cup boiling water
175g/6oz/¾ cup butter, at room
  temperature
350g/12oz/1½ cups soft dark
  brown sugar
3 eggs, at room temperature
225g/8oz/2 cups plain
  (all-purpose) flour

25ml/1½ tsp bicarbonate of soda
  (baking soda)
1.5ml/¼ tsp baking powder
175ml/6fl oz/¾ cup sour cream
pared orange rind, shredded and
  blanched, to decorate

For the frosting
285g/10½oz/1½ cups
  granulated sugar
2 egg whites
60ml/4 tbsp frozen orange juice
  concentrate
15ml/1 tbsp fresh lemon juice
grated rind of 1 orange

1 Preheat the oven to 180°C/350°F/Gas 4. Line two 23cm/9in cake tins (pans) with baking parchment and grease. In a bowl, mix the cocoa and the boiling water until smooth. Set aside.

2 With an electric whisk, cream the butter and sugar until light and fluffy. Add the eggs, one at a time, beating well.

3 When the cocoa mixture is lukewarm, stir into the butter mixture. Sift together the flour, bicarbonate of soda and baking powder twice. Fold into the cocoa mixture in three batches, alternately with the sour cream.

4 Pour into the tins. Bake for 30–35 minutes, until the cakes pull away from the sides. Stand for 15 minutes before turning out.

5 Make the frosting. Place all the ingredients in a bowl set over hot water. With an electric whisk, beat until the mixture holds soft peaks. Remove from the heat and continue beating until thick enough to spread. Sandwich the cake with frosting, then spread over the top and sides. Decorate with orange rind.

Pineapple Upside-Down Cake

Made with handy canned pineapple, this is a favourite year-round dessert. For an added splash of colour, place a halved candied cherry in the middle of each pineapple ring before cooking.

Serves 8
115g/4oz/½ cup butter
225g/8oz/1 cup muscovado
  (molasses) sugar

450g/16oz can pineapple rings,
  drained
4 eggs, separated
grated rind of 1 lemon
pinch of salt
90g/3½oz/½ cup granulated
  sugar
85g/3¼oz/¾ cup plain
  (all-purpose) flour
5ml/1 tsp baking powder
whipped cream, to serve

1 Preheat the oven to 180°C/350°F/Gas 4. Melt the butter in an ovenproof cast-iron frying pan, about 25cm/10in in diameter. Remove 15ml/1 tbsp of the melted butter and set aside.

2 Add the sugar to the frying pan and stir until blended. Place the drained pineapple slices on top in one layer. Set aside.

3 In a bowl, whisk together the egg yolks, reserved butter and lemon rind until smooth and well blended. Set aside.

4 With an electric whisk, beat the egg whites with the salt until stiff. Fold in the granulated sugar, 30ml/2 tbsp at a time. Fold in the egg yolk mixture.

5 Sift the flour and baking powder together. Fold into the egg mixture in three batches. Pour the batter over the pineapple and level the surface.

6 Bake for about 30 minutes or until a metal skewer inserted into the centre of the cake comes out clean.

7 While still hot, place an upside-down serving plate on top of the frying pan. Using oven gloves, firmly hold the pan and plate together, then flip over to turn out the cake. Serve hot or cold with whipped cream.

Devil's Food Cake Energy 537Kcal/2262kJ; Protein 6.5g; Carbohydrate 86.2g, of which sugars 68.5g; Fat 20.9g, of which saturates 12.5g; Cholesterol 105mg; Calcium 101mg; Fibre 1.3g; Sodium 200mg.
Upside-Down Cake Energy 358Kcal/1508kJ; Protein 4.6g; Carbohydrate 55.2g, of which sugars 47.1g; Fat 14.8g, of which saturates 8.3g; Cholesterol 126mg; Calcium 63mg; Fibre 1g; Sodium 126mg.

White Chocolate Cappuccino Gâteau

A sensational, rich gâteau, guaranteed to impress.

Serves 8

4 eggs
115g/4oz/generous ½ cup caster (superfine) sugar
15ml/1 tbsp strong black coffee
2.5ml/½ tsp vanilla extract
115g/4oz/1 cup plain (all-purpose) flour
75g/3oz white chocolate, coarsely grated

For the filling
120ml/4fl oz/½ cup double (heavy) cream or whipping cream
15ml/1 tbsp coffee liqueur

For the topping
15ml/1 tbsp coffee liqueur
1 quantity white chocolate frosting
white chocolate curls
cocoa powder (unsweetened) or ground cinnamon, for dusting

1 Preheat the oven to 180°C/350°F/Gas 4. Grease two 18cm/7in round sandwich cake tins (layer cake pans) and line the base of each with baking parchment.

2 Combine the eggs, caster sugar, coffee and vanilla extract in a large heatproof bowl. Place over a pan of hot water and whisk until pale and thick.

3 Sift half the flour over the mixture; fold in gently and evenly. Fold in the remaining flour with the grated white chocolate.

4 Divide the mixture between the prepared tins and smooth level. Bake for 20–25 minutes, until firm and golden brown, then turn out on to wire racks and leave to cool completely.

5 Make the filling. Whip the cream with the coffee liqueur in a bowl until it holds its shape. Spread over one of the cakes, then place the second layer on top.

6 Stir the coffee liqueur into the frosting. Spread over the top and sides of the cake, swirling with a palette knife. Top with curls of white chocolate and dust with cocoa or cinnamon. Transfer the cake to a serving plate and set aside until the frosting has set. Serve that day.

Death by Chocolate

One of the richest chocolate cakes ever.

Serves 16–20

225g/8oz dark (bittersweet) chocolate, broken into squares
115g/4oz/½ cup unsalted (sweet) butter
150ml/¼ pint/⅔ cup milk
225g/8oz/1 cup light muscovado (brown) sugar
10ml/2 tsp vanilla extract
2 eggs, separated
150ml/¼ pint/⅔ cup sour cream
225g/8oz/2 cups self-raising (self-rising) flour
5ml/1 tsp baking powder

For the filling
60ml/4 tbsp seedless raspberry jam
60ml/4 tbsp brandy
400g/14oz dark (bittersweet) chocolate, broken into squares
200g/7oz/scant 1 cup unsalted (sweet) butter

For the topping
250ml/8fl oz/1 cup double (heavy) cream
225g/8oz dark (bittersweet) chocolate, broken into squares
plain (semisweet) and white chocolate curls, to decorate
chocolate-dipped physalis, to serve (optional)

1 Preheat the oven to 180°C/350°F/Gas 4. Grease and base-line a deep 23cm/9in springform cake tin (pan). Place the chocolate, butter and milk in a pan. Heat gently until smooth. Remove from the heat, beat in the sugar and vanilla, then cool.

2 Beat the egg yolks and cream in a bowl, then beat into the chocolate mixture. Sift the flour and baking powder over the surface and fold in. Whisk the egg whites in a grease-free bowl until stiff; fold into the mixture.

3 Scrape into the prepared tin and bake for 45–55 minutes, or until firm. Cool in the tin for 15 minutes, then turn out and cool.

4 Slice the cold cake across the middle to make three even layers. In a small pan, warm the jam with 15ml/1 tbsp of the brandy, then brush over two of the layers. Heat the remaining brandy in a pan with the chocolate and butter, stirring, until smooth. Cool until beginning to thicken.

5 Spread the bottom layer of the cake with half the chocolate filling, taking care not to disturb the jam. Top with a second layer, jam side up, and spread with the remaining filling. Top with the final layer and press lightly. Leave to set.

6 Make the topping. Heat the cream and chocolate together in a pan over a low heat, stirring frequently until the chocolate has melted. Pour into a bowl, leave to cool, then whisk until the mixture begins to hold its shape.

7 Spread the top and sides of the cake with the chocolate topping. Decorate with chocolate curls and chocolate-dipped physalis, if you like.

> **Cook's Tip**
> For chocolate-coated physalis, melt the chocolate in a bowl, then dip in the fruit, holding them by their tops. Leave to set.

Cappuccino Gâteau Energy 337Kcal/1418kJ; Protein 5.3g; Carbohydrate 50.5g, of which sugars 39.5g; Fat 13.6g, of which saturates 7.4g; Cholesterol 116mg; Calcium 61mg; Fibre 0.7g; Sodium 41mg.
Death by Chocolate Energy 432Kcal/1809kJ; Protein 4.7g; Carbohydrate 49.9g, of which sugars 38.4g; Fat 24.7g, of which saturates 14.9g; Cholesterol 57mg; Calcium 99mg; Fibre 1.4g; Sodium 120mg.

Maple & Walnut Meringue Gâteau

This simple dessert is a real treat for all meringue lovers. Before serving the gâteau, allow it to thaw slightly in the refrigerator in order to enjoy the full flavour.

Serves 10–12
4 egg whites
200g/7oz/1 cup light muscovado (brown) sugar
150g/5oz/1¼ cups walnut pieces
600ml/1 pint/2½ cups double (heavy) cream
150ml/¼ pint/⅔ cup maple syrup, plus extra to serve

1 Preheat the oven to 140°C/275°F/Gas 1. Draw three 23cm/9in circles on separate sheets of baking parchment. Invert the sheets on to three baking sheets.

2 Whisk the egg whites in a grease-free bowl until stiff. Whisk in the sugar, about 15ml/1 tbsp at a time, whisking well after each addition until the meringue is stiff and glossy.

3 Spread the meringue on to the baking parchment to within 1cm/½in of the edge of each marked circle. Bake for about 1 hour or until crisp, swapping the baking sheets around halfway through cooking. Leave to cool.

4 Set aside 45ml/3 tbsp of the walnuts. Finely chop the remainder. Whip the cream with the maple syrup until it forms soft peaks. Fold in the chopped walnuts. Use about a third of the mixture to sandwich the meringues together on a flat, freezerproof serving plate.

5 Using a palette knife, spread the remaining cream mixture over the top and sides of the gâteau. Sprinkle with the reserved walnuts and freeze overnight.

6 Transfer the gâteau to the refrigerator about 1 hour before serving so that the cream filling softens slightly.

7 Just before serving, drizzle a little of the extra maple syrup over the gâteau. Serve in slices.

Black Forest Gâteau

This classic gâteau makes a great dinner-party dessert.

Serves 8–10
6 eggs
200g/7oz/1 cup caster (superfine) sugar
5ml/1 tsp vanilla extract
50g/2oz/½ cup plain (all-purpose) flour
50g/2oz/½ cup cocoa powder (unsweetened)
115g/4oz/½ cup unsalted (sweet) butter, melted

grated chocolate, chocolate curls and morello cherries, to decorate

For the filling and topping
60ml/4 tbsp Kirsch
600ml/1 pint/2½ cups double (heavy) cream
30ml/2 tbsp icing (confectioners') sugar
2.5ml/½ tsp vanilla extract
675g/1½lb jar pitted morello cherries, well drained

1 Preheat the oven to 180°C/350°F/Gas 4. Grease three 19cm/7½in sandwich cake tins (layer cake pans). Line the bottom of each with baking parchment. Combine the eggs with the sugar and vanilla in a bowl and beat until pale and very thick.

2 Sift the flour and cocoa powder over the mixture and fold in lightly with a metal spoon. Gently stir in the melted butter.

3 Divide the mixture among the prepared cake tins, smoothing them level. Bake for 15–18 minutes, until the cakes have risen and are springy to the touch. Leave to cool in the tins for about 5 minutes, then turn out and cool completely. Remove the lining.

4 Prick each layer all over with a skewer, then sprinkle with Kirsch. Using a hand-held electric mixer, whip the cream until it starts to thicken, then gradually beat in the icing sugar and vanilla extract until the mixture begins to hold its shape.

5 Spread one cake layer with flavoured cream and top with about half the cherries. Repeat with the second cake layer, then place on top of the first layer. Top with the third cake layer. Spread the remaining cream all over the cake. Press grated chocolate over the sides and decorate with curls and cherries.

Black Forest Energy 570Kcal/2371kJ; Protein 2.9g; Carbohydrate 44g, of which sugars 39.6g; Fat 42.8g, of which saturates 26.7g; Cholesterol 107mg; Calcium 67mg; Fibre 1.2g; Sodium 137mg.
Maple & Walnut Energy 441Kcal/1830kJ; Protein 3.7g; Carbohydrate 28.6g, of which sugars 28.5g; Fat 35.4g, of which saturates 17.4g; Cholesterol 69mg; Calcium 48mg; Fibre 0.4g; Sodium 67mg.

Apricot & Orange Roulade

Guests will be pleased to know that this elegant dessert has a very low fat content.

Serves 6
low-fat spread, for greasing
4 egg whites
115g/4oz/generous ½ cup golden caster (superfine) sugar
50g/2oz/½ cup plain (all-purpose) flour
finely grated rind of 1 small orange
45ml/3 tbsp orange juice

For the filling
115g/4oz/½ cup ready-to-eat dried apricots
150ml/¼ pint/⅔ cup orange juice
10ml/2 tsp icing (confectioners') sugar, for sprinkling
shreds of orange rind, to decorate

1 Preheat the oven to 200°C/400°F/Gas 6. Grease a 23 x 33cm/9 x 13in Swiss roll tin (jelly roll pan) and line it with baking parchment. Grease the paper.

2 Make the roulade. Pace the egg whites in a large clean bowl and whisk until they hold soft peaks. Gradually add the sugar, whisking vigorously between each addition.

3 Fold in the flour, orange rind and juice. Spoon the mixture into the prepared tin and spread it evenly.

4 Bake for 15–18 minutes, or until the sponge is firm and light golden in colour. Turn out on to a sheet of baking parchment and roll it up loosely from one short side. Leave to cool.

5 Roughly chop the dried apricots and put in a pan, with the orange juice. Cover the pan and leave to simmer until most of the liquid has been absorbed. Purée in a blender or food processor until smooth.

6 Unroll the roulade, spread the surface with the apricot mixture, then roll up. To decorate, arrange strips of paper diagonally across the roll, then sprinkle lightly with lines of icing sugar. Remove the paper, scatter the top of the roulade with orange rind and serve.

Gingerbread Upside-Down Pudding

A proper pudding goes down well on a cold winter's day. This one is quite quick and easy to make and looks very impressive.

Serves 4–6
sunflower oil, for brushing
15ml/1 tbsp soft brown sugar
4 medium peaches, halved and stoned (pitted), or canned peach halves
8 walnut halves

For the base
130g/4½oz/generous 1 cup wholemeal (whole-wheat) flour
2.5ml/½ tsp bicarbonate of soda (baking soda)
7.5ml/1½ tsp ground ginger
5ml/1 tsp ground cinnamon
115g/4oz/scant ½ cup muscovado (molasses) sugar
1 egg
120ml/4fl oz/½ cup skimmed milk
50ml/2fl oz/¼ cup sunflower oil

1 Preheat the oven to 180°C/350°F/Gas 4. For the topping, brush the base and sides of a 23cm/9in round springform cake tin (pan) with oil. Sprinkle the sugar over the base.

2 Arrange the peaches, cut side down, in the tin, placing a walnut half in each.

3 Sift together the flour, bicarbonate of soda, ginger and cinnamon, then stir in the sugar. Beat together the egg, milk and oil, then mix into the dry ingredients.

4 Pour the mixture evenly over the peaches and bake for 35–40 minutes, until firm to the touch. Turn out and serve hot.

Cook's Tips
• To turn out successfully, run the point of a sharp knife round the edge of the pudding, then place a serving plate upside-down on top. Holding the plate and tin (pan) firmly, invert. Release the sides of the tin and remove.
• To accentuate the ginger flavour, finely chop 15ml/1 tbsp drained stem ginger in syrup and add at the end of step 3.

Roulade Energy 164Kcal/697kJ; Protein 3.7g; Carbohydrate 39g, of which sugars 32.6g; Fat 0.3g, of which saturates 0g; Cholesterol 0mg; Calcium 42mg; Fibre 1.5g; Sodium 48mg.
Gingerbread Pud. Energy 272Kcal/1145kJ; Protein 4.8g; Carbohydrate 44.1g, of which sugars 27.5g; Fat 9.7g, of which saturates 1.4g; Cholesterol 33mg; Calcium 77mg; Fibre 1.5g; Sodium 23mg.

Hot Plum Batter Pudding

Other fruits can be used in place of plums, depending on the season. Canned black cherries are a convenient substitute to keep in the store cupboard.

Serves 4

450g/1lb ripe red plums, quartered and stoned (pitted)
200ml/7fl oz/scant 1 cup skimmed milk
60ml/4 tbsp skimmed milk powder
15ml/1 tbsp light muscovado (brown) sugar
5ml/1 tsp vanilla extract
75g/3oz/²⁄₃ cup self-raising (self-rising) flour
2 egg whites
icing (confectioners') sugar, to sprinkle
natural (plain) yogurt or crème fraîche, to serve

1 Preheat the oven to 220°C/425°F/Gas 7. Lightly oil a wide, shallow ovenproof dish and add the plums.

2 Pour the milk, milk powder, sugar, vanilla extract, flour and egg whites into a blender or food processor. Process the mixture to form a smooth batter.

3 Pour the batter over the plums in the dish. Bake for 25–30 minutes, or until the top is puffed and golden. Sprinkle with icing sugar and serve immediately with yogurt or crème fraîche.

Cook's Tips
• If you don't have a food processor, then place the dry ingredients for the batter in a large bowl and gradually whisk in the milk and egg whites.
• Flavoured cream would be delicious served with this dessert. Lightly whip double (heavy) cream, stir in a spoonful or two of your favourite liqueur and sweeten to taste.

Variation
Halved fresh or canned apricots are tasty instead of the plums, or try cherries, pre-soaked in a little kirsch for an added kick.

Glazed Apricot Sponge

Proper puddings can be extremely high in saturated fat, but this particular version uses the minimum of oil and no eggs. Fat-free natural or apricot yogurt would make a suitably healthy and tasty accompaniment to this delicious dessert.

Serves 4

10ml/2 tsp golden (light corn) syrup
411g/14½oz can apricot halves in fruit juice
150g/5oz/1¼ cups self-raising (self-rising) flour
75g/3oz/1½ cups fresh breadcrumbs
90g/3½oz/½ cup light muscovado (brown) sugar
5ml/1 tsp ground cinnamon
30ml/2 tbsp sunflower oil
175ml/6fl oz/¾ cup skimmed milk

1 Preheat the oven to 180°C/350°F/Gas 4. Lightly oil a 900ml/1½ pint/3¾ cup ovenproof bowl. Carefully spoon in the golden syrup.

2 Drain the apricots and reserve the juice. Arrange about 8 halves, rounded side up, in the bowl. Purée the rest of the apricots with the juice and set aside.

3 Mix together the flour, breadcrumbs, sugar and cinnamon in a mixing bowl, then beat in the oil and milk. Spoon into the ovenproof bowl on top of the apricots.

4 Bake the mixture for 50–55 minutes, or until firm to the touch and golden on top. Run a knife around the pudding to loosen it from the bowl, then turn it out on to a plate. Serve with the puréed fruit as an accompaniment.

Cook's tips
To make fresh breadcrumbs, use bread that is a couple of days old and process in a blender or food processor, or use a grater.

Plum Batter Pudding Energy 139Kcal/594kJ; Protein 5.5g; Carbohydrate 30.2g, of which sugars 16.3g; Fat 0.5g, of which saturates 0.1g; Cholesterol 2mg; Calcium 144mg; Fibre 2.4g; Sodium 123mg.
Apricot Sponge Energy 348Kcal/1485kJ; Protein 7.6g; Carbohydrate 79.1g, of which sugars 37.2g; Fat 2.4g, of which saturates 0.6g; Cholesterol 3mg; Calcium 242mg; Fibre 2.5g; Sodium 310mg.

Queen of Puddings

This hot pudding was developed from a seventeenth-century recipe by Queen Victoria's chefs and named in her honour.

Serves 4
75g/3oz/1½ cups fresh breadcrumbs
50g/2oz/¼ cup caster (superfine) sugar, plus 5ml/1 tsp
grated rind of 1 lemon
600ml/1 pint/2½ cups milk
4 eggs
45ml/3 tbsp raspberry jam, warmed

1 Preheat the oven to 160°C/325°F/Gas 3. Stir the breadcrumbs, half of the sugar and the lemon rind together in a bowl. Bring the milk to the boil in a pan, then stir into the breadcrumb mixture.

2 Separate three of the eggs and beat the yolks with the whole egg. Stir into the breadcrumb mixture, pour into a buttered baking dish and leave to stand for 30 minutes, then bake the pudding for 50–60 minutes, until set.

3 Whisk the three egg whites in a large, clean grease-free bowl until stiff but not dry, then gradually whisk in the remaining sugar until the mixture is thick and glossy, taking care that you do not overwhisk.

4 Spread the jam over the pudding, then spoon over the meringue to cover the top completely.

5 Sprinkle the remaining sugar over the meringue, then bake for a further 15 minutes, until the meringue is beginning to turn a light golden colour.

> **Cook's Tip**
> Ring the changes by using another flavoured jam, lemon curd, marmalade or fruit purée.

Christmas Pudding

Christmas day wouldn't seem the same without this traditional British dessert. It is absolutely delicious served with brandy or rum butter, whisky sauce, custard or whipped cream. Top with a decorative sprig of holly for a festive touch.

Serves 8
115g/4oz/½ cup butter, plus extra for greasing
225g/8oz/generous 1 cup soft dark brown sugar
50g/2oz/½ cup self-raising (self-rising) flour
5ml/1 tsp mixed spice (pumpkin pie spice)
1.5ml/¼ tsp grated nutmeg
2.5ml/½ tsp ground cinnamon
2 eggs
115g/4oz/2 cups fresh white breadcrumbs
175g/6oz/1 cup sultanas (golden raisins)
175g/6oz/generous 1 cup raisins
115g/4oz/½ cup currants
25g/1oz/3 tbsp mixed (candied) peel, chopped finely
25g/1oz/¼ cup chopped almonds
1 small cooking apple, peeled, cored and coarsely grated
finely grated rind of 1 orange or lemon
juice of 1 orange or lemon, made up to 150ml/¼ pint/⅔ cup with brandy, rum or sherry

1 Cut a disc of baking parchment to fit the base of one 1.2 litre/2 pint/5 cup heatproof bowl or two 600ml/1 pint/2½ cup heatproof bowls and butter each disc and bowl.

2 Whisk the butter and sugar together until soft. Beat in the flour, spices and eggs. Stir in the remaining ingredients thoroughly. The mixture should have a soft dropping consistency.

3 Turn the mixture into the greased bowl(s) and level the top with a spoon. Cover neatly with another disc of buttered baking parchment.

4 Make a pleat across the centre of a large piece of baking parchment and cover the bowl(s) with it, tying it in place with string under the rim. Cut off the excess paper. Pleat a piece of foil in the same way and cover the bowl(s) with it, tucking it around the bowl neatly, under the paper frill. Tie another piece of string around and across the top, as a handle.

5 Place the bowl(s) in a steamer over a pan of simmering water and steam for 6 hours. Alternatively, put into a large pan and pour round enough boiling water to come halfway up the bowl(s) and cover the pan with a tight-fitting lid. Check the water is simmering and remember to top it up with boiling water as it evaporates.

6 When the pudding(s) have cooked, leave to cool completely. Then remove the foil and paper. Wipe the bowls(s) clean and replace the paper and foil with clean pieces, ready for reheating.

> **Cook's Tip**
> To reheat, steam for 2 hours. Turn on to a plate and leave to stand for 5 minutes, before removing the bowl (the steam will rise to the top and help to loosen the pudding). The dish can be made up to a month in advance; store in a cool, dry place.

Queen of Puddings Energy 297Kcal/1259kJ; Protein 13.7g; Carbohydrate 45g, of which sugars 31g; Fat 8.5g, of which saturates 3.2g; Cholesterol 199mg; Calcium 242mg; Fibre 0.4g; Sodium 281mg.
Christmas Pudding Energy 530Kcal/2236kJ; Protein 6.3g; Carbohydrate 89.9g, of which sugars 74.4g; Fat 15.6g, of which saturates 8g; Cholesterol 78mg; Calcium 116mg; Fibre 2.2g; Sodium 259mg.

Chestnut Pudding

This is an Italian speciality, made during the months of October and November, when fresh sweet chestnuts are gathered.

Serves 4–5
450g/1lb fresh sweet chestnuts
300ml/½ pint/1¼ cups milk
115g/4oz/generous ½ cup caster (superfine) sugar

2 eggs, separated, at room temperature
25g/1oz/¼ cup cocoa powder (unsweetened)
2.5ml/½ tsp vanilla extract
50g/2oz/½ cup icing (confectioners') sugar, sifted
whipped cream and marrons glacés (candied chestnuts), to decorate

1 Cut a cross in the side of the chestnuts, then drop them into a pan of boiling water. Cook for 5–6 minutes. Remove with a slotted spoon and peel while still warm.

2 Place the peeled chestnuts in a heavy or non-stick pan with the milk and half of the caster sugar. Cook over low heat, stirring occasionally, until soft. Remove from the heat and allow to cool, then press the pan contents through a sieve (strainer).

3 Preheat the oven to 180°C/350°F/Gas 4. Beat the egg yolks with the remaining caster sugar until the mixture is pale yellow and fluffy. Beat in the cocoa powder and the vanilla.

4 In a separate clean bowl, whisk the egg whites with a wire whisk or electric whisk until they form soft peaks. Gradually beat in the sifted icing sugar and continue beating until the mixture forms stiff peaks.

5 Fold the chestnut and egg yolk mixtures together. Fold in the egg whites. Turn the mixture into one large or several individual buttered ovenproof moulds or bowls. Place on a baking sheet and bake in the oven for 12–20 minutes, depending on the size.

6 Remove the moulds or bowls from the oven. Allow to cool for 10 minutes then carefully turn out. Serve decorated with whipped cream and marrons glacés.

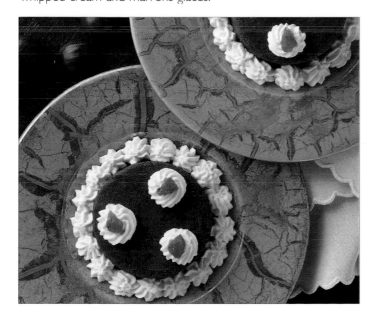

Bread Pudding with Pecan Nuts

A version of the British classic bread pudding, deliciously flavoured with pecan nuts and orange rind.

Serves 6
400ml/14fl oz/1⅔ cups milk
400ml/14fl oz/1⅔ cups single (light) or whipping cream
150g/5oz/¾ cup caster (superfine) sugar

3 eggs, beaten to mix
10ml/2 tsp grated orange rind
5ml/1 tsp vanilla extract
24 slices day-old French bread, 1cm/½in thick
75g/3oz/½ cup toasted pecan nuts, chopped
icing (confectioners') sugar, for sprinkling
whipped cream or sour cream and maple syrup, to serve

1 Put 350ml/12fl oz/1½ cups each of the milk and cream in a pan. Add the sugar. Warm over low heat, stirring to dissolve the sugar. Remove from the heat and cool. Add the eggs, orange rind and vanilla and mix well.

2 Arrange half of the bread slices in a buttered 23–25cm/9–10in baking dish. Sprinkle two-thirds of the pecans over the bread. Arrange the remaining bread slices on top and sprinkle over the rest of the pecans.

3 Pour the egg mixture evenly over the bread slices. Soak for 30 minutes. Press the top layer of bread down into the liquid once or twice.

4 Preheat the oven to 180°C/350°F/Gas 4. If the top layer of bread slices looks dry and all the liquid has been absorbed, moisten with the remaining milk and cream.

5 Place the baking dish in a roasting pan. Add enough boiling water to the pan to come halfway up the sides of the dish. Transfer to the oven and bake for 40 minutes or until the pudding is set and golden brown on top.

6 Sprinkle the top with sifted icing sugar and serve warm, with whipped cream or sour cream and maple syrup.

Chestnut Pudding Energy 356Kcal/1506kJ; Protein 7.4g; Carbohydrate 70.8g, of which sugars 43.6g; Fat 6.8g, of which saturates 2.4g; Cholesterol 80mg; Calcium 149mg; Fibre 4.3g; Sodium 113mg.
Bread Pudding Energy 731Kcal/3085kJ; Protein 20.9g; Carbohydrate 106.3g, of which sugars 35g; Fat 27.9g, of which saturates 10.8g; Cholesterol 136mg; Calcium 336mg; Fibre 3.8g; Sodium 906mg.

Cabinet Pudding

This rich custard is baked with dried fruit and sponge cake to make a delightful old-fashioned dessert. You can leave out the brandy if you wish, but it definitely adds a touch of something special to the dish.

Serves 4
25g/1oz/2½ tbsp chopped raisins
30ml/2 tbsp brandy (optional)
butter, for greasing
25g/1oz/2½ tbsp glacé
    (candied) fruit
25g/1oz/2½ tbsp angelica,
    chopped
2 trifle sponge cakes, diced
50g/2oz ratafia biscuits
    (almond macaroons)
2 eggs
2 egg yolks
30ml/2 tbsp sugar
450ml/¾ pint/scant 2 cups single
    (light) cream or milk
a few drops of vanilla extract

1 Place the raisins in a bowl with the brandy, if using, and leave to soak for several hours.

2 Grease a 750ml/1¼ pint/3 cup charlotte mould or round ovenproof dish with butter and arrange some of the cherries and angelica in the base.

3 Mix the remaining cherries and angelica with the sponge cakes, ratafias and raisins. Mix in the brandy, if using, and spoon into the mould or dish.

4 Lightly whisk together the eggs, egg yolks and sugar. Bring the cream or milk just to the boil in a pan, then stir into the egg mixture with the vanilla extract.

5 Strain the egg mixture into the mould or dish, then leave to stand for 15–30 minutes.

6 Preheat the oven to 160°C/325°F/Gas 3. Place the mould in a roasting pan, cover with baking parchment and pour in boiling water so that it comes halfway up the side of the mould or dish. Bake for 1 hour, or until the custard is set. Leave to stand for 2–3 minutes, then loosen the edge with a knife and turn out on to a warm plate, to serve.

Chocolate, Date & Walnut Pudding

This tempting pudding is not steamed in the traditional way, but baked in the oven. The result is still completely irresistible.

Serves 4
25g/1oz/¼ cup chopped walnuts
25g/1oz/2 tbsp chopped dates
2 eggs, separated
5ml/1 tsp vanilla extract
30ml/2 tbsp golden caster
    (superfine) sugar
45ml/3 tbsp plain wholemeal (all-
    purpose whole-wheat) flour
15ml/1 tbsp cocoa powder
    (unsweetened)
30ml/2 tbsp skimmed milk

1 Preheat the oven to 180°C/350°F/Gas 4. Grease and base-line with baking parchment a 1.2 litre/2 pint/5 cup ovenproof bowl. Spoon in the walnuts and dates.

2 Combine the egg yolks, vanilla extract and sugar in a heatproof bowl. Place over a pan of hot water.

3 Whisk the egg whites to soft peaks. Whisk the egg yolk mixture until it is thick and pale, then remove the bowl from the heat. Sift the flour and cocoa over the mixture and fold them in with a metal spoon. Stir in the milk, to soften the mixture, then fold in the egg whites.

4 Spoon the mixture over the walnuts and dates in the prepared bowl and bake for 40–45 minutes or until the pudding is well risen and firm to the touch. Run a knife around the pudding to loosen it from the bowl, and then turn it out on to a plate and serve immediately.

Cook's Tips
• Pudding fans won't be satisfied without custard to accompany this dessert. Why not serve a real custard, Crème Anglaise, made using cream, egg yolks, caster (superfine) sugar and a few drops of vanilla extract?
• If you wish, the cocoa can be omitted and the sponge mix flavoured with grated orange rind instead.

Cab. Pudding Energy 436Kcal/1818kJ; Protein 11.5g; Carbohydrate 34.2g, of which sugars 27.6g; Fat 29.2g, of which saturates 15.8g; Cholesterol 326mg; Calcium 164mg; Fibre 0.7g; Sodium 119mg.
Choc., Date & Wal. Energy 171Kcal/716kJ; Protein 6.2g; Carbohydrate 19.5g, of which sugars 10.5g; Fat 8.2g, of which saturates 1.7g; Cholesterol 96mg; Calcium 55mg; Fibre 1.1g; Sodium 76mg.

Rich Chocolate Brioche Bake

This dessert is amazingly easy to make and doesn't require many ingredients. Richly flavoured and quite delicious, it's the perfect dish for mid-week entertaining, when you are pushed for time. Serve with a platter of sliced tropical fruit as a foil to the richness of the dish.

Serves 4

40g/1½oz/3 tbsp unsalted (sweet) butter, plus extra for greasing
200g/7oz plain (semisweet) chocolate, chopped into small pieces
60ml/4 tbsp bitter marmalade
4 individual brioches, cut into halves, or 1 large brioche loaf, cut into thick slices
3 eggs
300ml/½ pint/1¼ cups milk
300ml/½ pint/1¼ cups single (light) cream
30ml/2 tbsp demerara (raw) sugar
crème fraîche, to serve

1 Preheat the oven to 180°C/350°F/Gas 4. Using the extra butter, lightly grease a shallow ovenproof dish.

2 Melt the chocolate with the marmalade and butter in a heatproof bowl over just simmering water, stirring the mixture occasionally, until smooth.

3 Spread the melted chocolate mixture over the brioche slices, then carefully arrange them in the dish so that the slices overlap in neat rows.

4 Beat the eggs in a large bowl, then add the milk and cream and mix well. Transfer to a jug (pitcher) and pour evenly over the slices.

5 Sprinkle the mixture with the demerara sugar and bake for 40–50 minutes, until the custard has set lightly and the brioche slices are golden brown. Serve immediately, topped with dollops of crème fraîche.

Sticky Toffee Pudding

Filling and warming, this tasty variation on a classic pudding will soon become a firm family favourite.

Serves 6

115g/4oz/1 cup toasted walnuts, chopped
175g/6oz/¾ cup butter
175g/6oz/scant 1 cup soft brown sugar
60ml/4 tbsp single (light) cream
30ml/2 tbsp freshly squeezed lemon juice
2 eggs, beaten
115g/4oz/1 cup self-raising (self-rising) flour

1 Prepare a steamer or half fill a pan with water and bring it to the boil. Grease a 900ml/1½ pint/3¾ cup heatproof bowl and add half the walnuts.

2 Heat 50g/2oz/4 tbsp of the butter with 50g/2oz/4 tbsp of the sugar, the cream and 15ml/1 tbsp of the lemon juice in a small pan, stirring until smooth. Pour half the sauce into the greased bowl, then swirl to coat it a little way up the sides. Reserve the remaining sauce.

3 Beat the remaining butter and sugar until light and fluffy, then gradually beat in the eggs. Fold in the flour and the remaining nuts and lemon juice and spoon into the bowl.

4 Cover the bowl with baking parchment with a pleat folded in the centre, then tie securely with string. Steam the pudding for about 1¼ hours, topping up the boiling water as required, until it is set in the centre.

5 Just before serving, gently warm the remaining sauce. To serve, run a knife around the edge of the pudding to loosen it, then turn out on to a warm plate and pour over the sauce.

Cook's Tip
Putting a pleat in the paper cover allows room for the pudding to rise. Secure tightly to prevent water or steam entering.

Sticky Toffee Pudding Energy 571Kcal/2378kJ; Protein 7.3g; Carbohydrate 46g, of which sugars 31.6g; Fat 41.1g, of which saturates 18g; Cholesterol 131mg; Calcium 124mg; Fibre 1.3g; Sodium 275mg.
Brioche Bake Energy 987Kcal/4143kJ; Protein 25.9g; Carbohydrate 127.8g, of which sugars 59.1g; Fat 45g, of which saturates 25.4g; Cholesterol 213mg; Calcium 460mg; Fibre 4.4g; Sodium 1060mg.

Fruit & Spice Bread Pudding

Made with brown bread and skimmed milk, this is a very healthy and utterly delicious version of an old favourite.

Serves 4
6 medium slices wholemeal (whole-wheat) bread
low-fat spread, for greasing
50g/2oz apricot or strawberry jam

50g/2oz/⅓ cup sultanas (golden raisins)
50g/2oz/¼ cup ready-to-eat dried apricots, chopped
50g/2oz/¼ cup soft light brown sugar
5ml/1 tsp mixed (apple pie) spice
2 eggs
600ml/1 pint/2½ cups skimmed milk
finely grated rind of 1 lemon

1 Preheat the oven to 160°C/325°F/Gas 3. Lightly grease an ovenproof dish with the spread.

2 Remove and discard the crusts from the bread. Spread the bread slices with jam and cut into small triangles.

3 Place half the bread triangles in the greased ovenproof dish, arranging them in neat rows and overlapping the pointed ends.

4 Mix together the sultanas, apricots, sugar and spice and sprinkle half the fruit mixture over the bread in the dish. Top with the remaining bread triangles and then sprinkle over the remaining fruit.

5 Beat the eggs, milk and lemon rind together in a jug (pitcher) and pour over the bread. Set aside for about 30 minutes, to allow the bread to absorb some of the liquid.

6 Bake the pudding in the oven for 45–60 minutes, until lightly set and golden brown. Serve hot or cold.

> **Cook's Tip**
> If you like, serve with fat-free yogurt as an accompaniment.

Peaches with Amaretti Stuffing

Peaches are both plentiful and luscious all over Italy. They are sometimes prepared hot, as in this traditional dish, which also adds the distinctive Italian signature of amaretti. Use properly ripened, good quality peaches – forced, over-hard supermarket fruit can produce a disappointing result.

Serves 4
4 ripe fresh peaches
juice of ½ lemon
65g/2½oz/⅔ cup amaretti, crushed
30ml/2 tbsp Marsala, brandy or peach brandy
25g/1oz/2 tbsp butter, at room temperature
2.5ml/½ tsp vanilla extract
30ml/2 tbsp granulated sugar
1 egg yolk

1 Preheat the oven to 180°C/350°F/Gas 4. Wash the peaches. Cut them in half and remove the stones (pits). Enlarge the hollow left by the stones with a small spoon.

2 Sprinkle the peach halves with the lemon juice.

3 Soften the amaretti crumbs in the Marsala or brandy for a few minutes.

4 Beat the butter until soft. Stir in the amaretti mixture and all the remaining ingredients.

5 Arrange the peach halves in a baking dish in one layer, hollow side upwards.

6 Divide the amaretti mixture into 8 parts, and fill the hollows, mounding the stuffing up in the centre.

7 Bake for 35–40 minutes. Serve hot or cold.

> **Cook's Tip**
> Serve these peaches with Zabaglione – made with the same wine or spirit – for a sensational dinner party dessert.

Bread Pudding Energy 303Kcal/1287kJ; Protein 12.6g; Carbohydrate 58.1g, of which sugars 39.1g; Fat 4.1g, of which saturates 1g; Cholesterol 101mg; Calcium 267mg; Fibre 1.7g; Sodium 319mg.
Peaches with Stuffing Energy 215Kcal/905kJ; Protein 2.8g; Carbohydrate 29.1g, of which sugars 22.1g; Fat 8.7g, of which saturates 4.6g; Cholesterol 64mg; Calcium 40mg; Fibre 1.9g; Sodium 95mg.

Spiced Peach Crumble

Fruit crumbles of various kinds have long been a traditional British family dessert. This peach crumble recipe offers a twist to the tradition, with rolled oats added for extra taste and crunchiness.

Serves 6

1.3kg/3lb ripe but firm peaches, peeled, stoned (pitted) and sliced
50g/2oz/¼ cup caster (superfine) sugar
2.5ml/½ tsp ground cinnamon
5ml/1 tsp lemon juice
whipped cream or vanilla ice cream, for serving (optional)

For the topping

115g/4oz/1 cup plain (all-purpose) flour
1.5ml/¼ tsp ground cinnamon
1.5ml/¼ tsp ground allspice
75g/3oz/scant 1 cup rolled oats
175g/6oz/¾ cup soft light brown sugar
115g/4oz/½ cup butter

1 Preheat the oven to 190°C/375°F/Gas 5. Make the topping for the fruit crumble. Sift the flour and the spices into a large mixing bowl.

2 Add the oats and sugar and stir to combine thoroughly. Cut or rub in the butter until the mixture resembles coarse breadcrumbs.

3 Toss the peaches with the sugar, cinnamon and lemon juice and place in a 20–23cm/8–9in diameter ovenproof dish.

4 Sprinkle the topping over the fruit in an even layer. Bake for 30–35 minutes.

5 Serve with cream or ice cream, if you like.

Variation

Try using fresh apricots instead of peaches, but leave the skins on the apricots. This dish also works well if you substitute nutmeg for cinnamon.

Rich Chocolate & Coffee Pudding

This heavenly dessert boasts a rich sponge topping with a luscious sauce underneath.

Serves 6

90g/3½oz/¾ cup plain (all-purpose) flour
10ml/2 tsp baking powder
pinch of salt
50g/2oz/¼ cup butter or margarine
25g/1oz plain (semisweet) chocolate, chopped into small pieces
115g/4oz/generous ½ cup caster (superfine) sugar
75ml/2½fl oz/⅓ cup milk
1.5ml/¼ tsp vanilla extract
whipped cream, to serve

For the topping

30ml/2 tbsp instant coffee powder or granules
325ml/11fl oz/1⅓ cups hot water
90g/3½oz/½ cup soft dark brown sugar
65g/2½oz/5 tbsp caster (superfine) sugar
30ml/2 tbsp cocoa powder (unsweetened)

1 Preheat the oven to 180°C/350°F/Gas 4. Grease a 23cm/9in square non-stick baking tin (pan).

2 Sift the flour, baking powder and salt into a small bowl. Set aside.

3 Melt the butter or margarine, chocolate and caster sugar in a heatproof bowl set over a pan of simmering water, or in a double boiler, stirring occasionally. Remove the bowl from the heat.

4 Add the flour mixture and stir well. Stir in the milk and vanilla extract. Mix well, then pour into the prepared tin.

5 Make the topping. Dissolve the coffee in the water in a bowl. Allow to cool. Mix the brown sugar, caster sugar and cocoa powder in a bowl. Sprinkle the mixture over the pudding mixture in the tin.

6 Pour the coffee evenly over the surface. Bake for 40 minutes or until the pudding is risen and set on top. The coffee mixture will have formed a delicious creamy sauce underneath. Serve immediately with whipped cream.

Peach Crumble Energy 495Kcal/2090kJ; Protein 6.2g; Carbohydrate 84g, of which sugars 60.3g; Fat 17.4g, of which saturates 10g; Cholesterol 41mg; Calcium 76mg; Fibre 5.2g; Sodium 126mg.
Choc. & Coffee Pudding Energy 325Kcal/1371kJ; Protein 3g; Carbohydrate 60.6g, of which sugars 50.5g; Fat 9.5g, of which saturates 5.8g; Cholesterol 19mg; Calcium 66mg; Fibre 1.1g; Sodium 107mg.

Greek Honey & Lemon Cake

Capture the flavour of Greece with this luscious cake, drenched in honey and lemon juice. The semolina in the recipe gives the cake an excellent texture.

Makes 16 slices
40g/1½oz/3 tbsp sunflower
    margarine
60ml/4 tbsp clear honey
finely grated rind and juice
    of 1 lemon
150ml/½ pint/⅔ cup skimmed
    milk
150g/5oz/1¼ cups plain
    (all-purpose) flour
7.5ml/1½ tsp baking powder
2.5ml/½ tsp grated nutmeg
50g/2oz/⅓ cup semolina
2 egg whites
10ml/2 tsp sesame seeds

1 Preheat the oven to 200°C/400°F/Gas 6. Lightly oil a 19cm/7½in square deep cake tin (pan) and line the base with baking parchment.

2 Place the margarine and 45ml/3 tbsp of the honey in a pan and heat gently until melted. Reserve 15ml/1 tbsp lemon juice, then stir in the rest with the lemon rind and milk.

3 Stir together the flour, baking powder and nutmeg in a large mixing bowl, then add the milk mixture with the semolina. Beat well together.

4 Whisk the egg whites until they form soft peaks, then fold evenly into the semolina mixture.

5 Spoon into the tin and sprinkle with sesame seeds. Bake for 25–30 minutes, until golden brown.

6 Mix the reserved honey and lemon juice and drizzle over the cake while warm. Cool in the tin, then cut into fingers to serve.

> **Cook's Tip**
> Use Greek honey for an authentic touch, or use a good-quality, fragrant, flower-flavoured honey.

Banana Ginger Parkin

This wholesome, moist parkin is totally scrumptious. The icing sets it off nicely, but you can leave this out to reduce the calorie content.

Makes 12 squares
200g/7oz/1¾ cups plain (all-
    purpose) flour
10ml/2 tsp bicarbonate of soda
    (baking soda)
10ml/2 tsp ground ginger
150g/5oz/1¼ cups medium
    oatmeal
60ml/4 tbsp dark muscovado
    (molasses) sugar
75g/3oz/6 tbsp sunflower
    margarine
150g/5oz/⅔ cup golden (light
    corn) syrup
1 egg, beaten
3 ripe bananas, mashed
75g/3oz/¾ cup icing
    (confectioners') sugar
preserved stem ginger, to decorate
    (optional)

1 Preheat the oven to 160°C/325°F/Gas 3. Grease and line an 18 x 28cm/7 x 11in cake tin (pan).

2 Sift together the flour, bicarbonate of soda and ginger into a mixing bowl, then stir in the oatmeal. Melt the sugar, margarine and syrup in a pan, then stir into the flour mixture. Beat in the egg and mashed bananas.

3 Spoon the mixture into the prepared tin and bake for about 1 hour, or until firm to the touch. Allow to cool in the tin, then turn out and cut into even-size squares.

4 Sift the icing sugar into a bowl and stir in just enough water to make a smooth, runny icing. Drizzle the icing over each square and top with pieces of stem ginger, if you like.

> **Cook's Tips**
> • This nutritious cake is ideal for packed lunches as it doesn't break up too easily.
> • The parkin improves with keeping – store in a tightly covered container for up to two months.

Honey & Lemon Cake Energy 80Kcal/339kJ; Protein 2g; Carbohydrate 13g, of which sugars 3.4g; Fat 2.6g, of which saturates 0.5g; Cholesterol 1mg; Calcium 30mg; Fibre 0.4g; Sodium 33mg.
Parkin Energy 478Kcal/2025kJ; Protein 6.7g; Carbohydrate 101.7g, of which sugars 74.2g; Fat 7.6g, of which saturates 1.4g; Cholesterol 16mg; Calcium 56mg; Fibre 4.1g; Sodium 97mg.

Chocolate Petits Fours

Serve these dainty biscuits (cookies) as a stylish way to finish a meal. If you do not have any amaretto liqueur, they will work well without it. Alternatively, you can substitute the same quantity of brandy or rum.

Serves 8
350g/12oz carton chocolate chip cookie dough
115g/4oz plain (semisweet) chocolate
30ml/2 tbsp Amaretto di Saronno liqueur
50g/2oz/¼ cup butter

1 Preheat the oven according to the instructions on the cookie dough packet. Roll out the cookie dough on a floured surface to 1cm/½in thick. Using a 2.5cm/1in cutter, stamp out as many rounds from the dough as possible and transfer them to a lightly greased baking sheet. Bake for about 8 minutes, or until cooked through. Transfer to a wire rack to cool completely.

2 Make the filling. Break the chocolate into small pieces and place in a heatproof bowl with the amaretto liqueur and butter. Sit the bowl over a pan of gently simmering water and stir occasionally, until the chocolate has melted. Remove from the heat and set aside to cool.

3 Spread a small amount of the filling on the flat bottom of one of the cookies and sandwich together with another. Repeat until all the cookies have been used.

Cherry Chocolate Brownies

This is a modern, quick version of the classic Black Forest gâteau. Choose really good-quality bottled fruits because this will make all the difference to the end result. Look out for bottled fruit at Christmas time in particular, when supermarket shelves are packed with different varieties.

Serves 4
4 chocolate brownies
300ml/½ pint/1¼ cups double (heavy) cream
20–24 bottled cherries in Kirsch
icing (confectioners') sugar, to decorate (optional)

1 Using a sharp knife, carefully cut the brownies in half horizontally to make two thin slices. Place one brownie square on each of four serving plates.

2 Pour the cream into a large bowl and whip until soft but not stiff, then divide half the whipped cream between the four brownie squares.

3 Divide half the cherries among the cream-topped brownies, then place the remaining brownie halves on top of the cherries. Press down lightly.

4 Spoon the remaining cream on top of the brownies, then top each one with more cherries. Dust with a little icing sugar, if you like, and serve immediately.

Banana Orange Loaf

For the best banana flavour and a really good, moist texture, make sure the bananas are very ripe

Makes 1 loaf
90g/3½oz/generous ¾ cup wholemeal (whole-wheat) flour
90g/3½oz/generous ¾ cup plain (all-purpose) flour
5ml/1 tsp baking powder
5ml/1 tsp mixed (pumpkin pie) spice
45ml/3 tbsp chopped hazelnuts, toasted
2 large ripe bananas
1 egg
30ml/2 tbsp sunflower oil
30ml/2 tbsp clear honey
finely grated rind and juice of 1 small orange
4 orange slices, halved
10ml/2 tsp icing (confectioners') sugar

1 Preheat the oven to 180°C/350°F/Gas 4. Brush a 1 litre/¾ pint/4 cup loaf tin (pan) with sunflower oil and line the base with baking parchment.

2 Sift the flours with the baking powder and spice into a bowl.

3 Stir the hazelnuts into the dry ingredients. Peel and mash the bananas in a separate bowl and beat in the egg, oil, honey and the orange rind and juice. Stir the banana mixture evenly into the dry ingredients.

4 Spoon the mixture into the prepared tin and smooth the top. Bake for 40–45 minutes, or until firm and golden brown. Turn out and cool on a wire rack.

5 Sprinkle the orange slices with the icing sugar and grill (broil) until golden. Use to decorate the cake.

Cook's Tip
If you plan to keep the loaf for more than two or three days, omit the orange slices. Brush the cake with honey and sprinkle with chopped hazelnuts.

Petit Fours Energy 337Kcal/1410kJ; Protein 3.3g; Carbohydrate 38.9g, of which sugars 24.1g; Fat 19.2g, of which saturates 10.3g; Cholesterol 15mg; Calcium 42mg; Fibre 1.2g; Sodium 192mg.
Brownies Energy 632Kcal/2619kJ; Protein 5g; Carbohydrate 31.1g, of which sugars 20.3g; Fat 53.5g, of which saturates 25.1g; Cholesterol 103mg; Calcium 78mg; Fibre 0.2g; Sodium 234mg.
Banana Loaf Energy 1465Kcal/6161kJ; Protein 35.1g; Carbohydrate 209.9g, of which sugars 80.2g; Fat 59.9g, of which saturates 7g; Cholesterol 190mg; Calcium 271mg; Fibre 16g; Sodium 84mg.

Chocolate, Banana & Toffee Pie

As an alternative to the coffee topping, just decorate the pie with whipped cream and extra banana slices.

Serves 6

65g/2½oz/5 tbsp unsalted
   (sweet) butter, melted
250g/9oz milk chocolate digestive
   biscuits (graham crackers),
   crushed
chocolate curls, to decorate

For the filling

397g/13½oz can condensed milk
150g/5oz plain (semisweet)
   chocolate, chopped
120ml/4fl oz/½ cup crème fraîche
15ml/1 tbsp golden (light corn)
   syrup

For the topping

2 bananas
250ml/8fl oz/1 cup crème fraîche
10ml/2 tsp strong black coffee

1 Mix the butter with the biscuit crumbs. Press on to the base and sides of a 23cm/9in loose-based flan tin (tart pan). Chill.

2 Make the filling. Place the unopened can of condensed milk in a deep pan of boiling water, making sure that it is completely covered. Lower the heat and simmer, covered for 2 hours, topping up the water as necessary. The can must remain covered at all times.

3 Remove the pan from the heat and set aside, covered, until the can has cooled down completely in the water. Do not attempt to open the can until it is completely cold.

4 Gently melt the chocolate with the crème fraîche and golden syrup in a heatproof bowl over a pan of simmering water. Stir in the caramelized condensed milk and beat together until thoroughly combined. Pour the chocolate filling into the biscuit crust and spread it evenly.

5 Slice the bananas evenly and arrange them over the chocolate filling in an attractive pattern.

6 Stir the crème fraîche and coffee together in a bowl, then spoon the mixture over the bananas. Sprinkle the chocolate curls on top.

Rhubarb Pie

This pie is as attractive as it is delicious.

Serves 6

175g/6oz/1½ cups plain
   (all-purpose) flour
2.5ml/½ tsp salt
10ml/2 tsp caster
   (superfine) sugar
75g/3oz/6 tbsp cold butter or
   margarine
30ml/2 tbsp single (light) cream

For the filling

1kg/2¼lb fresh rhubarb, cut into
   2.5cm/1in slices
30ml/2 tbsp cornflour
   (cornstarch)
1 egg
275g/10oz/1½ cups caster
   (superfine) sugar
15ml/1 tbsp grated orange rind

1 Make the pastry. Sift the flour, salt and sugar into a bowl. Add the butter or margarine and rub in until the mix resembles breadcrumbs. Sprinkle the flour mixture with enough chilled water, about 45ml/3 tbsp, to bind the ingredients into a dough that just holds together. If the dough is too crumbly, mix in a little more chilled water. Gather the dough into a ball, flatten into a round, place in a plastic bag and chill for 20 minutes.

2 Roll out the pastry between two sheets of baking parchment to 3mm/⅛in thick. Use to line a 23cm/9in pie dish or tin (pan). Trim around the edge, leaving a 1cm/½in overhang. Fold the overhang under the edge and flute. Chill the pastry case (pie shell) and trimmings for 30 minutes.

3 Make the filling. Put the rhubarb in a bowl, sprinkle with the cornflour and toss to coat. Preheat the oven to 220°C/425°F/Gas 7. Beat the egg with the sugar in a bowl until blended, then mix in the orange rind. Stir the sugar mixture into the rhubarb and mix well, then spoon the fruit into the prepared pastry case.

4 Roll out the pastry trimmings and make decorative shapes with a cutter. Arrange on top of the pie. Brush the shapes and the edge of the case with cream. Bake for 30 minutes. Reduce the temperature to 160°C/325°F/Gas 3 and bake for 15–20 minutes more, until the pastry is golden brown and the rhubarb is tender.

Toffee Pie Energy 900Kcal/3758kJ; Protein 11.5g; Carbohydrate 90g, of which sugars 73.2g; Fat 57.4g, of which saturates 35.8g; Cholesterol 139mg; Calcium 275mg; Fibre 1.8g; Sodium 368mg.
Rhubarb Pie Energy 431Kcal/1823kJ; Protein 5.8g; Carbohydrate 78.4g, of which sugars 51.6g; Fat 12.7g, of which saturates 7.4g; Cholesterol 61mg; Calcium 233mg; Fibre 3.3g; Sodium 100mg.

Cherry Pie

The woven lattice is the perfect finishing touch, although you can cheat and use a lattice pastry roller if you prefer.

Serves 8
900g/2lb fresh Morello cherries, pitted, or 2 x 450g/1lb cans or jars, drained and pitted
65g/2½oz/generous ¾ cup caster (superfine) sugar
25g/1oz/¼ cup plain (all-purpose) flour
25ml/1½ tbsp fresh lemon juice
1.5ml/¼ tsp almond extract
25g/1oz/2 tbsp butter or margarine

For the pastry
225g/8oz/2 cups plain (all-purpose) flour
5ml/1 tsp salt
175g/6oz/1 cup lard or vegetable fat
60–75ml/4–5 tbsp chilled water

1 Make the pastry. Sift the flour and salt into a mixing bowl. Using a pastry blender, cut in the fat until the mixture resembles coarse breadcrumbs.

2 Sprinkle in the chilled water, a tablespoon at a time, tossing lightly with your fingertips or a fork, until the pastry comes together to form a ball.

3 Preheat the oven to 220°C/425°F/Gas 7. Divide the pastry in half and shape each half into a ball. On a lightly floured surface, roll out one of the balls to a circle about 30cm/12in in diameter.

4 Use the rolled-out dough to line a 23cm/9in pie tin (pan), easing the pastry in and being careful not to stretch it. Using scissors or a knife, trim off the excess pastry, leaving a 1cm/½in overhang around the pie tin.

5 Roll out the remaining pastry to 3mm/⅛in thick. Cut out eleven strips 1cm/½in wide.

6 Combine the cherries, sugar, flour, lemon juice and almond extract in a mixing bowl. Spoon the mixture into the pastry case (pie shell) and dot the top with the butter or margarine.

7 Make the lattice. Place five of the pastry strips evenly across the filling. Fold every other strip back. Lay the first strip across in the opposite direction. Continue in this pattern, folding back every other strip each time you add a cross strip.

8 Trim the ends of the lattice strips even with the case overhang. Press together so that the edge rests on the pie-tin rim. With your thumbs, flute the edge. Chill for 15 minutes.

9 Bake the pie for 30 minutes, covering the edge of the pastry case with foil, if necessary, to prevent over-browning. Allow to cool, in the tin, on a wire rack.

> **Cook's Tip**
> Morello cherries are the sour tasting type. Dark red and juicy, they are particularly good for cooked dishes.

Apple & Cranberry Lattice Pie

Use fresh or frozen cranberries for this classic American pie.

Serves 8
grated rind of 1 orange
45ml/3 tbsp fresh orange juice
2 large, tart cooking apples
115g/4oz/1 cup cranberries
65g/2½oz/½ cup raisins
25g/1oz/¼ cup walnuts, chopped
225g/8oz/1 cup granulated sugar
115g/4oz/½ cup dark brown sugar
15ml/1 tbsp quick-cooking tapioca

For the pastry
225g/8oz/2 cups plain (all-purpose) flour
2.5ml/½ tsp salt
75g/3oz/6 tbsp cold butter, diced
60ml/4 tbsp cold lard, cut into pieces
15ml/1 tbsp granulated sugar, for sprinkling

1 Make the pastry. Sift the flour and salt into a bowl. Add the butter and lard and rub in until the mixture resembles coarse crumbs. With a fork, stir in just enough iced water to bind the dough. Gather into two equal balls, wrap in baking parchment, and chill for at least 20 minutes.

2 Put the orange rind and juice into a mixing bowl. Peel and core the apples; grate into the bowl. Stir in the cranberries, raisins, walnuts, granulated sugar, brown sugar and tapioca.

3 Place a baking sheet in the oven and preheat to 200°C/400°F/Gas 6.

4 On a lightly floured surface, roll out one ball of dough to about 3mm/⅛in thick. Transfer to a 23cm/9in pie tin (pan) and trim the edge. Spoon the cranberry and apple mixture into the shell.

5 Roll out the remaining dough to a circle about 28cm/11in in diameter. With a serrated pastry wheel, cut the dough into ten strips, 2cm/¾in wide. Place five strips horizontally across the top of the tart at 2.5cm/1in intervals. Weave in six vertical strips. Trim the edges. Sprinkle the top with the sugar.

6 Bake for 20 minutes. Reduce the heat to 180°C/350°F/Gas 4 and bake for 15 minutes until the crust is golden.

Cherry Pie Energy 437Kcal/1830kJ; Protein 3.6g; Carbohydrate 53.6g, of which sugars 29.8g; Fat 24.6g, of which saturates 10.5g; Cholesterol 27mg; Calcium 66mg; Fibre 1.7g; Sodium 30mg.
Lattice Pie Energy 485Kcal/2044kJ; Protein 3.8g; Carbohydrate 79.2g, of which sugars 57.8g; Fat 19.3g, of which saturates 9.1g; Cholesterol 31mg; Calcium 74mg; Fibre 2g; Sodium 79mg.

Filo Chiffon Pie

Filo pastry is low in fat and is very easy to use. Keep a pack in the freezer, ready to make impressive desserts like this one.

Serves 3
500g/1¼lb pink rhubarb
5ml/1 tsp mixed spice (apple pie spice)
finely grated rind and juice of 1 orange
15ml/1 tbsp caster (superfine) sugar
15g/½oz/1 tbsp butter
3 sheets filo pastry

1 Preheat the oven to 200°C/400°F/Gas 6. Trim the leaves and ends from the rhubarb sticks and chop them in to 2.5cm/1in pieces. Place in a bowl.

2 Add the mixed spice, orange rind and juice and sugar and toss well to coat evenly. Transfer the rhubarb to a 1 litre/1¾ pint/4 cup pie dish.

3 Melt the butter and brush it over the pastry sheets. Lift the pastry sheets on to the pie dish, butter-side up, and crumple to form a chiffon effect, covering the pie completely.

4 Place the dish on a baking sheet and bake in the oven for 20 minutes, until golden brown. Reduce the heat to 180°C/350°F/Gas 4 and bake for a further 10–15 minutes, until the rhubarb is tender. Serve warm.

> **Cook's Tip**
> *When buying rhubarb, choose young, slender, pink stems, as these will be the most tender.*

> **Variation**
> *Other fruit, such as apples, pears or peaches, can be used in this pie – try it with whatever is in season.*

Peach Leaf Pie

Juicy, lightly spiced peach slices are covered with a crust made entirely from individual pastry leaves to make this spectacular pie.

Serves 8
1.2kg/2½lb ripe peaches
juice of 1 lemon
115g/4oz/½ cup granulated sugar
45ml/3 tbsp cornflour (cornstarch)
1.5ml/¼ tsp grated nutmeg
2.5ml/½ tsp ground cinnamon
25g/1oz/2 tbsp butter, diced
1 egg, beaten with 15ml/1 tbsp water, to glaze

For the pastry
225g/8oz/2 cups plain (all-purpose) flour
4ml/¾ tsp salt
115g/4oz/½ cup cold butter, diced
40g/1½oz/3 tbsp white vegetable fat, diced
75–90ml/5–6 tbsp chilled water

1 Make the pastry. Sift the flour and salt into a large mixing bowl. Add the butter and vegetable fat, and rub in with your fingertips or cut in with a pastry blender until the mixture resembles coarse breadcrumbs.

2 Sprinkle over the dry ingredients just enough of the water to bind the mixture and use a fork to bring it together to form a soft dough. Gather the dough into two balls, one slightly larger than the other. Wrap separately in clear film (plastic wrap) and chill for 30 minutes.

3 Meanwhile, put a baking sheet in the oven and preheat to 220°C/425°F/Gas 7.

4 Drop a few peaches at a time into a large pan of boiling water, leave for 20 seconds, then transfer to a bowl of cold water. When the peaches are cool, peel off the skins. Slice the peaches and mix with the lemon juice, sugar, cornflour and spices in a bowl. Set aside.

5 On a lightly floured surface, roll out the larger piece of pastry to a thickness of 3mm/⅛in. Use to line a 23cm/9in pie plate. Chill until required.

6 Roll out the second piece of pastry and cut out leaf shapes about 7.5cm/3in long. Cut out enough to completely cover the top of the dish. Mark veins with a knife.

7 Brush the base of the pastry case with egg glaze. Add the peach mixture, piling it into a dome in the centre. Dot the surface with the diced butter.

8 To assemble the pie top, start from the outside edge. Make a ring of leaves around the edge, attaching each leaf to the pastry base with a dab of egg glaze. Place a second ring of leaves above, staggering the positions. Continue with rows of leaves until the pie is covered. Brush with egg glaze.

9 Bake the pie on the hot baking sheet for about 10 minutes. Lower the oven temperature to 180°C/350°F/Gas 4 and continue to bake for 35–40 minutes more, or until golden. Serve hot with cream, if you wish.

Chiffon Pie Energy 109Kcal/461kJ; Protein 2.6g; Carbohydrate 15.8g, of which sugars 8.2g; Fat 4.4g, of which saturates 2.6g; Cholesterol 11mg; Calcium 174mg; Fibre 2.7g; Sodium 38mg.
Peach Leaf Pie Energy 390Kcal/1638kJ; Protein 4.4g; Carbohydrate 53.8g, of which sugars 27.2g; Fat 19g, of which saturates 10.7g; Cholesterol 52mg; Calcium 62mg; Fibre 3.2g; Sodium 152mg.

Peach & Blueberry Pie

This pie features an unusual combination of fruits.

Serves 8
225g/8oz/2 cups plain
  (all-purpose) flour
pinch of salt
10ml/2 tsp sugar
150g/5oz/²⁄₃ cup cold butter
1 egg yolk
30ml/2 tbsp milk, to glaze

For the filling
450g/1lb fresh peaches, peeled,
  stoned (pitted) and sliced
275g/10oz/2 cups blueberries
150g/5oz/¾ cup caster
  (superfine) sugar
30ml/2 tbsp lemon juice
40g/1½oz/⅓ cup plain
  (all-purpose) flour
large pinch of grated nutmeg
25g/1oz/2 tbsp butter, diced

1 Sift the flour, salt and sugar into a bowl and rub in the butter. Mix the egg yolk with 50ml/2fl oz/¼ cup water, sprinkle over the mixture and mix with a fork until the dough holds together. Add a little more water if necessary. Gather the dough into a ball and flatten into a round. Place in a plastic bag and chill for 20 minutes.

2 Roll out two-thirds of the pastry between sheets of baking parchment to 3mm/⅛in thick. Use to line a 23cm/9in pie dish. Trim the edge, leaving a 1cm/½in overhang. Fold the overhang under and press the edge to the rim of the pie dish.

3 Roll out the trimmings and remaining pastry to 5mm/¼in thick. Cut into 1cm/½in wide strips. Chill them and the pastry case (pie shell) for 20 minutes. Preheat the oven to 200°C/400°F/Gas 6.

4 Line the pastry case with baking parchment and fill with baking beans. Bake for 7–10 minutes, until just set. Remove the paper and beans. Prick the base with a fork, return to the oven and bake for 5 minutes more. Leave to cool slightly. Leave the oven on.

5 Make the filling. Combine the peaches, blueberries, sugar, lemon juice, flour and nutmeg. Spoon into the dish. Dot with the butter.

6 Weave a lattice top with the strips, pressing the ends in place. Brush with the milk. Bake for 15 minutes. Lower the temperature to 180°C/350°F/Gas 4 and bake for 30 minutes more.

Peach & Brandy Pie

This fragrant fruit pie is simple but delicious.

450g/1lb puff pastry
vanilla ice cream, to serve

Serves 8
6 large, firm ripe peaches
40g/1½oz/3 tbsp butter
45ml/3 tbsp brandy
75g/3oz/6 tbsp caster (superfine)
  sugar

For the glaze
1 egg
5ml/1 tsp water
15ml/1 tbsp granulated sugar

1 Immerse the peaches in boiling water for about 30 seconds. Lift out with a slotted spoon, dip in cold water, then peel off the skins. Carefully halve and stone (pit) the peaches, then cut into slices.

2 Melt the butter in a frying pan, add the peaches and sprinkle with the brandy and sugar. Cook for 4 minutes, shaking the pan frequently, or until the the peaches are tender. Set the pan aside.

3 Cut the pastry into two pieces, one very slightly larger than the other. Roll out on a floured surface and cut the larger piece into a 30cm/12in round and the smaller one into a 28cm/11in round. Place on separate baking sheets lined with baking parchment. Cover with clear film (plastic wrap). Chill for 30 minutes.

4 Preheat the oven to 200°C/400°F/Gas 6. Remove the clear film from the pastry rounds. Spoon the peaches into the middle of the larger round and spread them out to within about 5cm/2in of the edge. Place the smaller round on top, shaping it in a mound over the peaches. Brush the edge of the larger pastry round with water, then fold this over the top pastry round. Press the edges to seal. Twist the edges together to make a pattern all the way round.

5 Make the glaze by mixing the egg and water together. Lightly brush it over the pastry and sprinkle evenly with the granulated sugar. Make five or six small crescent-shape slashes on the top of the pastry, radiating from the centre towards the edge. Bake the pie for about 45 minutes, or until the pastry is golden brown. Serve warm in slices with vanilla ice cream.

Peach & Blueberry Pie Energy 391Kcal/1640kJ; Protein 4.7g; Carbohydrate 53g, of which sugars 27.7g; Fat 19.3g, of which saturates 11.7g; Cholesterol 72mg; Calcium 86mg; Fibre 2.9g; Sodium 139mg.
Peach & Brandy Energy 343Kcal/1437kJ; Protein 5.2g; Carbohydrate 39.2g, of which sugars 19.1g; Fat 18.7g, of which saturates 2.8g; Cholesterol 34mg; Calcium 50mg; Fibre 1.7g; Sodium 215mg.

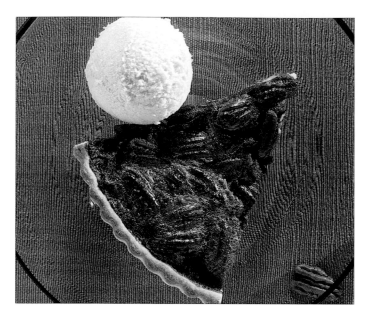

Key Lime Pie

This American dish hails
from the Florida Keys.

Makes 10 slices
225g/8oz/2 cups plain
   (all-purpose) flour
115g/4oz/¹/₂ cup chilled
   butter, diced
25g/1oz/2 tbsp caster
   (superfine) sugar
2 egg yolks
pinch of salt
30ml/2 tbsp cold water
shredded, thinly pared lime rind
   and mint leaves, to decorate

For the filling
4 eggs, separated
400g/14oz can condensed milk
grated rind and juice of 3 limes
a few drops of green food
   colouring (optional)
25g/1oz/2 tbsp caster
   (superfine) sugar

For the topping
300ml/¹/₂ pint/1¹/₄ cups double
   (heavy) cream
2 or 3 limes, thinly sliced

1 Sift the flour into a bowl and rub in the butter until the mixture resembles breadcrumbs. Add the sugar, egg yolks, salt and water. Mix to a soft dough. Roll out the pastry on a lightly floured surface and use to line a deep 21cm/8¹/₂in fluted flan tin (tart pan), letting excess pastry hang over the edge. Prick the pastry base. Chill for 30 minutes. Preheat the oven to 200°C/400°F/Gas 6. Trim off the excess pastry and line the pastry case (pie shell) with parchment and baking beans. Bake blind for 10 minutes. Remove the paper and beans and return the pastry case to the oven for 10 minutes.

2 Meanwhile, make the filling. Beat the egg yolks in a bowl until light and creamy, then beat in the condensed milk, lime rind and juice. Add the food colouring, if using, and beat until the mixture is thick. In a grease-free bowl, whisk the egg whites to stiff peaks. Whisk in the caster sugar, then fold into the lime mixture.

3 Lower the oven to 160°C/325°F/Gas 3. Pour the filling into the pastry case. Bake for 20–25 minutes, until it has set and starts to brown. Cool, then chill. Before serving, whip the cream and spoon it around the edge of the pie. Cut the lime slices once from the centre to the edge, twist each one and arrange on the cream. Decorate with lime rind and mint.

Mississippi Pecan Pie

This fabulous dessert
started life in the United
States but has become an
international favourite.

Serves 6–8
115g/4oz/1 cup plain
   (all-purpose) flour
50g/2oz/4 tbsp butter, cubed
25g/1oz/2 tbsp caster
   (superfine) sugar
1 egg yolk
30ml/2 tbsp water

For the filling
175g/6oz/¹/₂ cup golden (light
   corn) syrup
50g/2oz/¹/₄ cup dark muscovado
   (molasses) sugar
50g/2oz/4 tbsp butter
3 eggs, lightly beaten
2.5ml/¹/₂ tsp vanilla extract
150g/5oz/1¹/₄ cups pecan nuts
fresh cream or ice cream, to serve

1 Place the flour in a bowl and add the butter. Rub in the butter with your fingertips until the mixture resembles breadcrumbs, then stir in the sugar, egg yolk and the water. Mix to a dough and knead lightly on a floured surface until smooth.

2 Roll out the pastry and use to line a 20cm/8in loose-based fluted flan tin (tart pan). Prick the base, then line with baking parchment and fill with baking beans. Chill for 30 minutes. Preheat the oven to 200°C/400°F/Gas 6.

3 Bake the pastry case (pie shell) for 10 minutes. Remove the paper and beans and bake for a further 5 minutes. Reduce the oven temperature to 180°C/350°F/Gas 4.

4 Meanwhile, heat the syrup, sugar and butter in a pan until the sugar dissolves. Remove from the heat and cool slightly. Whisk in the eggs and vanilla extract and stir in the pecans. Pour into the pastry case and bake for 35–40 minutes, until the filling is set. Serve with cream or ice cream.

> **Cook's Tip**
> *Cooking the pastry before filling stops it from turning soggy.*

Pecan Pie Energy 409Kcal/1705kJ; Protein 6g; Carbohydrate 39.4g, of which sugars 28.2g; Fat 26.4g, of which saturates 8.4g; Cholesterol 123mg; Calcium 56mg; Fibre 1.3g; Sodium 163mg.
Key Lime Pie Energy 510Kcal/2126kJ; Protein 9.2g; Carbohydrate 46.6g, of which sugars 29.4g; Fat 33.2g, of which saturates 19.5g; Cholesterol 196mg; Calcium 182mg; Fibre 0.7g; Sodium 163mg.

Apple Pie

An English and American classic, delicious on its own or with a dollop of cream.

1.5ml/¼ tsp grated nutmeg
1.5ml/¼ tsp salt
50g/2oz/4 tbsp butter, diced

Serves 8
900g/2lb tart cooking apples
25g/1oz/¼ cup plain
   (all-purpose) flour
90g/3½oz/½ cup sugar
25ml/1½ tbsp fresh lemon juice
2.5ml/½ tsp ground cinnamon
2.5ml/½ tsp ground allspice
1.5ml/¼ tsp ground ginger

For the pastry
225g/8oz/2 cups plain
   (all-purpose) flour
5ml/1 tsp salt
75g/3oz/6 tbsp cold butter, cut
   into pieces
50g/2oz/4 tbsp cold lard, cut
   into pieces
60–120ml/4–8 tbsp iced water

1 Make the pastry. Sift the flour and salt into a bowl. Add the butter and lard and cut in with a pastry blender or rub with your fingertips until the mixture resembles coarse breadcrumbs. Stir in just enough iced water to bind the dough. Form into two balls, wrap in clear film (plastic wrap) and chill for 20 minutes.

2 On a lightly floured surface, roll out one dough ball to 3mm/⅛in thick. Transfer to a 23cm/9in pie tin (pan) and trim the edge. Place a baking sheet in the centre of the oven and preheat to 220°C/425°F/Gas 7.

3 Peel, core and slice the apples into a bowl. Toss with the flour, sugar, lemon juice, spices and salt. Spoon into the pastry case (pie shell) and dot with butter.

4 Roll out the remaining dough. Place on top of the pie and trim to leave a 2cm/¾in overhang. Fold the overhang under the bottom dough and press to seal. Crimp the edge. Roll out the leftover pastry and cut out leaf shapes and roll balls. Arrange on top of the pie. Cut steam vents.

5 Bake for 10 minutes. Reduce the heat to 180°C/350°F/Gas 4 and bake for 40–45 minutes more until golden. If the pie browns too quickly, protect the top with foil.

Apple & Orange Pie

Oranges add an evocative Mediterranean twist to an Anglo-American favourite.

caster (superfine) sugar,
   for sprinkling

Serves 4–6
3 navel oranges
1kg/2¼lb cooking apples, peeled,
   cored and thickly sliced
30ml/2 tbsp demerara
   (raw) sugar
beaten egg, to glaze

For the pastry
275g/10oz/2½ cups plain
   (all-purpose) flour
2.5ml/½ tsp salt
150g/5oz/10 tbsp chilled
   butter, diced
about 45ml/4 tbsp chilled
   water

1 Make the pastry. Sift the flour and salt into a large bowl. Rub in the butter with your fingertips, until the mixture resembles fine breadcrumbs. Mix in the water and knead lightly to form a firm dough. Wrap the dough in clear film (plastic wrap) and chill for at least 30 minutes.

2 Roll out the pastry on a lightly floured work surface to a shape 2cm/¾in larger than the top of a 1.2 litre/2 pint/5 cup pie dish. Cut off a narrow strip around the edge of the pastry, brush it with a little cold water and firmly attach it to the rim of the pie dish.

3 Preheat the oven to 190°C/375°F/Gas 5. Using a sharp knife, cut a thin slice of peel and pith from both ends of each orange. Place cut side down on a plate and cut off the peel and pith in strips. Remove any bits of remaining pith. Cut out each segment leaving the membrane behind. Squeeze the remaining juice from the membrane.

4 Mix together the orange segments and juice, the apples and sugar in the pie dish. Place a pie funnel in the centre of the dish. Dampen the pastry strip on the rim of the dish and cover with the pastry. Press the edges to the pastry strip.

5 Brush the top with beaten egg to glaze. Bake for 35 minutes, or until golden. Sprinkle with caster sugar before serving.

Apple Pie Energy 364Kcal/1528kJ; Protein 3.5g; Carbohydrate 46.6g, of which sugars 22.3g; Fat 19.6g, of which saturates 10.7g; Cholesterol 39mg; Calcium 58mg; Fibre 2.8g; Sodium 344mg.
Apple & Orange Pie Energy 444Kcal/1865kJ; Protein 5.7g; Carbohydrate 61.2g, of which sugars 26.3g; Fat 21.4g, of which saturates 13.1g; Cholesterol 53mg; Calcium 108mg; Fibre 5.2g; Sodium 324mg.

Basque Apple Pie

The pastry for this Spanish pie has a cake-like texture.

Serves 6
215g/7½oz/scant 2 cups plain
    (all-purpose) flour, plus extra
    for rolling
5ml/1 tsp baking powder
pinch of salt
115g/4oz/½ cup cold unsalted

(sweet) butter, cubed, plus
    extra for greasing
finely grated rind of ½ lemon
75g/3oz/6 tbsp caster (superfine)
    sugar, plus extra
    for sprinkling
2 small (US medium) eggs
3 eating apples, peeled, cored
    and cubed
ground cinnamon, for sprinkling

1 Sift the flour, baking powder and salt into a food processor. Add the butter and grated lemon rind and process briefly to combine, then add the sugar, 1 whole egg and the yolk of the second egg to the flour mixture and process to make a soft dough.

2 Divide the dough into two pieces, one portion nearly double the size of the other. Pat into two flat cakes. Wrap tightly in clear film (plastic wrap) and chill for at least 2 hours until firm.

3 Preheat the oven to 180°C/350°F/Gas 4. Place a baking sheet in the oven and grease a 20cm/8in loose-based flan tin (tart pan). Place the larger piece of dough on a lightly floured piece of clear film and cover with another piece of film. Roll out to a 25cm/10in round. Remove the film, transfer to the tin and press into the tin so that it stands just clear of the top.

4 Pack the tin with the apples and sprinkle with cinnamon. Roll out the second piece of dough in the same way, to exactly the same size as the tin. Lay the dough on top of the apples and fold the overlapping edges of the bottom piece of dough inward. Gently press the edges together with a fork, to seal.

5 Prick the dough a few times, brush with egg white and sprinkle with sugar. Place on the hot baking sheet and bake for 20 minutes. Reduce the temperature to 160°C/325°F/Gas 3 for a further 25–30 minutes until golden. Cool in the tin for 30 minutes, then remove from the tin. Cool on a wire rack.

Cider Pie

Few can resist this delectable pie, with its rich cider filling. Suggest the season with pretty pastry decorations of apples, dotted around the edge of the pie.

Serves 6
600ml/1 pint/2½ cups cider
    (hard cider)
15g/½oz/1 tbsp butter
250ml/8fl oz/1 cup maple syrup
60ml/4 tbsp water

2 eggs, at room temperature,
    separated and yolks beaten
5ml/1 tsp grated nutmeg
icing (confectioners') sugar,
    for dusting

For the pastry
175g/6oz/1½ cups plain
    (all-purpose) flour
1.5ml/¼ tsp salt
10ml/2 tsp granulated sugar
115g/4oz/½ cup cold butter,
    diced
about 60ml/4 tbsp chilled water

1 Make the pastry. Sift the flour, salt and sugar into a mixing bowl. Rub or cut in the butter until the mixture resembles fine breadcrumbs.

2 Sprinkle the chilled water over the flour mixture. Combine with a fork until the dough holds together. If the dough is too crumbly, add a little more water. Gather the dough into a ball and flatten into a round. Wrap in clear film (plastic wrap) and chill for 30 minutes.

3 Meanwhile, pour the cider into a pan and boil until only 175ml/6fl oz/¾ cup, or approximately one-third, remains, then set aside to cool.

4 Roll out the pastry between two large sheets of baking parchment or clear film to 3mm/⅛in thick. Use to line a 23cm/9in pie dish.

5 Trim the edge, leaving a 1cm/½in overhang. Fold the overhang under to form a rim. Using a fork, press the rim down and scallop the edge. Chill for at least 20 minutes. Preheat the oven to 180°C/350°F/Gas 4.

6 Place the butter, maple syrup, water and reduced cider in a pan and simmer gently for 5–6 minutes. Cool slightly, then whisk in the beaten egg yolks.

7 Place the egg whites in a large bowl, and whisk vigorously until they form stiff peaks. Using a wooden spoon, gently fold in the cider mixture.

8 Pour the filling into the pastry case (pie shell) so that it fills the case evenly. Lightly dust with the grated nutmeg. Bake for 30–35 minutes, or until the filling is firmly set and golden. Dust with icing sugar and serve immediately.

> **Cook's Tip**
> Cut apple shapes from the pastry trimmings, bake them for 10 minutes alongside the pie, then arrange on top of the baked pie before dusting with icing sugar.

Basque Apple Pie Energy 232Kcal/984kJ; Protein 5.7g; Carbohydrate 45.4g, of which sugars 18.1g; Fat 4.4g, of which saturates 1.9g; Cholesterol 69mg; Calcium 69mg; Fibre 1.9g; Sodium 41mg.
Cider Pie Energy 452Kcal/1897kJ; Protein 5.1g; Carbohydrate 60.1g, of which sugars 37.8g; Fat 20g, of which saturates 11.9g; Cholesterol 110mg; Calcium 70mg; Fibre 0.9g; Sodium 275mg.

Black Bottom Pie

A totally wicked rum and chocolate creation.

Serves 6–8
250g/9oz/2¼ cups plain (all-purpose) flour
150g/5oz/10 tbsp unsalted (sweet) butter
2 egg yolks
15–30ml/1–2 tbsp chilled water

For the filling
3 eggs, separated
20ml/4 tsp cornflour (cornstarch)

75g/3oz/6 tbsp golden caster (superfine) sugar
400ml/14fl oz/1⅔ cups milk
150g/5oz plain (semisweet) chocolate, chopped into small pieces
5ml/1 tsp vanilla extract
1 sachet powdered gelatine
45ml/3 tbsp water
30ml/2 tbsp dark rum
175ml/6fl oz/¾ cup whipping cream
chocolate curls, to decorate

1 Sift the flour into a bowl and rub in the butter until the mixture resembles coarse breadcrumbs. Stir in the egg yolks with just enough chilled water to bind the mixture to a soft dough. Roll out on a lightly floured surface and line a deep 23cm/9in flan tin (tart pan). Chill for about 30 minutes.

2 Preheat the oven to 190°C/375°F/Gas 5. Prick the pastry all over with a fork, cover with baking parchment weighed down with baking beans and bake blind for 10 minutes. Remove the baking beans and paper, return the pastry case (pie shell) to the oven and bake for 10 minutes, until golden. Cool in the tin.

3 Make the filling. Mix the egg yolks, cornflour and 25g/1oz/2 tbsp of the sugar in a bowl. Heat the milk in a pan until almost boiling, then beat into the egg mixture. Return to the clean pan and stir over a low heat until the custard has thickened and is smooth. Pour half the custard into a bowl.

4 Put the chocolate in a heatproof bowl. Place over a pan of barely simmering water until the chocolate has melted, stirring occasionally until smooth. Stir the melted chocolate into the custard in the bowl, with the vanilla extract.

5 Spread the chocolate filling in the pastry case and cover closely with dampened clear film (plastic wrap) to prevent a skin forming. Allow to cool, then chill until set.

6 Sprinkle the gelatine over the water in a bowl, leave until spongy, then place the bowl over a pan of simmering water until all the gelatine has dissolved. Stir into the remaining custard, then add the rum.

7 Whisk the egg whites in a clean, grease-free bowl until peaks form. Whisk in the remaining sugar, a little at a time, until stiff, then fold the egg whites quickly but evenly into the rum-flavoured custard.

8 Spoon the custard over the chocolate layer in the pastry shell. Level the mixture, making sure that none of the chocolate custard is visible. Chill the pie until the top layer has set, then remove the pie from the tin. Whip the cream, spread it over the top and sprinkle with chocolate curls, to decorate.

Coconut Cream Pie

A delicately flavoured tart, suitable for any occasion.

Serves 8
200g/7oz/2½ cups desiccated (dry unsweetened) coconut
115g/4oz/generous ½ cup caster (superfine) sugar
60ml/4 tbsp cornflour (cornstarch)
pinch of salt
600ml/1 pint/2½ cups milk
50ml/2fl oz/¼ cup whipping cream

2 egg yolks
25g/1oz/2 tbsp unsalted (sweet) butter
10ml/2 tsp vanilla extract

For the pastry
115g/4oz/1 cup plain (all-purpose) flour
1.5ml/¼ tsp salt
40g/1½oz/3 tbsp cold butter, cut into pieces
25g/1oz/2 tbsp cold lard
30–45ml/2–3 tbsp chilled water

1 Make the pastry. Sift the flour and salt into a bowl. Add the butter and lard and cut in with a pastry blender or two knives until the mixture resembles coarse breadcrumbs. With a fork, stir in just enough water to bind the dough. Gather into a ball, wrap in baking parchment and chill for at least 20 minutes.

2 Preheat the oven to 220°C/425°F/Gas 7. Roll out the dough to 3mm/⅛in thick. Transfer to a 23cm/9in flan tin (tart pan). Trim and flute the edges. Prick the base. Line with baking parchment and fill with baking beans. Bake for 10–12 minutes. Remove the paper and beans, reduce the heat to 180°C/350°F/Gas 4 and bake for a further 10–15 minutes until brown.

3 Spread 75g/3oz/1 cup of the coconut on a baking sheet. Toast in the oven for 6–8 minutes, stirring often, until golden. Set aside.

4 Put the sugar, cornflour and salt in a pan. In a bowl, whisk together the milk, cream and egg yolks. Add the egg mixture to the pan. Cook over low heat, stirring constantly, until the mixture comes to the boil. Boil for 1 minute, then remove from the heat. Add the butter, vanilla and remaining coconut.

5 Pour into the pastry case (pie shell). When the filling is cool, sprinkle the toasted coconut in a ring in the centre.

Black Bottom Energy 545Kcal/2276kJ; Protein 9.3g; Carbohydrate 51.3g, of which sugars 25.1g; Fat 34.2g, of which saturates 20g; Cholesterol 189mg; Calcium 118mg; Fibre 1.4g; Sodium 173mg.
Coconut Cream Energy 445Kcal/1857kJ; Protein 6.3g; Carbohydrate 38.4g, of which sugars 20.6g; Fat 30.7g, of which saturates 21.7g; Cholesterol 82mg; Calcium 136mg; Fibre 3.9g; Sodium 98mg.

Blueberry Pie

American blueberries or European bilberries can be used for this scrumptious pie. You may need to add a little more sugar if you are lucky enough to find native bilberries.

Serves 6

2 x 225g/8oz ready-rolled shortcrust pastry sheets, thawed if frozen

800g/1³⁄₄lb/7 cups blueberries
75g/3oz/6 tbsp caster (superfine) sugar, plus extra for sprinkling
45ml/3 tbsp cornflour (cornstarch)
grated rind and juice of ¹⁄₂ orange
grated rind of ¹⁄₂ lemon
2.5ml/¹⁄₂ tsp ground cinnamon
15g/¹⁄₂oz/1 tbsp unsalted (sweet) butter, diced
beaten egg, to glaze
whipped cream, to serve

1 Preheat the oven to 200°C/400°F/Gas 6. Use one sheet of pastry to line a 23cm/9in pie dish, leaving the excess pastry hanging over the edges.

2 Mix the blueberries, caster sugar, cornflour, orange rind and juice, lemon rind and cinnamon in a large bowl. Spoon into the pastry case and dot with the butter. Dampen the rim of the pastry case (pie shell) with a little water and top with the remaining pastry sheet.

3 Cut the pastry edge at 2.5cm/1in intervals, then fold each section over on itself to form a triangle and create a sunflower edge. Trim off the excess pastry and cut out decorations from the trimmings. Stick them to the pastry lid with a little of the beaten egg.

4 Glaze the pastry with the egg and sprinkle with caster sugar. Bake for 30–35 minutes or until golden. Serve warm or cold with whipped cream.

> **Variation**
> Substitute a crumble topping for the pastry lid. The contrast with the juicy blueberry filling is sensational.

Lemon Meringue Pie

A lovely lemon-filled tart, heaped with soft meringue, this classic British dessert never fails to please.

Serves 6

115g/4oz/1 cup plain (all-purpose) flour
pinch of salt
50g/2oz/¹⁄₄ cup butter
50g/2oz/¹⁄₄ cup lard
15ml/1 tbsp caster (superfine) sugar
about 15ml/1 tbsp iced water

For the filling
3 large (US extra large) egg yolks
25g/1oz/2 tbsp caster (superfine) sugar
grated rind and juice of 1 lemon
25g/1oz/¹⁄₂ cup fresh white breadcrumbs
250ml/8fl oz/1 cup milk

For the topping
3 large (US extra large) egg whites
115g/4oz/generous ¹⁄₂ cup caster (superfine) sugar

1 Sift the flour and salt into a bowl. Rub in the butter and lard until the mixture resembles fine breadcrumbs. Stir in the sugar and add enough iced water to make a soft dough. Roll out the pastry on a lightly floured surface and line a 21cm/8¹⁄₂in pie plate or tin (pan). Chill until required.

2 Meanwhile make the filling. Place all the ingredients in a bowl, mix lightly and leave to soak for 1 hour.

3 Preheat the oven to 200°C/400°F/Gas 6. Beat the filling until smooth and pour into the chilled pastry case (pie shell). Bake for 20 minutes or until the filling has just set and the pastry is golden. Remove from the oven and cool, in the tin, on a wire rack for 30 minutes or until a skin has formed on the surface. Lower the oven temperature to 180°C/350°F/Gas 4.

4 Make the topping. Whisk the egg whites in a grease-free bowl until they form stiff peaks. Whisk in the caster sugar to form a glossy meringue. Spoon on top of the set lemon filling and spread to completely cover. Swirl the meringue slightly.

5 Bake the pie for 20–25 minutes or until the meringue is crisp and golden brown. Cool slightly on a wire rack before serving.

Blueberry Pie Energy 458Kcal/1915kJ; Protein 4.7g; Carbohydrate 60g, of which sugars 20.4g; Fat 23.8g, of which saturates 1.3g; Cholesterol 5mg; Calcium 95mg; Fibre 5.6g; Sodium 143mg.
Lemon Meringue Pie Energy 357Kcal/1497kJ; Protein 6.8g; Carbohydrate 42.8g, of which sugars 25.1g; Fat 18.9g, of which saturates 9g; Cholesterol 129mg; Calcium 108mg; Fibre 0.7g; Sodium 137mg.

Boston Banoffee Pie

A great American creation, you simply press the biscuity pastry into the tin, rather than rolling it out. Just add the fudge-toffee filling and sliced banana topping and it'll prove irresistible.

Serves 6
115g/4oz/½ cup butter, diced
200g/7oz can skimmed, sweetened condensed milk
115g/4oz/scant ½ cup soft brown sugar
30ml/2 tbsp golden (light corn) syrup
2 small bananas, sliced
a little lemon juice
whipped cream, to decorate
5ml/1 tsp grated plain (semisweet) chocolate

For the pastry
150g/5oz/1¼ cups plain (all-purpose) flour
115g/4oz/½ cup butter, diced
50g/2oz/¼ cup caster (superfine) sugar

1 Make the pastry. Preheat the oven to 160°C/325°F/Gas 3. In a food processor, process the flour and diced butter until it forms crumbs. Stir in the caster sugar and mix to form a soft, pliable dough.

2 Press into a 20cm/8in loose-based flan tin (tart pan). Bake for 30 minutes.

3 Make the filling. Place the butter in a pan with the condensed milk, brown sugar and syrup. Heat gently, stirring, until the butter has melted and the sugar has completely dissolved.

4 Bring the mixture to a gentle boil, then cook for 7–10 minutes, stirring constantly, until the mixture thickens and turns a light caramel colour.

5 Pour the hot caramel filling into the pastry case (pie shell) and leave until completely cold.

6 Sprinkle the banana slices with lemon juice and arrange in overlapping circles on top of the filling, leaving a gap in the centre. Pipe a generous swirl of whipped cream in the centre and sprinkle with the grated chocolate.

American Pumpkin Pie

This spicy sweet pie is served at Thanksgiving, or at Hallowe'en to use the pulp from the hollowed-out pumpkin lanterns.

Serves 8
900g/2lb piece of pumpkin flesh
2 large (US extra large) eggs
75g/3oz/6 tbsp soft light brown sugar
60ml/4 tbsp golden (light corn) syrup
250ml/8fl oz/1 cup double (heavy) cream
15ml/1 tbsp mixed (pumpkin pie) spice
2.5ml/½ tsp salt
icing (confectioners') sugar, for dusting

For the pastry
200g/7oz/1¾ cups plain (all-purpose) flour
2.5ml/½ tsp salt
90g/3½oz/scant ½ cup butter, diced
1 egg yolk
15ml/1 tbsp chilled water

1 Make the pastry. Sift the flour and salt into a mixing bowl. Rub or cut in the butter until the mixture resembles fine breadcrumbs, then mix in the egg yolk and enough chilled water to make a soft dough. Roll into a ball, then wrap it in clear film (plastic wrap) and chill for at least 30 minutes.

2 Cut the pumpkin flesh into cubes and place in a heavy pan. Cover with water, bring to the boil and simmer for 15–20 minutes until tender. Mash the pumpkin until smooth, then spoon into a sieve (strainer) and set over a bowl to drain.

3 Preheat the oven to 200°C/400°F/Gas 6. Roll out the pastry and use to line a 23cm/9in loose-based flan tin (tart pan). Prick the base all over with a fork. Line with foil and baking beans. Chill the pastry case (pie shell) for 15 minutes. Bake for 10 minutes. Remove the foil and beans and bake for a further 5 minutes.

4 Lower the oven temperature to 190°C/375°F/Gas 5. Turn the pumpkin pulp into a mixing bowl and beat in the eggs, sugar, syrup, cream, spice and salt until smooth. Pour into the pastry case. Bake for 40 minutes, or until the filling has set. Dust the surface with icing sugar and serve at room temperature.

Banoffee Pie Energy 608Kcal/2547kJ; Protein 6.1g; Carbohydrate 78.5g, of which sugars 58.9g; Fat 32g, of which saturates 20.1g; Cholesterol 82mg; Calcium 169mg; Fibre 1.1g; Sodium 299mg.
Pumpkin Pie Energy 416Kcal/1736kJ; Protein 5.3g; Carbohydrate 38.2g, of which sugars 18.6g; Fat 28g, of which saturates 16.9g; Cholesterol 114mg; Calcium 98mg; Fibre 1.9g; Sodium 360mg.

Italian Chocolate Ricotta Pie

Savour the full richness of Italy with this de luxe tart.

Serves 6

225g/8oz/2 cups plain
 (all-purpose) flour
30ml/2 tbsp cocoa powder
 (unsweetened)
50g/2oz/¼ cup caster
 (superfine) sugar
115g/4oz/½ cup unsalted
 (sweet) butter
60ml/4 tbsp dry sherry

For the filling

2 egg yolks
115g/4oz/generous ½ cup caster
 (superfine) sugar
500g/1¼lb/2½ cups ricotta
 cheese
finely grated rind of 1 lemon
90ml/6 tbsp dark chocolate
 chips
75ml/5 tbsp mixed (candied)
 chopped peel
45ml/3 tbsp chopped
 angelica

1 Sift the flour and cocoa into a bowl. Stir in the sugar. Rub in the butter with your fingers. Work in the sherry to form a firm dough.

2 Preheat the oven to 200°C/400°F/Gas 6. Roll out three-quarters of the pastry on a lightly floured surface and line a 24cm/9½in loose-based flan tin (tart pan).

3 Make the filling. Beat the egg yolks and sugar in a bowl, then beat in the ricotta to mix thoroughly. Stir in the lemon rind, chocolate chips, mixed peel and angelica.

4 Scrape the ricotta mixture into the pastry case (pie shell) and level the surface. Roll out the remaining pastry and cut into strips. Arrange these in a lattice over the pie.

5 Bake for 15 minutes. Lower the oven temperature to 180°C/350°F/Gas 4 and cook for a further 30–35 minutes, until golden brown and firm. Cool the pie in the tin, then serve.

> **Cook's Tip**
> This dish is best served at room temperature, so if made in advance, chill it, then bring to room temperature before serving.

Shoofly Pie

A wonderful sweet pie from the American Deep South.

Serves 8

115g/4oz/1 cup plain
 (all-purpose) flour
115g/4oz/scant ½ cup soft dark
 brown sugar
1.5ml/¼ tsp each salt, ground
 ginger, cinnamon, mace, and
 nutmeg
75g/3oz/6 tbsp cold butter, diced

2 eggs
185g/6½oz/½ cup black treacle
 (molasses)
120ml/4fl oz/½ cup boiling water
1.5ml/½ tsp bicarbonate of soda
 (baking soda)

For the pastry

115g/4oz/½ cup cream cheese
115g/4oz/½ cup butter, diced
115g/4oz/1 cup plain
 (all-purpose) flour

1 Preheat the oven to 190°C/375°F/Gas 5. Meanwhile make the pastry. Put the cream cheese and butter in a mixing bowl. Sift over the flour. Rub in with your fingertips or cut in with a pastry blender to bind the dough together. Wrap in clear film (plastic wrap) and chill for at least 30 minutes.

2 Make the filling. Mix the flour, brown sugar, salt, spices and butter in a bowl. Rub in with your fingertips until the mixture resembles coarse breadcrumbs, then set aside.

3 Roll out the dough thinly on a lightly floured surface to a thickness of about 3mm/⅛in and use to line a 23cm/9in pie plate. Trim and flute the pastry edges. Spoon one-third of the filling mixture into the pastry case (pie shell).

4 Whisk the eggs with the treacle in a large bowl. Put a baking sheet in the oven to preheat.

5 Pour the boiling water into a small bowl and stir in the bicarbonate of soda; it will foam. Pour immediately into the egg mixture and whisk to blend. Pour into the pastry case and sprinkle the remaining filling mixture over the top in an even layer.

6 Place the pie on the hot baking sheet and bake for about 35 minutes, or until browned. Leave to cool and serve warm.

Ricotta Pie Energy 701Kcal/2938kJ; Protein 14.2g; Carbohydrate 83.4g, of which sugars 54.1g; Fat 35.6g, of which saturates 21.3g; Cholesterol 144mg; Calcium 115mg; Fibre 3g; Sodium 223mg.
Shoofly Pie Energy 472Kcal/1975kJ; Protein 5.2g; Carbohydrate 53g, of which sugars 31g; Fat 28.1g, of which saturates 17.1g; Cholesterol 112mg; Calcium 201mg; Fibre 0.9g; Sodium 248mg.

Butternut Squash & Maple Pie

This American-style pie has a crisp shortcrust pastry case and a creamy filling, sweetened with maple syrup and flavoured with fresh ginger and a dash of brandy.

Serves 10
1 small butternut squash
60ml/4 tbsp water
2.5cm/1in piece fresh root ginger, peeled and grated
275g/10oz shortcrust pastry
120ml/4fl oz/½ cup double (heavy) cream
90ml/6 tbsp maple syrup
40g/1½oz/3 tbsp light muscovado (brown) sugar
3 eggs, lightly beaten
30ml/2 tbsp brandy
1.5ml/¼ tsp grated nutmeg
beaten egg, to glaze

1 Halve the squash, peel and scoop out the seeds. Cut the flesh into cubes and put in a pan with the water. Cover and cook gently for 15 minutes. Uncover, stir in the ginger and cook for a further 5 minutes until the liquid has evaporated and the squash is tender. Cool slightly, then purée in a food processor.

2 Roll out the pastry and use to line a 23cm/9in flan tin (tart pan). Re-roll the trimmings, then cut into maple leaf shapes. Brush the edge of the pastry case with beaten egg and attach the leaf shapes at regular intervals to make a decorative rim. Cover with clear film (plastic wrap) and chill for 30 minutes.

3 Put a heavy baking sheet in the oven and preheat to 200°C/400°F/Gas 6. Prick the pastry base, line with foil and fill with baking beans. Bake blind on the baking sheet for 12 minutes.

4 Remove the foil and beans and bake for a further 5 minutes. Brush the base of the pastry case with beaten egg and return to the oven for about 3 minutes. Lower the oven temperature to 180°C/350°F/Gas 4.

5 Mix 200g/7oz/scant 1 cup of the butternut purée with the cream, syrup, sugar, eggs, brandy and nutmeg. (Discard any remaining purée.) Pour into the pastry case. Bake for about 30 minutes, until the filling is lightly set. Cool slightly and serve.

Mississippi Mud Pie

This is the ultimate in chocolate desserts.

Serves 6–8
3 eggs, separated
20ml/4 tsp cornflour (cornstarch)
75g/3oz/6 tbsp sugar
400ml/14fl oz/1²/₃ cups milk
150g/5oz plain (semisweet) chocolate, broken up
5ml/1 tsp vanilla extract
15ml/1 tbsp powdered gelatine
45ml/3 tbsp water
30ml/2 tbsp dark rum
175ml/6fl oz/¾ cup double (heavy) cream, whipped
a few chocolate curls, to decorate

For the pastry
250g/9oz/2¼ cups plain (all-purpose) flour
150g/5oz/10 tbsp butter, diced
2 egg yolks
15–30ml/1–2 tbsp chilled water

1 Make the pastry. Sift the flour into a bowl. Rub in the butter until "breadcrumbs" form. Stir in the yolks with enough chilled water to make a soft dough. Roll out and use to line a deep 23cm/9in flan tin (pie pan). Chill for 30 minutes. Preheat the oven to 190°C/375°F/Gas 5. Prick the pastry, line with foil and beans, and bake blind for 10 minutes. Remove the foil and beans, and return to the oven for 10 minutes until the pastry is crisp and golden. Cool.

2 Mix the yolks, cornflour and 30ml/2 tbsp of the sugar in a bowl. In a pan, bring the milk almost to a boil, then beat into the egg mixture. Return to the cleaned pan and stir over a low heat until the custard thickens. Pour half into a bowl. Melt the chocolate in a heatproof bowl set over a pan of hot water, then add to the custard in the bowl. Mix in the vanilla extract. Spread in the pastry case, cover with parchment to prevent a skin forming, cool, then chill until set. Sprinkle the gelatine over the water in a small bowl, leave until spongy, then place over a pan of simmering water until the gelatine dissolves. Stir into the remaining custard, with the rum.

3 Whisk the egg whites until stiff peaks form, whisk in the rest of the sugar, then fold into the gelatine and custard mix before it sets.

4 Spoon over the chocolate custard to cover. Chill until set, then remove from the tin. Spread whipped cream over the top, decorate with chocolate curls and serve immediately.

Squash & Maple Pie Energy 266Kcal/1109kJ; Protein 4g; Carbohydrate 26.2g, of which sugars 13.7g; Fat 16.1g, of which saturates 4.6g; Cholesterol 74mg; Calcium 56mg; Fibre 1.4g; Sodium 92mg.
Mud Pie Energy 571Kcal/2385kJ; Protein 9.4g; Carbohydrate 53.5g, of which sugars 22.7g; Fat 36.2g, of which saturates 21.2g; Cholesterol 196mg; Calcium 160mg; Fibre 1.3g; Sodium 180mg.

Chocolate Chiffon Pie

Decorate with chocolate curls for a pretty finish.

Serves 8

175g/6oz plain (semisweet) chocolate squares, chopped
25g/1oz dark (bittersweet) chocolate, chopped
250ml/8fl oz/1 cup milk
15ml/1 tbsp powdered gelatine
130g/4½oz/⅔ cup sugar

2 eggs, separated
5ml/1 tsp vanilla extract
350ml/12fl oz/1½ cups whipping cream
pinch of salt
whipped cream, to decorate

For the crust

75g/3oz/1½ cups digestive biscuit (graham cracker) crumbs
75g/3oz/6 tbsp butter, melted

1 Place a baking sheet in the oven and preheat to 180°C/350°F/Gas 4. Make the crust. Mix the biscuit crumbs and butter in a bowl. Press the crumbs evenly over the base and sides of a 23cm/9in pie tin (pan). Bake for 8 minutes. Allow to cool.

2 Grind the chocolate in a food processor or blender. Set aside. Place the milk in the top of a double boiler or in a heatproof bowl. Sprinkle over the gelatine. Let stand for 5 minutes to soften.

3 Set the top of the double boiler or heatproof bowl over hot water. Add 50g/2oz/¼ cup of the sugar, the chocolate and egg yolks. Stir until dissolved. Add the vanilla extract.

4 Place the top of the double boiler or the heatproof bowl in a bowl of ice and stir until the mixture reaches room temperature. Remove from the ice and set aside.

5 Whip the cream lightly. Set aside. With an electric whisk, beat the egg whites and salt until they hold soft peaks. Add the remaining sugar and beat only enough to blend. Fold a dollop of egg whites into the chocolate mixture, then pour back into the whites and gently fold in.

6 Fold in the cream and pour into the tin. Freeze for about 5 minutes until just set. If the centre sinks, fill with any remaining mixture. Chill for 3–4 hours. Decorate with whipped cream.

Chocolate, Pear & Pecan Pie

A classic pie gets a tempting new twist.

Serves 8–10

3 small pears, peeled
150ml/¼ pint/⅔ cup water
165g/5½oz/¾ cup caster (superfine) sugar
pared rind of 1 lemon
50g/2oz plain (semisweet) chocolate, broken into pieces
50g/2oz/¼ cup butter, diced
225g/8oz/scant ¾ cup golden (light corn) syrup

3 eggs, beaten
5ml/1 tsp vanilla extract
150g/5oz/1¼ cups pecan nuts, chopped

For the pastry

175g/6oz/1½ cups plain (all-purpose) flour
115g/4oz/½ cup butter, diced
25g/1oz/2 tbsp caster (superfine) sugar
1 egg yolk, lightly beaten with 10ml/2 tsp chilled water

1 Sift the flour into a bowl, rub in the butter and stir in the sugar. Add the egg yolk and mix to a dough, adding more water if necessary. Knead lightly, wrap and chill for 30 minutes.

2 Roll out the pastry and use to line a 23cm/9in flan tin (tart pan). Chill for 20 minutes. Preheat the oven to 200°F/400°C/Gas 6. Line the pie case (shell) with foil, fill with baking beans and bake for 10 minutes. Lift out the foil and beans and bake for 5 minutes more. Set aside to cool.

3 Halve and core the pears. Bring the water, 50g/2oz/¼ cup of the sugar and the lemon rind to the boil. Add the pears, cover and simmer for 10 minutes. Remove the pears from the pan.

4 Melt the chocolate over simmering water, beat in the butter and set aside. Heat the remaining sugar and syrup until the sugar has dissolved. Bring to the boil and simmer for 2 minutes. Whisk the eggs into the chocolate mixture until combined, then whisk in the syrup mixture. Stir in the vanilla and nuts.

5 Slice the pear halves lengthways without cutting all the way through. Arrange them in the pastry case and pour in the nut mixture. Bake for 25–30 minutes. Cool and serve sliced.

Choc. Chiffon Energy 509Kcal/2120kJ; Protein 5.5g; Carbohydrate 43.2g, of which sugars 37.8g; Fat 36.2g, of which saturates 21.7g; Cholesterol 121mg; Calcium 98mg; Fibre 0.8g; Sodium 158mg.
Choc., Pear & Pecan Energy 499Kcal/2090kJ; Protein 5.8g; Carbohydrate 59.9g, of which sugars 46.3g; Fat 28g, of which saturates 11g; Cholesterol 113mg; Calcium 68mg; Fibre 2.4g; Sodium 186mg.

Crunchy-Topped Coffee Meringue Pie

For a special treat, try this sweet pastry case filled with coffee custard and topped with meringue – crisp on the outside and soft and chewy underneath.

Serves 6
30ml/2 tbsp ground coffee
350ml/12fl oz/1½ cups milk
25g/1oz/¼ cup cornflour
   (cornstarch)
130g/4½oz/⅔ cup caster
   (superfine) sugar
4 egg yolks
15g/½oz/l tbsp butter

For the pastry
175g/6oz/1½ cups plain
   (all-purpose) flour
15ml/1 tbsp icing (confectioners')
   sugar
75g/3oz/6 tbsp butter, diced
1 egg yolk
finely grated rind of ½ orange
15ml/1 tbsp orange juice

For the meringue
3 egg whites
1.5ml/¼ tsp cream of tartar
150g/5oz/¾ cup caster
   (superfine) sugar
15ml/1 tbsp demerara (raw)
   sugar
25g/1oz/¼ cup skinned hazelnuts

1 Preheat the oven to 200°C/400°F/Gas 6. Make the pastry. Sift the flour and icing sugar into a bowl. Rub or cut in the butter until the mixture resembles fine breadcrumbs. Add the egg yolk, orange rind and juice and mix to form a firm dough. Wrap in clear film (plastic wrap) and chill for 20 minutes.

2 Roll out the pastry and use to line a 23cm/9in loose-based flan tin (tart pan). Cover again with clear film and chill for 30 minutes more.

3 Prick the pastry all over with a fork, line with foil, fill with baking beans and bake for about 10 minutes. Remove the foil and beans and bake for a further 5 minutes. Lower the oven temperature to 160°C/325°F/Gas 3.

4 Put the coffee in a small bowl. Heat 250ml/8fl oz/1 cup of the milk until near-boiling and pour over the coffee. Leave to infuse (steep) for 4–5 minutes, then strain. Blend the cornflour and sugar with the remaining milk in a pan and whisk in the coffee-flavoured milk.

5 Bring the mixture to the boil, stirring until thickened. Remove from the heat.

6 In a bowl, beat the egg yolks. Stir a little of the coffee mixture into the egg yolks, then add to the remaining coffee mixture in the pan with the butter. Cook the filling over a low heat for 4 minutes, or until very thick. Pour the coffee filling into the pastry case.

7 Make the meringue. Whisk the egg whites and cream of tartar in a small bowl until stiff peaks form. Whisk in the caster sugar, a spoonful at a time.

8 Spoon the meringue over the filling and spread right up to the edge of the pastry, swirling into peaks. Sprinkle with demerara sugar and hazelnuts, leaving some whole and chopping others into pieces. Bake for 30–35 minutes, or until the topping is golden brown and crisp. Serve warm or cold.

Plum Crumble Pie

Polenta adds a wonderful golden hue and crunchiness to the crumble topping for this pie, making a perfect contrast to the ripe, juicy plum filling.

Serves 6–8
10ml/2 tsp caster (superfine)
   sugar
15ml/1 tbsp polenta
450g/1lb dark plums
25g/1oz/¼ cup rolled oats
15ml/1 tbsp demerara (raw)
   sugar
custard or cream, to serve

For the pastry
115g/4oz/1 cup plain
   (all-purpose) flour, sifted
115g/4oz/1 cup wholemeal
   (whole-wheat) flour
150g/5oz/¾ cup caster
   (superfine) sugar
115g/4oz/1 cup polenta
5ml/1 tsp baking powder
pinch of salt
150g/5oz/10 tbsp butter, diced
1 egg, beaten
15ml/1 tbsp olive oil
about 60ml/4 tbsp chilled water

1 Make the pastry. Mix the dry ingredients in a large bowl. Rub or cut in the butter until the mixture resembles fine breadcrumbs. Stir in the egg, olive oil and chilled water to form a dough.

2 Grease a 23cm/9in springform cake tin (pan). Press two-thirds of the dough evenly over the base and sides of the tin. Wrap the remaining dough in clear film (plastic wrap) and chill.

3 Preheat the oven to 180°C/350°F/Gas 4. Sprinkle the sugar and polenta into the pastry case. Cut the plums in half and remove the stones (pits), then place the plums, cut side down, on top of the polenta base.

4 Unwrap the chilled dough, crumble with your fingers into a mixing bowl, then add the oats and mix lightly. Sprinkle the mixture over the plums. Sprinkle the demerara sugar on top.

5 Bake the pie for 50 minutes, or until golden. Leave for 15 minutes before removing the pie from the tin. Leave to cool for a few minutes before serving in slices with custard or cream.

Coffee Meringue Energy 540Kcal/2274kJ; Protein 9.5g; Carbohydrate 83.6g, of which sugars 57.4g; Fat 21g, of which saturates 10g; Cholesterol 203mg; Calcium 168mg; Fibre 1.2g; Sodium 160mg.
Plum Crumble Energy 426Kcal/1787kJ; Protein 6.4g; Carbohydrate 60.5g, of which sugars 26.5g; Fat 18.9g, of which saturates 10.2g; Cholesterol 64mg; Calcium 53mg; Fibre 3.2g; Sodium 127mg.

Chocolate Pecan Pie

A delicious version of an American favourite, this pie is great for any occasion.

Serves 6

200g/7oz/1¾ cups plain (all-purpose) flour
75ml/5 tbsp caster (superfine) sugar
90g/3½oz/scant ½ cup unsalted (sweet) butter, softened
1 egg, beaten
finely grated rind of 1 orange

For the filling

200g/7oz/¾ cup golden (light corn) syrup
45ml/3 tbsp light muscovado (brown) sugar
150g/5oz plain (semisweet) chocolate, chopped into small pieces
50g/2oz/¼ cup butter
3 eggs, beaten
5ml/1 tsp vanilla extract
175g/6oz/1½ cups shelled pecan nuts

1 Sift the flour into a bowl and stir in the sugar. Work in the butter evenly with your fingertips until combined.

2 Beat the egg and orange rind in a bowl, then stir into the mixture to make a firm dough. Add a little water if the mixture is too dry, and knead briefly.

3 Roll out the pastry on a lightly floured surface and use to line a deep, 20cm/8in loose-based flan tin (tart pan). Chill for about 30 minutes.

4 Preheat the oven to 180°C/350°F/Gas 4. Make the filling. Melt the syrup, sugar, chocolate and butter in a small pan.

5 Remove the pan from the heat and beat in the eggs and vanilla extract. Sprinkle the pecan nuts into the pastry case and carefully pour over the chocolate mixture.

6 Place the tin on a baking sheet and bake the pie for 50–60 minutes or until the filling is set.

7 Leave the pie in the tin for 10 minutes, then remove the tin's sides and transfer to a plate. Serve the pie on its own, or with a little single (light) cream.

Chocolate Almond Meringue Pie

This dreamy dessert offers a velvety chocolate filling on a light orange pastry case, topped with fluffy meringue.

Serves 6

175g/6oz/1½ cups plain (all-purpose) flour
50g/2oz/⅓ cup ground rice
150g/5oz/10 tbsp unsalted (sweet) butter
finely grated rind of 1 orange
1 egg yolk
flaked almonds and melted chocolate, to decorate

For the filling

150g/5oz plain (semisweet) chocolate, broken into squares
50g/2oz/¼ cup unsalted butter, softened
75g/3oz/6 tbsp caster (superfine) sugar
10ml/2 tsp cornflour (cornstarch)
4 egg yolks
75g/3oz/¾ cup ground almonds

For the meringue

3 egg whites
150g/5oz/¾ cup caster (superfine) sugar

1 Sift the flour and ground rice into a bowl. Rub in the butter to resemble breadcrumbs. Stir in the orange rind. Add the egg yolk; bring the dough together. Roll out and use to line a 23cm/9in round flan tin (tart pan). Chill for 30 minutes.

2 Preheat the oven to 190°C/375°F/Gas 5. Prick the pastry base all over with a fork, cover with baking parchment, weighed down with baking beans, and bake blind for 10 minutes. Remove the pastry case; take out the baking beans and paper.

3 Make the filling. Melt the chocolate in a heatproof bowl over hot water. Cream the butter with the sugar in a bowl, then beat in the cornflour and egg yolks. Fold in the almonds, then the chocolate. Spread in the pastry case. Bake for 10 minutes more.

4 Make the meringue. Whisk the egg whites until stiff, then gradually add half the sugar. Fold in the remaining sugar. Spoon the meringue over the chocolate filling, lifting it up with the back of the spoon to form peaks. Reduce the oven temperature to 180°C/350°F/Gas 4 and bake the pie for 15–20 minutes or until the topping is pale gold. Serve, sprinkled with almonds and drizzled with melted chocolate.

Choc. Pecan Pie Energy 843Kcal/3524kJ; Protein 11.6g; Carbohydrate 90.8g, of which sugars 64.8g; Fat 50.8g, of which saturates 19.1g; Cholesterol 178mg; Calcium 112mg; Fibre 3g; Sodium 282mg.
Meringue Pie Energy 792Kcal/3312kJ; Protein 11.4g; Carbohydrate 87g, of which sugars 56g; Fat 46.4g, of which saturates 23.5g; Cholesterol 241mg; Calcium 128mg; Fibre 2.6g; Sodium 248mg.

Rhubarb Meringue Pie

Tangy rhubarb contrasts
beautifully with meringue.

Serves 6
675g/1½lb rhubarb, chopped
250g/9oz/1¼ cup caster
   (superfine) sugar
grated rind and juice of 3 oranges
3 eggs, separated
75ml/5 tbsp cornflour (cornstarch)

For the pastry
200g/7oz/1¾ cups plain
   (all-purpose) flour
25g/1oz/¼ cup ground walnuts
115g/4oz/½ cup butter, diced
30ml/2 tbsp sugar
1 egg yolk, beaten with
   15ml/1 tbsp water

1 To make the pastry, sift the flour into a bowl and add the
walnuts. Rub in the butter until the mixture resembles very fine
breadcrumbs. Stir in the sugar and egg yolk mixture to make a
firm dough. Knead lightly, wrap and chill for 30 minutes.

2 Preheat the oven to 190°C/375°F/Gas 5. Roll out the pastry
on a lightly floured surface and use to line a 23cm/9in fluted
flan tin (tart pan). Prick the base all over with a fork. Line the
pastry with foil and baking beans, then bake for 15 minutes.

3 Meanwhile, to make the filling, put the chopped rhubarb in a
large pan with 75g/3oz/6 tbsp of the sugar. Add the orange
rind. Cover and cook over a low heat until tender.

4 Remove the foil and beans from the pastry case, then brush
all over with a little egg yolk. Bake the pastry case for about
15 minutes, or until the pastry is crisp and golden.

5 Mix together the cornflour and the orange juice in a mixing
bowl. Remove the rhubarb from the heat, stir in the cornflour
mixture, then return the pan to the heat and bring to the boil,
stirring constantly. Cook for 1–2 minutes more. Cool slightly,
then beat in the remaining egg yolks. Pour into the pastry case.

6 Whisk the egg whites until they form soft peaks, then whisk
in the remaining sugar, 15ml/1 tbsp at a time. Swirl over the
filling and bake for 25 minutes until the meringue is golden.

Apple, Raisin & Maple Pies

Calvados accentuates the
apple flavour of these
elegant puff pastry pies.

Serves 4
350g/12oz puff pastry
beaten egg or milk, to glaze
whipped cream, flavoured with
   orange liqueur and sprinkled
   with grated orange rind, to serve

For the filling
75g/3oz/6 tbsp soft light
   brown sugar
30ml/2 tbsp lemon juice
45ml/3 tbsp maple syrup
150ml/¼ pint/⅔ cup water
45ml/3 tbsp Calvados
6 small eating apples, halved,
   peeled and cored
75g/3oz/½ cup raisins

1 Make the filling. Mix the sugar, lemon juice, maple syrup and
water in a pan. Heat over medium heat until the sugar has
dissolved, then bring to the boil and cook until reduced by half.
Stir in the Calvados.

2 Cut four of the apples into eight even segments. Add the
apple pieces to the syrup and simmer for 5–8 minutes until just
tender. Lift the apple pieces out of the syrup using a slotted
spoon and set them aside.

3 Chop the remaining apples and add to the syrup with the
raisins. Simmer until the mixture is thick, then cool.

4 Preheat the oven to 200°C/400°F/Gas 6. Roll out the pastry
on a floured surface and stamp out eight 15cm/6in rounds with
a fluted cutter. Use half the pastry to line four 10cm/4in
individual flan tins (mini tart pans). Spoon in the raisin mixture
and level the surface.

5 Arrange the apple segments on top of the raisin mixture.
Brush the edge of each pastry case with egg or milk and cover
with a pastry lid. Trim, seal and flute the edges.

6 Cut attractive shapes from the pastry trimmings and use to
decorate the pies. Brush over the tops with beaten egg or milk,
then bake for 30–35 minutes until golden. Serve hot, with the
liqueur-flavoured cream.

Rhubarb Pie Energy 567Kcal/2388kJ; Protein 8.4g; Carbohydrate 89.5g, of which sugars 52.6g; Fat 22.1g, of which saturates 11.1g; Cholesterol 136mg; Calcium 202mg; Fibre 2.8g; Sodium 168mg.
Apple, Raisin & Maple Energy 545Kcal/2294kJ; Protein 5.8g; Carbohydrate 82.8g, of which sugars 51.6g; Fat 21.6g, of which saturates 0g; Cholesterol 0mg; Calcium 75mg; Fibre 2g; Sodium 316mg.

Nectarine Puff Pastry Tarts

These simple, fresh fruit pastries are easy to put together, but the puff pastry gives them an elegant look. You could use peaches, apples or pears instead of the nectarines.

Serves 6
15g/½oz/1 tbsp butter, plus extra
  for greasing
225g/8oz rough puff or puff
  pastry
450g/1lb nectarines
25g/1oz/2 tbsp caster (superfine)
  sugar
freshly grated nutmeg
crème fraîche or lightly whipped
  cream, to serve (optional)

1 Lightly grease a large baking sheet and sprinkle very lightly with water.

2 On a lightly floured surface, roll out the rough puff pastry to a large rectangle, measuring about 40 x 25cm/16 x 10in, and cut into six smaller rectangles.

3 Transfer the pastry to the baking sheet. Using the back of a small knife, scallop the edges of each piece of pastry. Then, using the tip of the knife, score a line 1cm/½in from the edge of each rectangle to form a border.

4 Chill the shapes for 30 minutes. Meanwhile, preheat the oven to 200°C/400°F/Gas 6.

5 Halve the nectarines and remove the stones (pits), then cut the fruit into thin slices. Arrange the nectarine slices neatly in the centre of the pastry rectangles, leaving the border uncovered. Sprinkle the fruit with the caster sugar and a little freshly grated nutmeg.

6 Bake for 12–15 minutes until the edges of each pastry case (pie shell) are puffed up and the fruit is tender.

7 Transfer the tarts to a wire rack to cool slightly, then serve warm with crème fraîche or whipped cream, if you like.

Crunchy Apple & Almond Flan

A tasty apple tart with a delicious crunchy topping.

Serves 8
115g/4oz/1 cup plain
  (all-purpose) flour
1.5ml/¼ tsp mixed spice (apple
  pie spice)
50g/2oz/¼ cup butter, diced
50g/2oz/¼ cup demerara
  (raw) sugar
50g/2oz/½ cup flaked (sliced)
  almonds
675g/1½lb cooking apples

25g/1oz/3 tbsp raisins
sifted icing (confectioners') sugar,
  for dusting

For the pastry
175g/6oz/1½ cups plain
  (all-purpose) flour
75g/3oz/6 tbsp butter, diced
25g/1oz/¼ cup ground almonds
25g/1oz/2 tbsp caster (superfine)
  sugar
1 egg yolk
15ml/1 tbsp cold water
1.5ml/¼ tsp almond extract

1 Make the pastry. Put the flour in a mixing bowl and rub in the butter until it resembles fine breadcrumbs. Stir in the almonds and sugar. Whisk the egg yolk, water and almond extract together, then mix into the flour mixture to form a soft dough. Knead until smooth, wrap in clear film (plastic wrap) and leave in a cool place for 20 minutes.

2 Meanwhile, make the topping. Sift the flour and spice into a mixing bowl and rub in the butter. Stir in the sugar and almonds.

3 Roll out the pastry on a lightly floured surface and use to line a 23cm/9in loose-based flan tin (tart pan), making a lip around the top edge. Trim off the excess pastry. Chill for 15 minutes.

4 Place a baking sheet in the oven and preheat to 190°C/375°F/ Gas 5. Peel, core and thinly slice the apples. Arrange over the pastry in overlapping circles, then sprinkle over the raisins.

5 Cover the apples with the crunchy topping mixture, pressing it on lightly. Place the flan on the hot baking sheet and bake for 25–30 minutes, or until the top is golden brown and the apples are tender. Leave the flan to cool in the tin for 10 minutes. Serve warm or cold, dusted with sifted icing sugar.

Nectarine Tarts Energy 208Kcal/873kJ; Protein 3.2g; Carbohydrate 25.9g, of which sugars 12.5g; Fat 11.3g, of which saturates 1.3g; Cholesterol 5mg; Calcium 30mg; Fibre 0.9g; Sodium 133mg.
Apple & Almond Energy 380Kcal/1594kJ; Protein 6.2g; Carbohydrate 48.4g, of which sugars 20.5g; Fat 19.3g, of which saturates 8.8g; Cholesterol 59mg; Calcium 89mg; Fibre 3.2g; Sodium 102mg.

Chilled Chocolate & Date Slice

This richly flavoured dessert is wonderful served in wedges, accompanied by fresh orange segments.

Serves 6–8

115g/4oz/½ cup unsalted (sweet) butter, melted
225g/8oz ginger nut biscuits (gingersnaps) finely crushed
50g/2oz/⅔ cup stale sponge cake crumbs
75ml/5 tbsp orange juice

115g/4oz/⅔ cup stoned (pitted) dates
25g/1oz/¼ cup finely chopped nuts
175g/6oz dark (bittersweet) chocolate
300ml/½ pint/1¼ cups whipping cream
grated chocolate and icing (confectioners') sugar, to decorate
single (light) cream, to serve (optional)

1 Mix the butter and ginger biscuit crumbs in a bowl, then press the mixture on to the sides and base of an 18cm/7in loose-based flan tin (tart pan). Chill while making the filling.

2 Put the cake crumbs in a bowl. Pour over 60ml/4 tbsp of the orange juice, stir well with a wooden spoon and leave to soak. Put the dates in a pan and add the remaining orange juice. Warm the mixture over a low heat. Mash the warm dates thoroughly and stir in the cake crumbs, with the chopped nuts.

3 Mix the chocolate with 60ml/4 tbsp of the cream in a heatproof bowl. Place the bowl over a pan of barely simmering water and stir occasionally until melted. In a separate bowl, whip the rest of the cream to soft peaks, then fold in the melted chocolate.

4 Add the cooled date, crumb and nut mixture to the cream and chocolate and mix lightly but thoroughly. Pour into the tin. Using a spatula, level the mixture. Chill until just set, then mark the tart into portions, using a sharp knife dipped in hot water. Return the tart to the refrigerator and chill until firm.

5 To decorate, scatter the grated chocolate over the surface and dust with icing sugar. Serve with cream, if you wish.

Kiwi Ricotta Cheese Tart

It is well worth taking your time arranging the kiwi fruit topping in neat rows for this exotic tart – the results will be truly impressive.

Serves 8

50g/2oz/½ cup blanched almonds
90g/3½oz/½ cup plus 15ml/ 1 tbsp caster (superfine) sugar
900g/2lb/4 cups ricotta cheese
250ml/8fl oz/1 cup whipping cream
1 egg
3 egg yolks
15ml/1 tbsp plain (all-purpose) flour
pinch of salt

30ml/2 tbsp rum
grated rind of 1 lemon
40ml/2½ tbsp lemon juice
50ml/2fl oz/¼ cup clear honey
5 kiwi fruit

For the pastry

150g/5oz/1¼ cups plain (all-purpose) flour
15ml/1 tbsp caster (superfine) sugar
2.5ml/½ tsp salt
2.5ml/½ tsp baking powder
75g/3oz/6 tbsp cold butter, cut into small pieces
1 egg yolk
45–60ml/3–4 tbsp whipping cream

1 Make the pastry. Sift the flour, sugar, salt and baking powder into a bowl. Cut in the butter until the mixture resembles coarse crumbs. Mix the egg yolk and cream together. Stir in just enough to bind the dough.

2 Transfer to a lightly floured surface, flatten slightly, wrap in baking parchment and chill for 30 minutes. Preheat the oven to 220°C/425°F/Gas 7.

3 On a lightly floured surface, roll out the dough 3mm/⅛in thick and use to line a 23cm/9in springform tin (pan). Crimp the edge of the pastry.

4 Prick the base of the dough all over with a fork. Line with baking parchment and fill with baking beans. Bake for 10 minutes. Remove the paper and beans and bake for a further 6–8 minutes until golden. Allow to cool. Reduce the heat to 180°C/350°F/Gas 4.

5 Grind the almonds finely with 15ml/1 tbsp of the sugar in a food processor or blender.

6 With an electric whisk, beat the ricotta until creamy. Add the cream, egg, yolks, remaining sugar, flour, salt, rum, lemon rind and 30ml/2 tbsp of the lemon juice. Beat to combine. Stir in the ground almonds until well blended.

7 Pour the mixture into the pastry case (pie shell) and bake for about 1 hour until golden. Allow to cool, then chill, loosely covered, for 2–3 hours. Remove from the tin.

8 Combine the honey and remaining lemon juice for the glaze. Set aside.

9 Peel the kiwis. Halve them lengthways, then cut crossways into 5mm/¼in slices. Arrange the slices in rows across the top of the tart. Just before serving, brush with the glaze.

Chocolate & Date Energy 575Kcal/2394kJ; Protein 5.1g; Carbohydrate 51.3g, of which sugars 37.5g; Fat 40.2g, of which saturates 22.8g; Cholesterol 78mg; Calcium 87mg; Fibre 1.8g; Sodium 214mg.
Kiwi Ricotta Tart Energy 645Kcal/2686kJ; Protein 16.9g; Carbohydrate 41.1g, of which sugars 25.2g; Fat 46.2g, of which saturates 25.7g; Cholesterol 231mg; Calcium 93mg; Fibre 1.4g; Sodium 83mg.

Chocolate & Pine Nut Tart

Orange-flavoured pastry makes this a real winner.

Serves 8
200g/7oz/1¾ cups plain
  (all-purpose) flour
50g/2oz/¼ cup caster
  (superfine) sugar
pinch of salt
grated rind of ½ orange
115g/4oz/½ cup unsalted (sweet)
  butter, cut into small pieces
3 egg yolks, lightly beaten
15–30ml/1–2 tbsp chilled water

For the filling
2 eggs
45ml/3 tbsp caster
  (superfine) sugar
grated rind of 1 orange
15ml/1 tbsp orange liqueur
250ml/8fl oz/1 cup whipping cream
115g/4oz plain (semisweet)
  chocolate, cut into small pieces
75g/3oz/¾ cup pine nuts, toasted

For the decoration
thinly pared rind of 1 orange
50g/2oz/¼ cup granulated sugar

1 Process the flour, sugar, salt and orange rind in a food processor, add the butter and process again for 30 seconds. Add the yolks and pulse until the dough begins to stick together. If it seems dry, gradually add the water. Knead, then wrap and chill for 2–3 hours.

2 Grease a 23cm/9in loose-based flan tin (tart pan). Roll out the dough on a floured surface into a 28cm/11in round. Ease it into the tin and roll a rolling pin over the edge to trim. Prick the base. Chill for 1 hour. Preheat the oven to 200°C/400°F/Gas 6.

3 Line the pastry with foil, fill with baking beans and bake blind for 5 minutes. Remove the foil and beans and bake for 5 minutes more, then cool. Lower the temperature to 180°C/350°F/Gas 4.

4 Beat the eggs, sugar, orange rind and liqueur in a bowl. Stir in the cream. Sprinkle the chocolate and pine nuts over the base of the tart. Pour in the filling. Bake for 20–30 minutes, until golden.

5 Make the decoration. Cut the orange rind into strips. Dissolve the sugar in 120ml/4fl oz/½ cup water over a medium heat, add the rind and boil for 5 minutes. Remove from the heat and stir in 15ml/1 tbsp cold water. Brush the orange syrup over the tart and decorate with the caramelized strips. Serve warm.

Fruit Tartlets

The cream and fresh fruit topping contrast beautifully with the chocolate pastry.

Makes 8
215g/7½oz/¾ cup redcurrant or
  grape jelly
15ml/1 tbsp fresh lemon juice
175ml/6fl oz/¾ cup whipping
  cream
675g/1½lb fresh fruit, such as
  strawberries, raspberries, kiwi
  fruit, peaches, grapes or
  blueberries, peeled and sliced
  as necessary

For the pastry
150g/5oz/10 tbsp cold butter, cut
  into pieces
65g/2½oz/5 tbsp dark brown
  sugar
45ml/3 tbsp cocoa powder
  (unsweetened)
175g/6oz/1½ cups plain
  (all-purpose) flour
1 egg white

1 Make the pastry. Place the butter, brown sugar and cocoa in a medium pan over low heat. When the butter has melted, remove from the heat and sift over the flour. Stir with a wooden spoon to combine, then add just enough egg white to bind the mixture. Gather into a ball, wrap in baking parchment and chill for at least 30 minutes.

2 Preheat the oven to 180°C/350°F/Gas 4. Grease eight 7.5cm/3in tartlet tins (muffin pans). Roll out the dough between two sheets of baking parchment and stamp out eight 10cm/4in rounds with a fluted cutter.

3 Line the tartlet tins with dough rounds. Prick the pastry bases with a fork. Chill for 15 minutes.

4 Bake for 20–25 minutes until firm. Leave to cool, then remove from the tins.

5 Melt the jelly with the lemon juice. Brush a thin layer over the base of the tartlets. Whip the cream and spread a thin layer in the tartlet cases (shells). Arrange the fruit on top. Brush evenly with the glaze and serve.

Choc. & Pine Nut Energy 543Kcal/2261kJ; Protein 7.8g; Carbohydrate 42.7g, of which sugars 23.5g; Fat 38.6g, of which saturates 19.2g; Cholesterol 187mg; Calcium 84mg; Fibre 1.3g; Sodium 118mg.
Fruit Tartlets Energy 440Kcal/1841kJ; Protein 5.4g; Carbohydrate 49.3g, of which sugars 32g; Fat 26g, of which saturates 16.1g; Cholesterol 63mg; Calcium 83mg; Fibre 3.5g; Sodium 192mg.

Berry Brûlée Tarts

This quantity of pastry is enough for eight tartlets, so freeze half for another day. The brûlée topping is best added no more than two hours before serving.

Makes 4
250g/9oz/2¼ cups plain (all-purpose) flour
pinch of salt
25g/1oz/¼ cup ground almonds
15ml/1 tbsp icing (confectioners') sugar
150g/5oz/10 tbsp unsalted (sweet) butter, chilled and diced

1 egg yolk
about 45ml/3 tbsp cold water

For the filling
4 egg yolks
15ml/1 tbsp cornflour (cornstarch)
50g/2oz/¼ cup caster (superfine) sugar
a few drops of vanilla extract
300ml/½ pint/1¼ cups creamy milk
225g/8oz/2 cups mixed berry fruits, such as strawberries, raspberries and redcurrants
50g/2oz/½ cup icing (confectioners') sugar

1 Mix the flour, salt, ground almonds and icing sugar in a bowl. Rub in the butter by hand or in a food processor until the mixture resembles fine breadcrumbs. Add the egg yolk and enough cold water to form a dough. Knead the dough gently, then cut it in half and freeze half for use later.

2 Cut the remaining pastry into four equal pieces and roll out thinly on a lightly floured surface. Use the pastry rounds to line four individual tartlet tins (muffin pans), allowing the excess pastry to hang over the edges. Chill for 30 minutes.

3 Preheat the oven to 200°C/400°F/Gas 6. Line the pastry with baking parchment and fill with baking beans. Bake blind for 10 minutes. Remove the paper and beans and return the tartlet cases to the oven for 5 minutes until golden. Allow the pastry to cool, then carefully trim off the excess pastry.

4 Beat the egg yolks, cornflour, caster sugar and vanilla in a bowl. Warm the milk in a heavy pan, pour it on to the egg yolks, whisking constantly, then return the mixture to the cleaned out pan.

5 Heat, stirring, until the custard thickens, but do not let it boil. Remove from the heat, press a piece of clear film (plastic wrap) directly on the surface of the custard and allow to cool.

6 Scatter the berries in the tartlet cases and spoon over the custard. Chill the tarts for 2 hours.

7 To serve, sift icing sugar generously over the tops of the tartlets. Preheat the grill (broiler) to the highest setting. Place the tartlets under the hot grill until the sugar melts and caramelizes. Allow the topping to cool and harden for about 10 minutes before serving.

> **Cook's Tip**
> If you have a culinary blow torch – and are confident about operating it safely – use it to melt the brûlée topping easily.

Tangy Raspberry & Lemon Tartlets

Fresh raspberries and popular lemon curd are teamed up to create colourful, tangy tartlets. Buy the best lemon curd you can find.

Serves 4
175g/6oz ready-made shortcrust pastry, thawed if frozen
120ml/8 tbsp good quality lemon curd
115g/4oz/⅔ cup fresh raspberries
whipped cream, to serve

1 Preheat the oven to 190°C/375°F/Gas 5. Roll out the pastry and use to line four 9cm/3½in tartlet tins (muffin pans). Line each tin with a circle of baking parchment and fill with baking beans or uncooked rice.

2 Bake for 15–20 minutes, or until golden and cooked through. Remove the baking beans or rice and paper and take the pastry cases (pie shells) out of the tins. Leave to cool completely on a wire rack.

3 Set aside 12 raspberries for decoration and fold the remaining ones into the lemon curd. Spoon the mixture into the pastry cases and top with the reserved raspberries. Serve immediately with whipped cream.

> **Cook's Tips**
> • To save on last-minute preparation, you can make the pastry cases (pie shells) for these little tartlets in advance and store them in an airtight container until ready to serve.
> • For an attractive finish, dust the raspberry topping with sifted icing (confectioners') sugar and decorate with mint sprigs or finely shredded lemon rind.

> **Variation**
> Stir a little whipped cream into the lemon for a luxurious touch.

Berry Tarts Energy 713Kcal/3099kJ; Protein 13.6g; Carbohydrate 75.2g, of which sugars 20.6g; Fat 45g, of which saturates 23.8g; Cholesterol 342mg; Calcium 250mg; Fibre 4g; Sodium 282mg.
Raspberry & Lemon Energy 289Kcal/1214kJ; Protein 3.1g; Carbohydrate 40.6g, of which sugars 13.8g; Fat 13.9g, of which saturates 4.3g; Cholesterol 13mg; Calcium 47mg; Fibre 1.6g; Sodium 195mg.

Ricotta Cheesecake

This refreshing, Sicilian-style cheesecake makes good use of ricotta's firm texture. Here, the cheese is enriched with eggs and cream and enlivened with grated orange and lemon rind.

Serves 8
450g/1lb/2 cups ricotta cheese
120ml/4fl oz/½ cup double (heavy) cream
2 eggs
1 egg yolk
75g/3oz/6 tbsp caster (superfine) sugar
finely grated rind of 1 orange and 1 lemon, plus extra to decorate

For the pastry
175g/6oz/1½ cups plain (all-purpose) flour
45ml/3 tbsp caster (superfine) sugar
115g/4oz/½ cup chilled butter, diced
1 egg yolk

1 Make the pastry. Sift the flour and sugar on to a cold work surface. Make a well in the centre and add the butter and egg yolk. Work the flour into the butter and egg yolk.

2 Gather the dough together, reserve a quarter and press the rest into a 23cm/9in loose-based, fluted flan tin (tart pan) and chill. Preheat the oven to 190°C/375°F/Gas 5.

3 Beat the cheese with the cream, eggs and egg yolk, sugar and citrus rinds in a large bowl.

4 Prick the base of the pastry case, then line with foil and fill with baking beans. Bake for 15 minutes, transfer to a wire rack, remove the foil and beans and allow the pastry to cool in the tin.

5 Spoon the cheese and cream filling into the pastry case (pie shell) and level the surface. Roll out the reserved dough and cut into long, even strips. Arrange the strips on the top of the filling in a lattice pattern, sticking them in place with water.

6 Bake the cheesecake for 30–35 minutes until golden and set. Transfer to a wire rack and leave to cool, then remove the side of the tin. Transfer to a plate and decorate with citrus rind.

Marbled Chocolate Cheesecake

This attractive-looking dessert will be a big hit.

Serves 6
butter or margarine, for greasing
50g/2oz/½ cup cocoa powder (unsweetened)
75ml/5 tbsp hot water
900g/2lb/4 cups cream cheese, at room temperature
200g/7oz/1 cup caster (superfine) sugar
4 eggs
5ml/1 tsp vanilla extract
75g/3oz digestive biscuits (graham crackers), crushed

1 Preheat the oven to 180°C/350°F/Gas 4. Line a deep 20cm/8in cake tin (pan) with baking parchment. Grease the paper.

2 Sift the cocoa powder into a bowl. Pour over the hot water and stir to dissolve.

3 In another bowl, beat the cheese until smooth, then beat in the sugar, followed by the eggs, one at a time. Do not overmix.

4 Divide the mixture evenly between two bowls. Stir the chocolate mixture into one bowl, then add the vanilla extract to the remaining mixture.

5 Pour a cup or ladleful of the plain mixture into the centre of the tin; it will spread out into an even layer. Slowly pour over a cupful of chocolate mixture in the centre. Continue to alternate the cake mixtures in this way until both are used up. Draw a thin metal skewer through the cake mixture for a marbled effect.

6 Place the tin in a roasting pan and pour in hot water to come 4cm/1½in up the sides of the cake tin. Bake the cheesecake for about 1½ hours, until the top is golden. (The cake will rise during baking but will sink later.) Cool in the tin on a wire rack.

7 Run a knife around the inside edge of the cheesecake. Invert a flat plate over the tin and turn out the cake. Sprinkle the crushed biscuits evenly over the cake, gently invert another plate on top, and turn over again. Cover and chill for 3 hours, preferably overnight, before serving.

Ricotta Energy 449Kcal/1873kJ; Protein 9.9g; Carbohydrate 34.8g, of which sugars 18.1g; Fat 31.1g, of which saturates 18.4g; Cholesterol 173mg; Calcium 62mg; Fibre 0.7g; Sodium 112mg
Marbled Chocolate Energy 923Kcal/3828kJ; Protein 11.3g; Carbohydrate 44.4g, of which sugars 36.5g; Fat 79.3g, of which saturates 47.8g; Cholesterol 274mg; Calcium 206mg; Fibre 1.3g; Sodium 653mg.

Fresh Lemon Tart

Serve at room temperature to enjoy the zesty lemon flavour to the full.

Serves 6–8

350g/12oz ready-made rich
   sweet shortcrust pastry

For the filling
3 eggs
115g/4oz/½ cup caster
   (superfine) sugar
115g/4oz/1 cup ground almonds
105ml/7 tbsp double
   (heavy) cream
grated rind and juice of 2 lemons

For the topping
2 thin-skinned unwaxed lemons,
   thinly sliced
200g/7oz/1 cup caster
   (superfine) sugar
105ml/7 tbsp water

1 Roll out the pastry and line a deep 23cm/9in fluted flan tin (tart pan). Prick the base and chill for 30 minutes.

2 Preheat the oven to 200°C/400°F/Gas 6. Line the pastry with baking parchment and baking beans and bake blind for 10 minutes. Remove the paper and beans and return the pastry case to the oven for 5 minutes more.

3 Meanwhile, make the filling. Beat the eggs, caster sugar, almonds and cream in a bowl until smooth. Beat in the lemon rind and juice. Pour the filling into the pastry case. Lower the oven temperature to 190°C/375°F/Gas 5 and bake for 20 minutes or until the filling has set and the pastry is golden.

4 Make the topping. Place the lemon slices in a pan and pour over water to cover. Simmer for 15–20 minutes or until the skins are tender, then drain. Place the sugar in a pan and stir in the measured water. Heat gently until the sugar has dissolved, stirring constantly, then boil for 2 minutes. Add the lemon slices and cook for 10–15 minutes until the skins become candied.

5 Lift out the candied lemon slices and arrange them over the top of the tart. Return the syrup to the heat and boil until reduced to a thick glaze. Brush this over the tart and allow to cool completely before serving.

Pear Tarte Tatin with Cardamom

Cardamom is a spice that is equally at home in sweet and savoury dishes. It is delicious with pears, and brings out their flavour beautifully in this easy-to-make tart.

Serves 4–6
50g/2oz/¼ cup butter, softened
50g/2oz/¼ cup caster
   (superfine) sugar
seeds from 10 green
   cardamom pods
225g/8oz fresh ready-made
   puff pastry
3 ripe, large round pears
single (light) cream, to serve

1 Preheat the oven to 220°C/425°F/Gas 7. Spread the butter over the base of an 18cm/7in heavy ovenproof omelette pan. Sprinkle the butter with the sugar, then sprinkle the cardamom seeds evenly over the top.

2 On a lightly floured work surface, roll out the pastry to a circle slightly larger than the pan. Prick the pastry all over with a fork, place on a baking sheet and chill.

3 Peel the pears, cut in half lengthways and remove the cores. Arrange the pears, rounded side down, in the pan. Place over medium heat and cook until the sugar melts and begins to bubble with the juice from the pears.

4 Once the sugar has caramelized, remove the pan from the heat. Carefully place the pastry on top, tucking in the edges with a knife. Bake for 25 minutes.

5 Leave the tart in the pan for about 2 minutes until the juices have stopped bubbling.

6 Invert a serving plate over the pan then, wearing oven gloves to protect your hands, firmly hold the pan and plate together and quickly turn over, gently shaking them to release the tart. It may be necessary to slide a spatula underneath the pears to loosen them. Allow the tart to cool slightly, then serve warm, with single cream.

Lemon Tart Energy 528Kcal/2212kJ; Protein 7.8g; Carbohydrate 61.7g, of which sugars 42.3g; Fat 29.6g, of which saturates 5.6g; Cholesterol 89mg; Calcium 91mg; Fibre 1.9g; Sodium 104mg.
Tarte Tatin Energy 265Kcal/1106kJ; Protein 2.5g; Carbohydrate 30.1g, of which sugars 16.8g; Fat 16.1g, of which saturates 4.3g; Cholesterol 18mg; Calcium 36mg; Fibre 1.7g; Sodium 170mg.

Treacle Tart

An old-fashioned favourite, with its sticky filling and twisted lattice topping, this tart is perfect with custard.

Serves 4–6
260g/9½oz/generous ¾ cup golden (light corn) syrup
75g/3oz/1½ cups fresh white breadcrumbs
grated rind of I lemon
30ml/2 tbsp lemon juice

For the pastry
150g/5oz/1¼ cups plain (all-purpose) flour
2.5ml/½ tsp salt
130g/4½oz/9 tbsp chilled butter, diced
45–60ml/3–4 tbsp chilled water

I Make the pastry. Combine the flour and salt in a bowl. Rub or cut in the butter until the mixture resembles coarse breadcrumbs. With a fork, stir in just enough water to bind the dough. Gather into a smooth ball, knead lightly until smooth then wrap in clear film (plastic wrap) and chill for at least 20 minutes.

2 On a lightly floured surface, roll out the pastry to a thickness of 3mm/⅛in. Transfer to a 20cm/8in fluted flan tin (tart pan) and trim off the overhang. Chill the pastry case for 20 minutes. Reserve the pastry trimmings.

3 Put a baking sheet in the oven and preheat to 200°C/400°F/Gas 6. To make the filling, warm the syrup in a pan until it melts.

4 Remove the syrup from the heat and stir in the breadcrumbs and lemon rind. Leave to stand for 10 minutes, then add more breadcrumbs if the mixture is too thin and moist. Stir in the lemon juice, then spread the mixture evenly in the pastry case.

5 Roll out the pastry trimmings and cut into 10–12 thin strips. Twist the strips into spirals, then lay half of them on the filling. Arrange the remaining strips at right angles to form a lattice. Press the ends on to the rim.

6 Place the tart on the hot baking sheet and bake for 10 minutes. Lower the oven temperature to 190°C/375°F/Gas 5. Bake for 15 minutes more, until golden. Serve warm.

Bakewell Tart

Although the pastry base makes this a tart, in the English village of Bakewell, where it originated, it is traditionally called Bakewell Pudding.

Serves 4
225g/8oz puff pastry
30ml/2 tbsp raspberry or apricot jam
2 eggs, plus 2 egg yolks
115g/4oz/generous ½ cup caster (superfine) sugar
115g/4oz/½ cup butter, melted
50g/2oz/⅔ cup ground almonds
a few drops of almond extract
icing (confectioners') sugar, for dusting

I Preheat the oven to 200°C/400°F/Gas 6. Roll out the pastry on a lightly floured surface and use to line an 18cm/7in pie plate. Trim the edge.

2 Re-roll the pastry trimmings and cut out wide strips of pastry. Use these to decorate the edge of the pastry case by gently twisting them around the rim, joining the strips together as necessary. Prick the pastry case all over, then spread the jam over the base.

3 Whisk the eggs, egg yolks and sugar together in a bowl until the mixture is thick and pale.

4 Gently stir the melted butter, ground almonds and almond extract into the whisked egg mixture.

5 Pour the mixture into the pastry case and bake for 30 minutes, or until the filling is just set and is lightly browned. Dust with icing sugar before serving hot, warm or cold.

> **Cook's Tip**
> Since this pastry case is not baked blind before being filled, place a baking sheet in the oven while it preheats, then place the tart on the hot sheet. This will ensure that the base of the pastry case cooks right through.

Treacle Tart Energy 420Kcal/1764kJ; Protein 4.1g; Carbohydrate 63.5g, of which sugars 35.1g; Fat 18.4g, of which saturates 11.3g; Cholesterol 46mg; Calcium 62mg; Fibre 1.1g; Sodium 344mg.
Bakewell Tart Energy 700Kcal/2919kJ; Protein 10.8g; Carbohydrate 57.1g, of which sugars 36.7g; Fat 49.9g, of which saturates 17.1g; Cholesterol 257mg; Calcium 110mg; Fibre 0.9g; Sodium 394mg.

Prune Tart with Custard Filling

Armagnac makes a great partner for prunes but fresh orange juice works well, too.

Serves 6–8

225g/8oz/1 cup pitted prunes
50ml/2fl oz/¼ cup Armagnac or other brandy
4 egg yolks
300ml/½ pint/1¼ cups milk
a few drops of vanilla extract
15g/½oz/2 tbsp cornflour (cornstarch)
25g/1oz/¼ cup flaked (sliced) almonds

icing (confectioners') sugar, for dusting
thick cream, to serve

For the pastry

175g/6oz/1½ cups plain (all-purpose) flour, sifted, plus extra for dusting
pinch of salt
90g/3½oz/½ cup caster (superfine) sugar
115g/4oz/½ cup unsalted (sweet) butter, at room temperature
1 egg

1 Place the prunes in a bowl with the Armagnac and leave in a warm place to soak.

2 Place the flour, salt, 50g/2oz/¼ cup of the sugar, the butter and egg, reserving 5ml/1 tsp egg white, in a food processor and process until blended.

3 Turn out on a clean, lightly floured surface and bring the mixture together into a ball. Leave for 10 minutes to rest.

4 Flour a 28 x 18cm/11 x 7in loose-based flan tin (tart pan). Roll out the pastry and line the tin; don't worry if you have to push it into shape, as this pastry is soft and easy to mould. Chill for 10–20 minutes. Meanwhile, preheat the oven to 200°C/400°F/Gas 6.

5 Line the pastry case with baking parchment and fill with baking beans, then bake for 15 minutes. Remove the paper and beans, and bake for 10–15 minutes. Brush the base of the pastry with the reserved egg white while it is still hot. Set aside to cool slightly.

6 Bring the milk and vanilla extract to the boil. In a bowl, whisk the egg yolks and remaining sugar until thick, pale and fluffy, then whisk in the cornflour. Strain in the milk and whisk until there are no lumps.

7 Return to the pan and bring to the boil, whisking all the time to remove any lumps. Cook for about 2 minutes until thick and smooth, then set aside to cool. Press clear film (plastic wrap) on to the surface of the custard to prevent a skin forming.

8 Stir any prune liquid into the custard, then spread over the pastry case. Arrange the prunes on top, sprinkle with the flaked almonds and dust with icing sugar, and return to the oven for 10 minutes until golden and glazed. Remove from the oven and leave to cool. Serve hot or at room temperature with cream.

> **Cook's Tip**
> Let the prunes soak for at least an hour to absorb the brandy.

Blueberry Frangipane Flan

A lemon pastry case is filled with a sweet almond filling, dotted with blueberries.

Serves 6

30ml/2 tbsp ground coffee
45ml/3 tbsp milk
50g/2oz/¼ cup unsalted (sweet) butter
50g/2oz/¼ cup caster (superfine) sugar
1 egg
115g/4oz/1 cup ground almonds
15ml/1 tbsp plain

(all-purpose) flour, sifted
225g/8oz/2 cups blueberries
30ml/2 tbsp jam
15ml/1 tbsp brandy

For the pastry

175g/6oz/1½ cups plain (all-purpose) flour
115g/4oz/½ cup unsalted (sweet) butter or margarine
25g/1oz/2 tbsp caster (superfine) sugar
finely grated rind of ½ lemon
15ml/1 tbsp chilled water

1 Preheat the oven to 190°C/375°F/Gas 5. To make the pastry, sift the flour into a bowl and rub in the butter. Stir in the sugar and lemon rind, then add the water and mix to a firm dough. Wrap in clear film (plastic wrap) and chill for 20 minutes.

2 Roll out the pastry on a lightly floured work surface and use to line a 23cm/9in loose-based flan tin (tart pan). Line the pastry with baking parchment and baking beans and bake for 10 minutes. Remove the paper and beans and bake for a further 10 minutes. Remove from the oven.

3 Meanwhile, make the filling. Put the ground coffee in a bowl. Bring the milk almost to the boil, then pour over the coffee and leave to infuse for 4 minutes. Cream the butter and sugar until pale. Beat in the egg, then add the almonds and flour. Finely strain in the coffee-flavoured milk and fold in.

4 Spread the coffee mixture into the pastry case. Scatter the blueberries over and push down slightly into the mixture. Bake for 30 minutes, until firm, covering with foil after 20 minutes.

5 Heat the jam and brandy in a small pan until melted. Brush over the flan and remove from the tin.

Prune Tart Energy 362Kcal/1518kJ; Protein 71g; Carbohydrate 42.1g, of which sugars 23.6g; Fat 18.1g, of which saturates 9.1g; Cholesterol 157mg; Calcium 117mg; Fibre 2.5g; Sodium 122mg.
Flan Energy 523Kcal/2180kJ; Protein 8.9g; Carbohydrate 44.9g, of which sugars 20.2g; Fat 34.8g, of which saturates 15.6g; Cholesterol 91mg; Calcium 132mg; Fibre 3.6g; Sodium 188mg.

Red Grape & Cheese Tartlets

The natural partnership of fruit and cheese is the hallmark of this simple recipe. Look out for small, pale, mauve-coloured or red grapes. These are often seedless, and sweeter than large black varieties.

Makes 6
225g/8oz/1 cup curd (farmer's) cheese
150ml/¼ pint/⅔ cup double (heavy) cream
2.5ml/½ tsp vanilla extract
30ml/2 tbsp icing (confectioners') sugar
200g/7oz/2 cups red grapes, halved, seeded if necessary
60ml/4 tbsp apricot jam
15ml/1 tbsp water

For the pastry
200g/7oz/1¾ cups plain (all-purpose) flour
15ml/1 tbsp caster (superfine) sugar
150g/5oz/10 tbsp butter
2 egg yolks
15ml/1 tbsp chilled water

1 Make the pastry. Sift the flour and sugar into a mixing bowl. Rub or cut in the butter until the mixture resembles fine breadcrumbs. Add the egg yolks and water and mix to a dough. Knead lightly until smooth. Wrap in clear film (plastic wrap) and chill for 30 minutes.

2 Preheat the oven to 200°C/400°F/Gas 6. Roll out the pastry and use to line six deep 10cm/4in fluted tartlet tins (muffin pans). Prick the bases, line with foil and fill with baking beans. Bake for 10 minutes, remove the foil and beans, then bake for a further 5 minutes until golden. Remove the pastry cases (pie shells) from the tins and cool.

3 Meanwhile, beat the curd cheese with the double cream, vanilla extract and icing sugar in a small bowl. Divide the mixture among the pastry cases. Smooth the surface and arrange the halved grapes attractively on top.

4 Press the apricot jam through a sieve (strainer) into a small pan. Add the water and heat, stirring constantly, until smooth and glossy. Generously spoon the apricot glaze over the grapes. Leave to cool, then chill before serving.

Orange Sweetheart Tart

A real treat to eat, this tart has a crisp shortcrust pastry case, spread with apricot jam and filled with frangipane, then topped with tangy orange slices.

Serves 8
200g/7oz/1 cup sugar
250ml/8fl oz/1 cup fresh orange juice, strained
2 large navel oranges
75g/3oz/½ cup blanched almonds
50g/2oz/¼ cup butter
1 egg
15ml/1 tbsp plain (all-purpose) flour
45ml/3 tbsp apricot jam

For the pastry
175g/6oz/1½ cups plain (all-purpose) flour
2.5ml/½ tsp salt
75g/3oz/6 tbsp chilled butter, diced
45ml/3 tbsp chilled water

1 Make the pastry. Sift the flour and salt into a mixing bowl. Add the butter and rub in with your fingertips until the mixture resembles fine breadcrumbs. Sprinkle over the water and mix to a dough. Knead the dough on a lightly floured surface for a few seconds until smooth. Wrap the dough in clear film (plastic wrap) and chill for at least 30 minutes.

2 After the pastry has rested, roll it out on a floured surface to a thickness of about 5mm/¼in. Use to line a 20cm/8in heart-shaped tart tin (pan). Trim the pastry edges and chill again for a further 30 minutes.

3 Preheat the oven to 200°C/400°F/Gas 6, with a baking sheet placed in the centre. Line the pastry case (pie shell) with baking parchment or foil and fill with baking beans. Bake blind for 10 minutes. Remove the parchment or foil and beans and cook for 10 minutes more, or until it is light and golden.

4 Put 150g/5oz/¾ cup of the sugar into a heavy pan and pour in the orange juice. Bring to the boil, stirring until the sugar has dissolved, then boil steadily for about 10 minutes, or until the liquid is thick and syrupy.

5 Cut the unpeeled oranges into 5mm/¼in slices. Add to the syrup. Simmer for 10 minutes, or until glazed. Transfer the slices to a wire rack placed over a plate to dry, reserving the syrup. When the orange slices are cool, cut in half.

6 Grind the almonds finely in a food processor. With an electric whisk, cream the butter and remaining sugar until light. Beat in the egg and 30ml/2 tbsp of the orange syrup. Stir in the almonds, then add the flour.

7 Melt the jam over a low heat, then brush it evenly over the the pastry case. Pour in the ground almond mixture. Bake for 20 minutes, or until set. Leave to cool in the tin.

8 Starting at the top of the heart shape and working down to the point, arrange the orange slices on the surface of the tart in an overlapping pattern, cutting them to fit. Boil the remaining syrup until thick and brush on top to glaze. Leave to cool.

Grape & Cheese Energy 559Kcal/2330kJ; Protein 10.4g; Carbohydrate 45.1g, of which sugars 19.7g; Fat 39.3g, of which saturates 23.9g; Cholesterol 164mg; Calcium 123mg; Fibre 1.3g; Sodium
Orange Tart Energy 405Kcal/1699kJ; Protein 6.4g; Carbohydrate 53.7g, of which sugars 36.8g; Fat 19.8g, of which saturates 9g; Cholesterol 81mg; Calcium 90mg; Fibre 2g; Sodium 125mg. 351mg.

Plum & Almond Tart

Plums and marzipan are terrific together and here they are used as a delicious topping for light puff pastry. Simplicity itself to make, this tart is the perfect dessert for an informal gathering.

Serves 4

375g/13oz ready-rolled puff pastry, thawed if frozen
115g/4oz marzipan
6–8 plums, stoned (pitted) and sliced
icing (confectioners') sugar, for dusting
crème fraîche, to serve

1 Preheat the oven to 190°C/375°F/Gas 5. Unroll the pastry on to a large baking sheet. Using a small, sharp knife, score a border 5cm/2in from the edge of the pastry, without cutting all the way through.

2 Roll out the marzipan into a rectangle, to fit just within the pastry border, then lay it on top of the pastry, pressing down lightly with the tips of your fingers.

3 Sprinkle the sliced plums on top of the marzipan in an even layer and bake for 20–25 minutes, or until the pastry is risen and golden brown.

4 Carefully transfer the tart to a wire rack to cool slightly, then dust lightly with icing sugar. To serve, cut into squares or wedges and serve with crème fraîche.

> **Cook's Tip**
> Puff pastry is particularly light because the dough is folded and rolled a number of times, trapping air between the layers.

> **Variation**
> Apricots and peaches also have a natural affinity with almonds, so they can be successfully substituted for the plums.

Yellow Plum Tart

In this pretty tart, glazed yellow plums sit on top of a delectable almond filling.

Serves 8

175g/6oz/1½ cups plain (all-purpose) flour
pinch of salt
75g/3oz/6 tbsp butter, chilled
30ml/2 tbsp caster (superfine) sugar
a few drops of vanilla extract
45ml/3 tbsp chilled water
cream or custard, to serve

For the filling
75g/3oz/6 tbsp caster (superfine) sugar
75g/3oz/6 tbsp butter, softened
75g/3oz/¾ cup ground almonds
1 egg, beaten
30ml/2 tbsp plain (all-purpose) flour
450g/1lb yellow plums or greengages, halved and pitted

For the glaze
45ml/3 tbsp apricot jam
15ml/1 tbsp water

1 Sift the flour and salt into a bowl, then rub in the chilled butter until the mixture resembles fine breadcrumbs. Stir in the sugar, vanilla and enough water to make a soft dough. Knead the dough gently on a lightly floured surface until smooth, then wrap in clear film (plastic wrap) and chill for 10 minutes.

2 Preheat the oven to 200°C/400°F/Gas 6. Roll out the pastry and use to line a 23cm/9in fluted flan tin (tart pan), allowing the excess pastry to overhang the top. Prick the base with a fork and line with baking parchment and baking beans. Bake blind for 10 minutes, remove the paper and beans, then cook for a further 10 minutes. Allow to cool. Trim off any excess pastry.

3 Make the filling. Whisk or beat together all the ingredients except the plums. Spread over the pastry base. Arrange the plums on top, placing them cut side down. Make a glaze. Press the jam through a sieve (strainer) and heat with the water. Stir well, then brush a little of the glaze over the top of the fruit.

4 Bake for 50–60 minutes, until the almond filling is cooked and the plums are tender. Warm any remaining jam glaze and brush over the top. Cut into slices and serve with cream or custard.

Lemon & Lime Cheesecake

This tangy cheesecake is a citrus sensation.

Makes 8 slices
150g/5oz/1½ cups digestive biscuits (graham crackers)
40g/1½oz/3 tbsp butter

For the topping
grated rind and juice of 2 lemons
10ml/2 tsp powdered gelatine
250g/9oz/generous 1 cup ricotta cheese

75g/3oz/6 tbsp caster (superfine) sugar
150ml/¼ pint/⅔ cup double (heavy) cream
2 eggs, separated

For the lime syrup
pared rind and juice of 3 limes
75g/3oz/6 tbsp caster (superfine) sugar
5ml/1 tsp arrowroot mixed with 30ml/2 tbsp water
green food colouring (optional)

1 Lightly grease a 20cm/8in round springform cake tin (pan). Place the biscuits in a food processor or blender and process until they form fine crumbs. Melt the butter in a large pan, then stir in the crumbs until well coated. Spoon into the prepared cake tin, press the crumbs down well in an even layer, then chill.

2 Make the topping. Place the lemon rind and juice in a small pan and sprinkle over the gelatine. Leave for 5 minutes. Heat gently until the gelatine has dissolved, then set aside to cool slightly. Beat the ricotta cheese and sugar in a bowl. Stir in the cream and egg yolks, then whisk in the cooled gelatine mixture.

3 Whisk the egg whites in a grease-free bowl until they form soft peaks. Fold them into the cheese mixture. Spoon on to the biscuit base, level the surface and chill for 2–3 hours.

4 Meanwhile, make the lime syrup. Place the lime rind and juice and sugar in a small pan. Bring to the boil, stirring, then boil the syrup for 5 minutes. Stir in the arrowroot mixture and continue to stir until the syrup boils again and thickens slightly. Tint pale green with a little food colouring, if you like. Cool, then chill.

5 Spoon the lime syrup over the set cheesecake. Remove from the tin and cut into slices to serve.

Pomegranate Jewelled Cheesecake

This light cheesecake has a stunning pomegranate glaze.

Serves 8
225g/8oz oat biscuits (crackers)
75g/3oz/6 tbsp unsalted (sweet) butter, melted

For the filling
45ml/3 tbsp orange juice
15ml/1 tbsp powdered gelatine
250g/9oz/generous 1 cup mascarpone cheese
200g/7oz/scant 1 cup full-fat soft cheese

75g/3oz/⅔ cup icing (confectioners') sugar, sifted
200ml/7fl oz/scant 1 cup coconut cream
2 egg whites

For the topping
2 pomegranates, peeled and seeds separated
grated rind and juice of 1 orange
30ml/2 tbsp caster (superfine) sugar
15ml/1 tbsp arrowroot, mixed to a paste with 30ml/2 tbsp Kirsch
red food colouring (optional)

1 Grease a 23cm/9in springform cake tin (pan). Crumb the biscuits in a food processor or blender. Add the butter and process briefly. Spoon into the tin, press in well, then chill.

2 Make the filling. Pour the orange juice into a heatproof bowl, sprinkle the gelatine on top and set aside for 5 minutes. Place the bowl in a pan of hot water; stir until the gelatine dissolves.

3 In a bowl, beat together both cheeses and the icing sugar, then gradually beat in the coconut cream. Whisk the egg whites in a grease-free bowl to soft peaks. Quickly stir the melted gelatine into the coconut mixture and fold in the egg whites. Pour over the biscuit base, level and chill until set.

4 Make the topping. Place the pomegranate seeds in a pan and add the orange rind and juice and sugar. Bring to the boil, then lower the heat, cover and simmer for 5 minutes. Add the arrowroot paste and heat, stirring, until thickened. Stir in a few drops of food colouring, if using. Cool, stirring occasionally.

5 Pour the glaze over the top of the set cheesecake, then chill. Remove from the tin and cut into slices to serve.

Lemon & Lime Energy 366Kcal/1526kJ; Protein 6g; Carbohydrate 33.8g, of which sugars 23.5g; Fat 23.9g, of which saturates 13.8g; Cholesterol 105mg; Calcium 44mg; Fibre 0.4g; Sodium 166mg.
Pomegranate Energy 407Kcal/1702kJ; Protein 8.2g; Carbohydrate 37.3g, of which sugars 26.1g; Fat 26.1g, of which saturates 15.2g; Cholesterol 56mg; Calcium 57mg; Fibre 1.1g; Sodium 336mg.

Classic American Cheesecake

Popular throughout America, this type of cheesecake with a crumb base is simple to make and tastes wonderful. You can decorate the dish with fruit and serve it with cream, if you like, but it tastes delicious just as it is.

Serves 8
25g/1oz/½ cup digestive biscuit (graham cracker) crumbs
900g/2lb/4 cups cream cheese
250g/9oz/1¼ cups caster (superfine) sugar
grated rind of 1 lemon
45ml/3 tbsp fresh lemon juice
5ml/1 tsp vanilla extract
4 eggs, at room temperature

1 Preheat the oven to 160°C/325°F/Gas 3. Grease a 23cm/8in springform cake tin (pan). Place on a round of foil that is 13cm/5in larger than the diameter of the pan. Press the foil up the sides of the tin to seal tightly.

2 Sprinkle the crumbs in the base of the tin. Press to form an even layer.

3 With an electric whisk, beat the cream cheese until smooth. Add the sugar, lemon rind and juice and vanilla extract, and beat until blended. Beat in the eggs, one at a time. Beat just enough to blend thoroughly.

4 Pour the mixture into the prepared tin. Place the tin in a roasting pan and pour in enough hot water to come 2.5cm/1in up the side of the filled tin.

5 Bake for about 1½ hours until the top of the cake is golden brown. Remove from the roasting pan. Leave to cool in the tin.

6 Run a knife around the edge to loosen, then remove the rim of the tin. Chill for at least 4 hours before serving.

> **Cook's Tip**
> Make sure the foil is wrapped high enough up the tin's side.

American Chocolate Cheesecake

This popular variation of the American classic is made with a crunchy cinnamon and chocolate base.

Serves 10–12
175g/6oz plain (semisweet) chocolate, chopped
115g/4oz dark (bittersweet) chocolate, chopped
1.2kg/2½lb/5 cups cream cheese, at room temperature
200g/7oz/1 cup caster (superfine) sugar
10ml/2 tsp vanilla extract
4 eggs, at room temperature
175ml/6fl oz/¾ cup sour cream

For the base
75g/3oz/1½ cups chocolate biscuit (cookie) crumbs
75g/3oz/6 tbsp butter, melted
2.5ml/½ tsp ground cinnamon

1 Preheat the oven to 180°C/350°F/Gas 4. Grease a 23cm/9in springform cake tin (pan).

2 Make the base. Mix the chocolate wafer crumbs with the butter and cinnamon. Press evenly over the bottom of the tin.

3 Melt the plain and dark chocolate in the top of a double boiler, or in a heatproof bowl set over hot water. Set aside.

4 With an electric whisk, beat the cream cheese until smooth, then beat in the sugar and vanilla extract. Add the eggs, one at a time, scraping the bowl with a spatula when necessary.

5 Add the sour cream to the cheese mixture, then stir in the melted chocolate, mixing well.

6 Pour into the tin. Bake for 1 hour. Allow to cool in the tin, then remove from the tin. Chill before serving.

> **Variation**
> For a chocolate-orange cheesecake, replace the vanilla extract with finely grated orange rind. Serve with sliced oranges coated in a light sugar syrup, flavoured with shredded orange rind.

Cheesecake Energy 668Kcal/2772kJ; Protein 7g; Carbohydrate 34.8g, of which sugars 33.1g; Fat 56.9g, of which saturates 34.5g; Cholesterol 203mg; Calcium 144mg; Fibre 0.1g; Sodium 393mg.
Choc. Cheesecake Energy 717Kcal/2972kJ; Protein 5.2g; Carbohydrate 37.5g, of which sugars 34.9g; Fat 61.8g, of which saturates 38.4g; Cholesterol 118mg; Calcium 131mg; Fibre 0.7g; Sodium 362mg.

Baked Chocolate & Raisin Cheesecake

This classic cheesecake will disappear in a flash.

Serves 8–10
75g/3oz/⅔ cup plain (all-purpose) flour
45ml/3 tbsp cocoa powder (unsweetened)
75g/3oz/½ cup semolina
50g/2oz/¼ cup caster (superfine) sugar
115g/4oz/½ cup unsalted (sweet) butter, softened

For the filling
225g/8oz/1 cup cream cheese
120ml/4fl oz/½ cup natural

(plain) yogurt
2 eggs, beaten
75g/3oz/6 tbsp caster (superfine) sugar
finely grated rind of 1 lemon
75g/3oz/½ cup raisins
45ml/3 tbsp plain (semisweet) chocolate chips

For the topping
75g/3oz plain (semisweet) chocolate, chopped into small pieces
30ml/2 tbsp golden (light corn) syrup
40g/1½oz/3 tbsp butter

1 Preheat the oven to 150°C/300°F/Gas 2. Sift the flour and cocoa into a mixing bowl and stir in the semolina and sugar. Using your fingertips, work the butter into the flour mixture until it makes a firm dough.

2 Press the dough into the base of a 22cm/8½in springform tin (pan). Prick all over with a fork and bake in the oven for 15 minutes. Remove the tin but leave the oven on.

3 Make the filling. In a large bowl, beat the cream cheese with the yogurt, eggs and sugar until evenly mixed. Stir in the lemon rind, raisins and chocolate chips.

4 Smooth the cream cheese mixture over the chocolate base and bake for a further 35–45 minutes or until the filling is pale gold and just set. Cool in the tin on a wire rack.

5 Make the topping. Melt the chocolate, syrup and butter in a bowl over simmering water, then pour over the cheesecake. Leave until set. Remove the cheesecake from the tin and serve.

Blueberry-Hazelnut Cheesecake

Ground hazelnuts give this cheesecake an unusual base.

Serves 6–8
350g/12oz blueberries
15ml/1 tbsp clear honey
75g/3oz/6 tbsp granulated sugar
juice of 1 lemon
175g/6oz/¾ cup cream cheese, at room temperature
1 egg
5ml/1 tsp hazelnut liqueur (optional)

120ml/4fl oz/½ cup whipping cream

For the base
175g/6oz/1⅔ cups ground hazelnuts
75g/3oz/⅔ cup plain (all-purpose) flour
pinch of salt
50g/2oz/4 tbsp butter, plus extra for greasing
65g/2½oz/5 tbsp light muscovado (brown) sugar
1 egg yolk

1 Make the base. Put the hazelnuts in a large bowl. Sift in the flour and salt, then stir to mix. Set aside. Beat the butter with the sugar until light and fluffy. Beat in the egg yolk. Gradually fold in the nut mixture, in three batches, until well combined.

2 Press the dough into a greased 23cm/9in pie or tart dish, spread evenly against the sides. Form a rim around the top edge that is slightly thicker than the sides. Cover and chill for 30 minutes.

3 Preheat the oven to 180°C/350°F/Gas 4. Meanwhile, make the topping. Combine the blueberries, honey, 15ml/1 tbsp of the granulated sugar and 5ml/1 tsp of the lemon juice in a heavy pan. Cook for 5–7 minutes over low heat, stirring, until the berries have given off some liquid but retain their shape. Remove from the heat and set aside. Place the pastry base in the oven and bake for 15 minutes. Remove and allow to cool while making the filling.

4 In a bowl, beat the cream cheese with the remaining granulated sugar until light and fluffy. Add the egg, 15ml/1 tbsp of the lemon juice, the liqueur, if using, and the cream and beat until blended.

5 Pour the mixture into the pastry base. Bake for 25 minutes until just set. Cool on a wire rack, then cover and chill for at least 1 hour. Spread the blueberry mixture over the top.

Chocolate & Raisin Energy 441Kcal/1841kJ; Protein 5.8g; Carbohydrate 41.4g, of which sugars 29.3g; Fat 29.3g, of which saturates 17.7g; Cholesterol 93mg; Calcium 86mg; Fibre 1.4g; Sodium 243mg.
Blueberry-Hazelnut Energy 476Kcal/1978kJ; Protein 6.6g; Carbohydrate 31g, of which sugars 23.4g; Fat 37.1g, of which saturates 15g; Cholesterol 99mg; Calcium 109mg; Fibre 3.1g; Sodium 121mg.

Luxury White Chocolate Cheesecake

A luscious dessert for a special occasion.

Serves 16–20

150g/5oz (about 16–18) digestive biscuits (graham crackers)
50g/2oz/¹⁄₂ cup blanched hazelnuts, toasted
50g/2oz/¹⁄₄ cup unsalted (sweet) butter, melted, plus extra for greasing
2.5ml/¹⁄₂ tsp ground cinnamon
white chocolate curls, to decorate
cocoa powder (unsweetened), for dusting (optional)

For the filling

350g/12oz fine white chocolate, chopped into small pieces
120ml/4fl oz/¹⁄₂ cup whipping cream or double (heavy) cream
675g/1¹⁄₂lb/3 cups cream cheese, softened
50g/2oz/¹⁄₄ cup granulated sugar
4 eggs
30ml/2 tbsp hazelnut-flavoured liqueur or 15ml/1 tbsp vanilla extract

For the topping

450ml/³⁄₄ pint/scant 2 cups sour cream
50g/2oz/¹⁄₄ cup granulated sugar
15ml/1 tbsp hazelnut-flavoured liqueur or 5ml/1 tsp vanilla extract

Raspberry & White Chocolate Cheesecake

An unbeatable combination: raspberries teamed with mascarpone and white chocolate on a crunchy ginger and pecan nut base.

Serves 8

50g/2oz/4 tbsp unsalted (sweet) butter
225g/8oz/2¹⁄₃ cups ginger nut biscuits (gingersnaps), crushed
50g/2oz/¹⁄₂ cup chopped pecan nuts or walnuts

For the filling

275g/10oz/1¹⁄₄ cups mascarpone
175g/6oz/³⁄₄ cup fromage frais or soft white (farmer's) cheese
2 eggs, beaten
40g/1¹⁄₂oz/3 tbsp caster (superfine) sugar
250g/9oz white chocolate, broken into squares
225g/8oz/1¹⁄₃ cups fresh or frozen raspberries

For the topping

115g/4oz/¹⁄₂ cup mascarpone cheese
75g/3oz/¹⁄₃ cup fromage frais or soft white (farmer's) cheese
white chocolate curls and raspberries, to decorate

1 Preheat the oven to 180°C/350°F/Gas 4. Grease a deep 23cm/9in springform tin (pan).

2 Put the biscuits and hazelnuts in a food processor and process to form fine crumbs. Pour in the butter and cinnamon. Process just until blended. Using the back of a spoon, press on to the base and to within 1cm/¹⁄₂in of the top of the sides of the cake tin.

3 Bake the crumb crust for 5–7 minutes, until just set. Cool in the tin on a wire rack. Lower the oven temperature to 150°C/300°F/Gas 2 and place a baking sheet inside to heat up.

4 Make the filling. Melt the white chocolate and cream in a small pan over a low heat, until smooth, stirring frequently. Set aside to cool slightly.

5 Using an electric whisk, beat the cream cheese and sugar in a large bowl until smooth. Add the eggs one at a time, beating well. Slowly beat in the white chocolate mixture and liqueur or vanilla extract.

6 Pour the filling into the baked crust. Place the tin on the hot baking sheet. Bake for 45–55 minutes; do not allow the top to brown. Transfer to a wire rack while preparing the topping. Increase the oven temperature to 200°C/400°F/Gas 6.

7 Make the topping. In a small bowl whisk the sour cream, sugar and liqueur or vanilla extract until mixed. Pour over the cheesecake, spreading it evenly, and return to the oven. Bake for a further 5–7 minutes. Turn off the oven, but do not open the door for 1 hour.

8 Serve the cheesecake at room temperature, decorated with the white chocolate curls. Dust with cocoa powder, if you like.

1 Preheat the oven to 150°C/300°F/Gas 2. Melt the butter in a pan, then stir in the crushed biscuits and nuts. Press into the base of a 23cm/9in springform cake tin (pan).

2 Make the filling. Beat the mascarpone and fromage frais in a bowl, then beat in the eggs and caster sugar until evenly mixed.

3 Melt the white chocolate gently in a heatproof bowl over hot water. Stir the chocolate into the cheese mixture with the raspberries.

4 Turn into the prepared tin and spread evenly, then bake for about 1 hour or until just set. Switch off the oven, but do not remove the cheesecake. Leave it until cold and completely set.

5 Remove the cheesecake from the tin. Make the topping. Mix the mascarpone with the fromage frais and spread over the cheesecake. Decorate with chocolate curls and raspberries.

Luxury White Choc. Energy 421Kcal/1746kJ; Protein 5.3g; Carbohydrate 22.3g, of which sugars 18.1g; Fat 34.6g, of which saturates 20g; Cholesterol 98mg; Calcium 124mg; Fibre 0.3g; Sodium 206mg.
Rasp. & White Choc. Energy 551Kcal/2305kJ; Protein 12.8g; Carbohydrate 53.9g, of which sugars 41.4g; Fat 33.1g, of which saturates 17g; Cholesterol 88mg; Calcium 170mg; Fibre 1.4g; Sodium 195mg.

Apricot & Almond Tart

This dish shows how well almonds and apricots combine.

Serves 6

115g/4oz/½ cup butter or
 margarine
115g/4oz/generous ½ cup caster
 (superfine) sugar
1 egg, beaten
50g/2oz/⅓ cup ground rice
50g/2oz/½ cup ground almonds
few drops of almond extract
450g/1lb fresh apricots, halved and
 stoned (pitted)

sifted icing (confectioners') sugar,
 for dusting (optional)
apricot slices and fresh mint
 sprigs, to decorate (optional)

For the pastry

115g/4oz/1 cup brown rice flour
115g/4oz/1 cup cornmeal
115g/4oz/½ cup butter or
 margarine
25g/1oz/2 tbsp caster (superfine)
 sugar
1 egg yolk

1 Make the pastry. Place the rice flour and cornmeal in a large mixing bowl and stir to mix. Lightly rub in the butter or margarine until the mixture resembles fine breadcrumbs. Add the sugar, the egg yolk and enough chilled water to make a smooth, soft but not sticky dough. Wrap the dough in clear film (plastic wrap) and chill for 30 minutes.

2 Preheat the oven to 180°C/350°F/Gas 4. Line a 24cm/9½in loose-based flan tin (tart pan) with the pastry by pressing it gently over the base and up the sides, making sure that there are no holes in the pastry. Trim the edge of the pastry with a sharp knife.

3 Make the almond filling. Place the butter or margarine and sugar in a bowl and cream together with a wooden spoon until the mixture is light and fluffy. Gradually add the beaten egg to the mix, beating well after each addition. Fold in the ground rice and almonds and the almond extract and mix well to incorporate.

4 Spoon the mixture into the pastry case, spreading it evenly, then arrange the apricot halves cut side down on top. Place the tart on a baking sheet and bake for 40–45 minutes until the filling and pastry are cooked and lightly browned. Serve warm or cold, dusted with icing sugar and decorated with apricots and mint.

Strawberry Tart

This summery tart is best assembled just before serving, but you can bake the pastry case earlier in the day. You can also make the filling ahead of time so that the tart can be put together in just a few minutes – perfect for easy entertaining.

Serves 6

350g/12oz rough puff or puff
 pastry
225g/8oz/1 cup cream cheese
grated rind of ½ orange
30ml/2 tbsp orange liqueur or
 orange juice
45–60ml/3–4 tbsp icing
 (confectioners') sugar, plus
 extra for dusting (optional)
450g/1lb/4 cups strawberries,
 hulled

1 Roll out the pastry on a lightly floured surface to a thickness of about 3mm/⅛in and use to line a 28 × 10cm/11 × 4in tranche tin or shallow rectangular tin (pan). Trim the edges of the pastry neatly with a knife, then chill for 30 minutes. Preheat the oven to 200°C/400°F/Gas 6.

2 Prick the base of the pastry all over. Line with foil, fill with baking beans and bake for 15 minutes. Remove the foil and beans and bake for a further 10 minutes until the pastry is browned. Gently press down on the pastry base to deflate it, then leave to cool on a wire rack.

3 Using a hand-held electric whisk or food processor, beat well together the cream cheese, orange rind, liqueur or orange juice and icing sugar.

4 Spread the cheese filling in the pastry case (pie shell). Halve the strawberries and arrange them on top of the cheese filling. Dust with icing sugar, if you like, just before serving.

> **Cook's Tip**
> Ready-made puff pastry is available in most supermarkets. If you use the frozen version, thaw it thoroughly before using.

Apricot & Almond Energy 640Kcal/2670kJ; Protein 8.4g; Carbohydrate 66.2g, of which sugars 30.7g; Fat 39g, of which saturates 20.9g; Cholesterol 147mg; Calcium 89mg; Fibre 3.1g; Sodium 251mg.
Strawberry Energy 434Kcal/1805kJ; Protein 5.2g; Carbohydrate 34.4g, of which sugars 13.5g; Fat 32.2g, of which saturates 11.1g; Cholesterol 36mg; Calcium 87mg; Fibre 0.8g; Sodium 299mg.

Coffee Custard Tart

For sheer decadence, this creamy tart is hard to beat.

Serves 6–8
1 vanilla pod (bean)
30ml/2 tbsp ground coffee
300ml/½ pint/1¼ cups single (light) cream
150ml/¼ pint/⅔ cup milk
2 eggs, plus 2 egg yolks
50g/2oz/¼ cup caster (superfine) sugar

whipped cream, to serve

For the pastry
175g/6oz/1½ cups plain (all-purpose) flour
30ml/2 tbsp icing (confectioners') sugar
115g/4oz/½ cup butter, diced
75g/3oz/¾ cup walnuts, chopped
1 egg yolk
5ml/1 tsp vanilla extract
10ml/2 tsp chilled water

1 Make the pastry. Sift the flour and sugar into a mixing bowl. Rub or cut in the butter until the mixture resembles fine breadcrumbs. Stir in the walnuts.

2 In a small bowl, mix together the egg yolk, vanilla and water. Add to the flour mixture and mix to a smooth dough. Wrap in clear film (plastic wrap); chill for 20 minutes. Put a heavy baking sheet in the oven and preheat the oven to 200°C/400°F/Gas 6.

3 Roll out the pastry and use to line a 20cm/8in loose-based flan tin (tart pan). Trim the edges. Chill for 20 minutes.

4 Prick the pastry base all over with a fork. Line with foil and fill with baking beans. Place on the baking sheet and bake for 10 minutes. Remove the foil and beans, bake for 10 minutes more, then reduce the oven temperature to 150°C/300°F/Gas 2.

5 Meanwhile, split the vanilla pod and scrape out the seeds. Put both in a pan with the coffee, cream and milk. Heat until almost boiling, remove from the heat, cover and infuse for 10 minutes. Whisk the eggs, egg yolks and caster sugar together in a bowl.

6 Bring the coffee mixture back to the boil, then pour on to the egg mixture, stirring. Strain into the tin. Bake for 40–45 minutes until lightly set, then cool. Top with whirls of cream to serve.

Yorkshire Curd Tart

The distinguishing characteristic of Yorkshire curd tarts is allspice, or "clove pepper" as it was known locally. This tart tastes superb and does not taste too sweet.

grated rind and juice of 1 lemon
40g/1½oz/3 tbsp butter, melted
450g/1lb/2 cups curd (farmer's) cheese
75g/3oz/½ cup raisins
whipped cream, to serve (optional)

Serves 8
90g/3½oz/scant ½ cup soft light brown sugar
large pinch of ground allspice
3 eggs, beaten

For the pastry
225g/8oz/2 cups plain (all-purpose) flour
115g/4oz/½ cup butter, diced
1 egg yolk
15–30ml/1–2 tbsp chilled water

1 Make the pastry. Place the flour in a large mixing bowl and rub or cut in the butter until the mixture resembles fine breadcrumbs. Stir the egg yolk into the flour and add just enough of the water to bind the mixture together to form a dough.

2 Put the dough on a floured surface, knead lightly and briefly, then form into a ball. Roll out the pastry thinly and use to line a 20cm/8in fluted loose-based flan tin (tart pan). Cover with clear film (plastic wrap) and chill for about 15 minutes.

3 Preheat the oven to 190°C/375°F/Gas 5. Mix the sugar with the ground allspice in a bowl, then stir in the eggs, lemon rind and juice, butter, curd cheese and raisins. Mix well.

4 Pour the filling into the pastry case (pie shell), then bake for 40 minutes, or until the pastry is cooked and the filling is lightly set and golden brown. Cut the tart into wedges while it is still slightly warm, and serve with cream, if you like.

> **Cook's Tip**
> Although it is not traditional, mixed spice (apple pie spice) would make a good substitute for the ground allspice.

Coffee Custard Energy 408Kcal/1698kJ; Protein 8.1g; Carbohydrate 29.6g, of which sugars 12.8g; Fat 29.5g, of which saturates 13.8g; Cholesterol 176mg; Calcium 119mg; Fibre 1g; Sodium 129mg.
Yorkshire Curd Energy 419Kcal/1753kJ; Protein 14.1g; Carbohydrate 42.2g, of which sugars 20.8g; Fat 23.6g, of which saturates 13.9g; Cholesterol 151mg; Calcium 132mg; Fibre 1.1g; Sodium 398mg.

Chocolate Lemon Tart

In this easy-to-make recipe, the chocolate-flavoured pastry is pressed into the tin rather than rolled out, helping to speed up the preparation. With a simple lemon filling, this is a great dessert for the busy cook.

Serves 8–10

175g/6oz/1½ cups plain
   (all-purpose) flour
10ml/2 tsp cocoa powder
   (unsweetened)
25g/1oz/¼ cup icing
   (confectioners') sugar
2.5ml/½ tsp salt
115g/4oz/½ cup unsalted
   (sweet) butter or margarine,
   plus extra for greasing
15ml/1 tbsp water

For the filling

225g/8oz/1 cup caster
   (superfine) sugar
6 eggs
grated rind of 2 lemons
175ml/6fl oz/¾ cup freshly
   squeezed lemon juice
175ml/6fl oz/¾ cup double
   (heavy) or whipping cream
chocolate curls, to decorate

1 Grease a 25cm/10in loose-based flan tin (tart pan). Sift the flour, cocoa, icing sugar and salt into a bowl. Set aside.

2 Melt the butter or margarine and water in a pan over a low heat. Add the flour mixture and stir until the flour has absorbed all the liquid and the dough is smooth.

3 Press the dough evenly over the base and side of the prepared tin. Chill the pastry case (pie shell).

4 Preheat the oven to 190°C/375°F/Gas 5, and place a baking sheet inside to heat up. Make the filling. Whisk the caster sugar and eggs in a bowl until the sugar has dissolved. Add the lemon rind and juice and mix well. Stir in the cream. Taste and add more lemon juice or sugar if needed, for a sweet taste with a touch of tartness.

5 Pour the filling into the pastry shell and place the tin on the hot baking sheet. Bake for 20–25 minutes or until the filling is set. Cool the tart on a rack, then remove from the tin. Decorate with the chocolate curls and serve.

Rich Chocolate-Berry Tart

A gorgeous way to serve fresh summer berries.

Serves 10

115g/4oz/½ cup unsalted (sweet)
   butter, softened
90g/3½oz/½ cup caster
   (superfine) sugar
2.5ml/½ tsp salt
15ml/1 tbsp vanilla extract
50g/2oz/½ cup cocoa powder
   (unsweetened)
215g/7½oz/scant 2 cups plain
   (all-purpose) flour
450g/1lb fresh berries for topping

For the chocolate filling

475ml/16fl oz/2 cups double
   (heavy) cream
150g/5oz/½ cup seedless
   blackberry preserve
225g/8oz plain (semisweet)
   chocolate, chopped
25g/1oz/2 tbsp unsalted (sweet)
   butter

For the blackberry sauce

225g/8oz fresh or frozen
   blackberries or raspberries
15ml/1 tbsp lemon juice
25g/1oz/2 tbsp caster (superfine)
   sugar
30ml/2 tbsp blackberry liqueur

1 Make the pastry. Place the butter, sugar, salt and vanilla in a food processor and process until creamy. Add the cocoa and process for 1 minute. Add the flour all at once and process for 10–15 seconds, until just blended. Place a piece of clear film (plastic wrap) on a work surface. Turn out the dough on to the clear film. Use the clear film to help shape the dough into a flat disc and wrap tightly. Chill for 1 hour.

2 Lightly grease a 23cm/9in loose-based flan tin (tart pan). Roll out the dough between two sheets of clear film to a 28cm/11in round, about 5mm/¼in thick. Peel off the top sheet of clear film and invert the dough into the prepared tin. Ease the dough into the tin. Remove the clear film.

3 With floured fingers, press the dough on to the base and side of the tin, then roll a rolling pin over the edge of the tin to cut off any excess dough. Prick the base of the dough with a fork. Chill for 1 hour. Preheat the oven to 180°C/350°F/Gas 4. Line the pastry case (pie shell) with foil or baking paper and fill with baking beans. Bake for 10 minutes, then lift out the foil and beans and bake for 5 minutes more, until just set (the pastry may look underdone on the base, but will dry out). Place on a wire rack to cool completely.

4 Make the filling. Place the cream and blackberry preserve in a medium pan over medium heat and bring to the boil. Remove from the heat and add the chocolate, stirring until smooth. Stir in the butter and strain into the cooled tart, then level the surface. Leave the tart to cool completely.

5 Make the sauce. In a food processor, combine the blackberries, lemon juice and sugar and process until smooth. Strain into a small bowl and add the blackberry-flavour liqueur. If the sauce is too thick, thin with a little water.

6 To serve, remove the tart from the tin. Place on a serving plate and arrange the berries on the top of the tart. With a pastry brush, brush the berries with a little of the blackberry sauce to glaze lightly. Serve the remaining sauce separately.

Choc. Lemon Tart Energy 379Kcal/1585kJ; Protein 6.1g; Carbohydrate 40.5g, of which sugars 27g; Fat 22.6g, of which saturates 12.9g; Cholesterol 163mg; Calcium 68mg; Fibre 0.7g; Sodium 127mg.
Choc.-Berry Tart Energy 653Kcal/2722kJ; Protein 6g; Carbohydrate 58.9g, of which sugars 41.8g; Fat 44.9g, of which saturates 27.7g; Cholesterol 96mg; Calcium 95mg; Fibre 3.5g; Sodium 152mg.

Peach Tart with Almond Cream

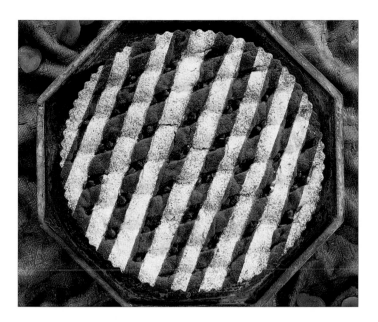

Peaches and almonds form a natural flavour partnership.

Serves 8–10

115g/4oz/²⁄₃ cup blanched
  almonds
30ml/2 tbsp plain
  (all-purpose) flour
90g/3½oz/scant ½ cup unsalted
  (sweet) butter, slightly soft
130g/4½oz/scant ¾ cup
  granulated sugar
1 egg
1 egg yolk

2.5ml/½ tsp vanilla extract or
  10ml/2 tsp rum
4 large ripe peaches, skinned

For the pastry

150g/5oz/1¼ cups plain
  (all-purpose) flour
4ml/¾ tsp salt
90g/3½oz/scant ½ cup cold
  unsalted (sweet) butter, cut into
  pieces
1 egg yolk
30–45ml/2–3 tbsp iced
  water

1 Make the pastry. Sift the flour and salt into a bowl. Add the butter and cut in with a pastry blender until the mixture resembles breadcrumbs. With a fork, stir in the egg yolk and just enough iced water to bind the dough. Gather into a ball, wrap in baking parchment and chill for at least 20 minutes. Place a baking sheet in the oven and preheat to 200°C/400°F/Gas 6.

2 On a lightly floured surface, roll out the pastry to 3mm/⅛in thick. Transfer to a 25cm/10in flan tin (tart pan). Trim the edge, prick the pastry base and chill.

3 Grind the almonds finely with the flour. With an electric whisk, cream the butter and 90g/3½oz/½ cup of the sugar until light and fluffy. Gradually beat in the egg and yolk. Stir in the almonds and vanilla or rum. Spread in the pastry case (pie shell).

4 Halve the peaches and remove the stones (pits). Cut crossways into thin slices and arrange on top of the almond cream like the spokes of a wheel. Press down gently to fan out. Bake for 10–15 minutes until the pastry begins to brown. Lower the heat to 180°C/350°F/Gas 4 and continue baking for about 15 minutes until the filling sets. Ten minutes before the end of the cooking time, sprinkle with the remaining sugar.

Chocolate Apricot Linzer Tart

This makes an excellent dinner party dessert.

Serves 10–12

50g/2oz/⅓ cup blanched
  almonds
115g/4oz/generous ½ cup caster
  (superfine) sugar
175g/6oz/1½ cups plain
  (all-purpose) flour
30ml/2 tbsp cocoa powder
  (unsweetened)
5ml/1 tsp ground cinnamon
2.5ml/½ tsp salt

5ml/1 tsp grated orange rind
225g/8oz/1 cup unsalted (sweet)
  butter, cut into small pieces
75g/3oz/½ cup chocolate chips
icing (confectioners') sugar,
  for dusting

For the apricot filling

350g/12oz/1½ cups dried
  apricots
120ml/4fl oz/½ cup orange juice
40g/1½oz/3 tbsp granulated sugar
50g/2oz/2 tbsp apricot jam
2.5ml/½ tsp almond extract

1 For the filling, simmer the apricots, orange juice and 175ml/6fl oz/¾ cup water, stirring, until the liquid is absorbed. Stir in the remaining ingredients. Strain into a bowl, cool, cover and chill.

2 Grease a 28cm/11in loose-based flan tin (tart pan). Grind the almonds and half the sugar in a food processor. Sift in the flour, cocoa, cinnamon and salt, add the remaining sugar and process. Add the rind and butter. Process for 15–20 seconds until the mixture resembles breadcrumbs. Add 30ml/2 tbsp iced water and pulse, adding a little more water until the dough holds together.

3 Turn out and knead the dough on a lightly floured surface. Halve and press one piece on to the base and sides of the tin. Prick the base with a fork. Chill for 20 minutes. Roll out the rest of the dough between sheets of clear film (plastic wrap) to a 28cm/11in round, then slide on to a baking sheet and chill for 30 minutes.

4 Preheat the oven to 180°C/350°F/Gas 4. Spread the filling in the pastry case (pie shell) and sprinkle with chocolate chips. Cut the dough round into 1cm/½in strips. Leave to soften, then place the strips over the filling, 1cm/½in apart, to form a lattice. Press the ends on to the side of the tart and trim. Bake for 35–40 minutes, until golden. Cool on a rack and dust with icing sugar.

Linzer Tart Energy 368Kcal/1539kJ; Protein 4.4g; Carbohydrate 44.3g, of which sugars 32.8g; Fat 20.4g, of which saturates 11.4g; Cholesterol 40mg; Calcium 69mg; Fibre 3.1g; Sodium 147mg.
Peach Tart Energy 350Kcal/1459kJ; Protein 5.9g; Carbohydrate 31.5g, of which sugars 17.5g; Fat 23.1g, of which saturates 10.4g; Cholesterol 98mg; Calcium 73mg; Fibre 2g; Sodium 121mg.

Raspberry Tart

A lovely, summery dessert, this glazed fruit tart really does taste as good as it looks.

Serves 8
4 egg yolks
65g/2¹/₂oz/5 tbsp granulated sugar
45g/1³/₄oz/3 tbsp plain
  (all-purpose) flour
300ml/¹/₂ pint/1¹/₄ cups milk
pinch of salt
2.5ml/¹/₂ tsp vanilla extract
450g/1lb/2¹/₂ cups fresh raspberries

75ml/5 tbsp redcurrant jelly
15ml/1 tbsp fresh orange juice

For the pastry
150g/5oz/1¹/₄ cups plain
  (all-purpose) flour
2.5ml/¹/₂ tsp baking powder
1.5ml/¹/₄ tsp salt
15ml/1 tbsp sugar
grated rind of ¹/₂ orange
90ml/6 tbsp cold butter, diced
1 egg yolk
45ml/3 tbsp whipping cream

1 Make the pastry. Sift the flour, baking powder and salt into a bowl. Stir in the sugar and orange rind. Add the butter and rub in until the mixture resembles coarse breadcrumbs. With a fork, stir in the egg yolk and just enough cream to bind the dough. Gather into a ball, wrap in clear film (plastic wrap) and chill.

2 Make the custard filling. Beat the egg yolks and sugar until thick and lemon-coloured. Gradually stir in the flour.

3 In a pan, bring the milk and salt just to the boil, and remove from the heat. Whisk into the egg yolk mixture, return to the pan, and continue whisking over medium-high heat until just bubbling for 3 minutes to thicken. Transfer at once to a bowl and stir in the vanilla. Cover closely with baking parchment.

4 Preheat the oven to 200°C/400°F/Gas 6. Roll out the dough on a lightly floured surface to 3mm/¹/₈in thick. Use to line a 25cm/10in flan tin (tart pan) and trim the edge. Prick the pastry case (pie shell) all over with a fork and line with baking parchment. Fill with baking beans and bake for 15 minutes. Remove the paper and beans. Bake for 6–8 minutes more until golden. Cool.

5 Spread the filling in the pastry case. Top with the raspberries. Melt the jelly and orange juice together and brush on to glaze.

Lemon & Orange Tart

A tasty combination of refreshing citrus fruit and crisp, nutty pastry, this useful tart can be served at any time of the year.

Serves 8–10
115g/4oz/1 cup plain
  (all-purpose) flour, sifted
115g/4oz/1 cup wholemeal
  (whole-wheat) flour

25g/1oz/3 tbsp ground hazelnuts
25g/1oz/¹/₄ cup icing
  (confectioners') sugar, sifted
pinch of salt
115g/4oz/¹/₂ cup unsalted
  (sweet) butter
30–45ml/2–3 tbsp water
60ml/4 tbsp lemon curd
300ml/¹/₂ pint/1¹/₄ cups whipped
  cream or fromage frais
4 oranges, peeled and thinly sliced

1 Place the flours, hazelnuts, sugar, salt and butter in a food processor and process in short bursts until the mixture resembles breadcrumbs. Add the cold water and process until the mixture comes together as a dough.

2 Turn out on to a lightly floured surface and knead gently until smooth. Roll out and line a 25cm/10in loose-based flan tin (tart pan). Ease the pastry gently into the corners without stretching it. Chill for 20 minutes. Preheat the oven to 190°C/375°F/Gas 5.

3 Line the pastry with baking parchment and fill with baking beans. Bake blind for 15 minutes, remove the paper and beans and continue cooking for a further 5–10 minutes, until the pastry is crisp. Allow to cool.

4 Whisk the lemon curd into the cream or fromage frais and spread over the base of the pastry. Arrange the orange slices on top of the filling in overlapping, concentric circles. Remove the tart from the tin, transfer to a serving plate and serve at room temperature.

Variation
Fresh raspberries or halved strawberries would also team up well with the lemon-flavoured filling.

Sticky Tart

This is quite a filling tart, so it is best served after a light main course.

Serves 4–6
250g/9oz/¾ cup golden
    (light corn) syrup
75g/3oz/1½ cups fresh white
    breadcrumbs
grated rind of 1 lemon
30ml/2 tbsp fresh lemon juice

For the pastry
150g/5oz/1¼ cups plain
    (all-purpose) flour
2.5ml/½ tsp salt
75g/3oz/6 tbsp cold butter or
    margarine, cut into pieces
45–60ml/3–4 tbsp iced water

1 Make the pastry. Combine the flour and salt in a bowl. Add the butter or margarine and rub in or cut in with a pastry blender until the mixture resembles coarse breadcrumbs.

2 With a fork, stir in just enough iced water to bind the mixture into a dough. Gather into a ball, wrap in baking parchment and chill for at least 20 minutes.

3 Roll out the dough on a lightly floured surface to 3mm/⅛in thick. Use to line a 20cm/8in loose-based flan tin (tart pan) and trim off the excess pastry. Chill for at least 20 minutes.

4 Place a baking sheet above the centre of the oven and heat to 200°C/400°F/Gas 6.

5 In a pan, warm the syrup until thin and runny. Remove from the heat and stir in the breadcrumbs and lemon rind. Set aside for 10 minutes to allow the bread to absorb the syrup.

6 Add more breadcrumbs if the mixture is thin. Stir in the lemon juice and spread evenly in the pastry case (pie shell).

7 Place the tart on the hot baking sheet and bake in the oven for 10 minutes. Lower the heat to 190°C/375°F/Gas 5. Continue to bake for about 15 minutes until the top is golden. Remove from the tin and serve warm or cold.

Chocolate Pear Tart

Serve slices of this tart drizzled with cream for a special treat.

Serves 8
115g/4oz plain (semisweet)
    chocolate, grated
3 large firm, ripe pears
1 egg
1 egg yolk
120ml/4fl oz/½ cup single
    (light) cream
2.5ml/½ tsp vanilla extract

40g/1½oz/3 tbsp caster
    (superfine) sugar

For the pastry
115g/4oz/1 cup plain
    (all-purpose) flour
pinch of salt
25g/1oz/2 tbsp caster
    (superfine) sugar
115g/4oz/½ cup cold unsalted
    (sweet) butter, cut into pieces
1 egg yolk
15ml/1 tbsp fresh lemon juice

1 Make the pastry. Sift the flour and salt into a bowl. Add the sugar and butter. Cut in with a pastry blender until the mixture resembles coarse crumbs. With a fork, stir in the egg yolk and lemon juice until the mixture forms a dough. Gather into a ball, wrap in baking parchment, and chill for at least 20 minutes.

2 Place a baking sheet in the oven and preheat to 200°C/400°F/Gas 6. On a lightly floured surface, roll out the dough to 3mm/⅛in thick and trim the edge. Use to line a 25cm/10in loose-based flan tin (tart pan).

3 Sprinkle the base of the pastry with the grated chocolate.

4 Peel, halve and core the pears. Cut in thin slices crossways, then fan them out slightly. Transfer the pear halves to the tart with the help of a metal spatula and arrange on top of the chocolate in a pattern resembling the spokes of a wheel.

5 Whisk together the egg and egg yolk, cream and vanilla extract. Spoon over the pears, then sprinkle with sugar.

6 Bake for 10 minutes. Reduce the heat to 180°C/350°F/Gas 4 and continue to cook for about 20 minutes until the custard is set and the pears begin to caramelize. Serve warm.

Sticky Tart Energy 347Kcal/1462kJ; Protein 4g; Carbohydrate 62.1g, of which sugars 33.7g; Fat 10.8g, of which saturates 6.6g; Cholesterol 27mg; Calcium 60mg; Fibre 1.1g; Sodium 284mg.
Choc. Pear Tart Energy 357Kcal/1492kJ; Protein 4.5g; Carbohydrate 39.9g, of which sugars 28.8g; Fat 21.1g, of which saturates 12.3g; Cholesterol 114mg; Calcium 66mg; Fibre 2.9g; Sodium 107mg.

Jam Tart

Jam tarts are popular in Italy and Britain, traditionally decorated with pastry strips.

Serves 6–8
200g/7oz/1¾ cups plain (all-purpose) flour
pinch of salt
50g/2oz/¼ cup granulated sugar
115g/4oz/½ cup butter or margarine, chilled
1 egg
1.5ml/¼ tsp grated lemon rind
350g/12oz/1¼ cups fruit jam, such as raspberry, apricot or strawberry
1 egg, lightly beaten with 30ml/ 2 tbsp whipping cream

1 Make the pastry. Put the flour, salt and sugar in a mixing bowl. Using a pastry blender or two knives, cut the butter into the dry ingredients until the mixture resembles coarse crumbs.

2 Beat the egg with the lemon rind in a cup, and pour it over the flour mixture. Combine with a fork until the dough holds together. If it is too crumbly, mix in 15–30ml/1–2 tbsp water.

3 Gather the dough into two balls, one slightly larger than the other, and flatten into discs. Wrap in waxed paper, and put in the refrigerator for at least 40 minutes.

4 Lightly grease a shallow 23cm/9in flan tin (tart pan), preferably with a removable base. Roll out the larger ball of pastry on a lightly floured surface to about 3mm/⅛in thick.

5 Roll the pastry around the rolling pin and transfer to the prepared tin. Trim the edges evenly with a small knife. Prick the bottom with a fork. Chill for at least 30 minutes.

6 Preheat the oven to 190°C/375°F/Gas 5. Spread jam thickly over the base of the pastry. Roll out the remaining pastry. Cut the pastry into strips about 1cm/½in wide. Arrange over the jam in a lattice pattern. Trim the edges of the strips, pressing them lightly on to the pastry case (pie shell).

7 Brush the pastry with the egg and cream mix. Bake for about 35 minutes, or until the pastry is golden. Cool before serving.

Pear & Almond Cream Tart

This tart is equally successful made with other kinds of fruit – variations can be seen in almost every good French pâtisserie.

Serves 6
350g/12oz shortcrust or sweet shortcrust pastry
3 firm pears
lemon juice
15ml/1 tbsp peach brandy or water
60ml/4 tbsp peach preserve, strained

For the almond cream filling
115g/4oz/¾ cup blanched whole almonds
50g/2oz/¼ cup caster (superfine) sugar
65g/2½oz/5 tbsp butter
1 egg, plus 1 egg white
few drops almond extract

1 Roll out the pastry thinly and use to line a 23cm/9in flan tin (tart pan). Chill the pastry case (pie shell). Meanwhile, make the filling. Put the almonds and sugar in a food processor and pulse until finely ground (not a paste). Add the butter and process until creamy. Add the egg, egg white and almond extract and mix well.

2 Place a baking sheet in the oven and preheat to 190°C/ 375°F/Gas 5. Peel the pears, halve them, remove the cores and rub with lemon juice. Put the pear halves, cut-side down, on a board and slice thinly crossways, keeping the slices together.

3 Pour the almond cream filling into the pastry case. Slide a metal spatula under one pear half and press the top with your fingers to fan out the slices. Transfer to the tart, placing the fruit on the filling like spokes of a wheel. If you like, remove a few slices from each half before arranging and use to fill in any gaps in the centre.

4 Place on the baking sheet and bake for 50–55 minutes until the filling is set and well browned. Cool on a rack.

5 Meanwhile, heat the brandy or water and the preserve in a small pan, then brush over the top of the hot tart to glaze. Serve the tart warm, or at room temperature.

Jam Tart Energy 340Kcal/1434kJ; Protein 3.4g; Carbohydrate 56.4g, of which sugars 37.3g; Fat 12.8g, of which saturates 7.7g; Cholesterol 54mg; Calcium 49mg; Fibre 0.8g; Sodium 117mg.
Pear Tart Energy 558Kcal/2326kJ; Protein 8.6g; Carbohydrate 50.3g, of which sugars 24.4g; Fat 37.2g, of which saturates 6.8g; Cholesterol 55mg; Calcium 92mg; Fibre 4.2g; Sodium 189mg.

Tarte Tatin

This upside-down apple tart was first made by two sisters at their restaurant in the Loire Valley in France.

Serves 8–10
225g/8oz puff or shortcrust pastry
10–12 large eating apples

lemon juice
115g/4oz/½ cup butter, cut into pieces
90g/3½oz/½ cup caster (superfine) sugar
1.5ml/½ tsp ground cinnamon
crème fraîche or whipped cream, to serve

1 On a lightly floured surface, roll out the pastry into a 28cm/11in round, less than 5mm/¼in thick. Transfer to a lightly floured baking sheet and chill.

2 Peel the apples, cut them in half lengthways and core. Sprinkle them generously with lemon juice.

3 Preheat the oven to 230°C/450°F/Gas 8. In a 25cm/10in tarte tatin tin (pan), cook the butter, sugar and cinnamon over medium heat until the sugar has dissolved, stirring occasionally. Continue cooking for 6–8 minutes, until the mixture turns a caramel colour. Remove from the heat and arrange the apple halves in the tin, fitting them in tightly since they will shrink.

4 Return the apple-filled tin to the heat and bring to a simmer over a medium heat for 20–25 minutes until the apples are tender and coloured. Remove the tin from the heat and cool slightly.

5 Place the pastry on top of the apple-filled pan and tuck the edges of the pastry inside the edge of the tin around the apples.

6 Pierce the pastry in two or three places, then bake for 25–30 minutes until the pastry is golden. Cool for 10–15 minutes.

7 To serve, run a sharp knife around edge of the tin to loosen the pastry. Cover with a serving plate and, holding them tightly, carefully invert the tin and plate together (do this over the sink in case any caramel drips). Lift off the tin and loosen any apples that stick with a spatula. Serve the tart warm with cream.

Tarte au Citron

This classic lemon tart is served in restaurants all over France. The rich, citrus flavour of the filling gives the tart a truly gourmet feel, making it the perfect dessert for a dinner party.

Serves 8–10
350g/12oz shortcrust or sweet shortcrust pastry
grated rind of 2 or 3 lemons
150ml/¼ pint/⅔ cup freshly squeezed lemon juice
90g/3½oz/½ cup caster (superfine) sugar
60ml/4 tbsp crème fraîche or double (heavy) cream
4 eggs, plus 3 egg yolks
icing (confectioners') sugar, for dusting

1 Preheat the oven to 190°C/375°F/Gas 5. Roll out the pastry thinly and use to line a 23cm/9in flan tin (tart pan). Prick the base of the pastry with a fork.

2 Line the pastry case (pie shell) with foil and fill with baking beans. Bake for about 15 minutes until the edges are set and dry. Remove the foil and beans and continue baking for a further 5–7 minutes until golden.

3 Place the lemon rind, juice and sugar in a bowl. Beat until combined and then gradually add the crème fraîche or double cream and beat until well blended.

4 Beat in the eggs, one at a time, then beat in the egg yolks and pour the filling into the pastry case. Bake for 15–20 minutes, until the filling is set. If the pastry begins to brown too much, cover the edges with foil.

5 Leave to cool and dust with a little icing sugar before serving.

> **Variation**
> Replace half the lemon juice and rind with orange juice and rind.

Tarte Tatin Energy 228Kcal/954kJ; Protein 1.6g; Carbohydrate 23.7g, of which sugars 15.7g; Fat 15g, of which saturates 6g; Cholesterol 25mg; Calcium 23mg; Fibre 1.1g; Sodium 141mg.
Tarte au Citron Energy 259Kcal/1082kJ; Protein 5.3g; Carbohydrate 26.2g, of which sugars 10.1g; Fat 15.6g, of which saturates 5.6g; Cholesterol 128mg; Calcium 55mg; Fibre 0.7g; Sodium 172mg.

Honey & Pine Nut Tart

Wonderful tarts of all
descriptions are to be found
throughout France, and
this recipe recalls the
flavours of the south.

Serves 6
115g/4oz/½ cup butter, diced
115g/4oz/generous ½ cup caster
   (superfine) sugar
3 eggs, beaten
175g/6oz/⅔ cup sunflower honey
grated rind and juice of 1 lemon
225g/8oz/2⅔ cups pine nuts

pinch of salt
icing (confectioners') sugar,
   for dusting

For the pastry
225g/8oz/2 cups plain
   (all-purpose) flour
115g/4oz/½ cup butter, diced
30ml/2 tbsp icing
   (confectioners') sugar
1 egg
15ml/1 tbsp chilled water
crème fraîche or vanilla ice
   cream, to serve (optional)

1 Preheat the oven to 180°C/350°F/Gas 4. Make the pastry. Sift
the flour into a large mixing bowl and rub or cut in the butter
until the mixture resembles fine breadcrumbs.

2 Stir in the icing sugar. Add the egg and water and mix to
form a soft dough. Knead lightly until smooth.

3 Roll out the pastry on a lightly floured surface and use to line
a 23cm/9in flan tin (tart pan). Prick the base with a fork, then
chill for 10 minutes. Line with baking parchment and fill with
baking beans. Bake for 10 minutes. Remove the paper and
beans and set the pastry case aside.

4 Cream the butter and caster sugar together until light and
fluffy. Beat in the eggs one at a time. In a small pan, gently heat
the honey until it melts, then add it to the butter mixture with
the lemon rind and juice. Mix well. Stir in the pine nuts and salt,
blending well, then pour the filling evenly into the pastry case.

5 Bake for about 45 minutes, or until the filling is lightly browned
and set. Leave the tart to cool slightly in the tin, then remove
and dust generously with icing sugar. Serve warm, or at room
temperature, with crème fraîche or vanilla ice cream, if you like.

Almond & Pine Nut Tart

Strange though it may seem,
this traditional tart is an
Italian version of the homely
Bakewell tart from
Derbyshire in England.

Serves 8
115g/4oz/½ cup butter, softened
115g/4oz/generous ½ cup caster
   (superfine) sugar
1 egg, plus 2 egg yolks
150g/5oz/1¼ cups ground
   almonds
115g/4oz/1⅓ cups pine nuts
60ml/4 tbsp seedless raspberry
   jam

icing (confectioners') sugar,
   for dusting

For the pastry
175g/6oz/1½ cups plain
   (all-purpose) flour
65g/2½oz/5 tbsp caster
   (superfine) sugar
1.5ml/¼ tsp baking powder
pinch of salt
115g/4oz/½ cup chilled
   butter, diced
1 egg yolk

1 Make the pastry. Sift the flour, sugar, baking powder and salt
on to a clean, dry cold surface or marble pastry board. Make a
well in the centre and put in the diced butter and egg yolk.
Gradually work the flour mixture into the butter and egg yolk,
using just your fingertips, until you have a soft, pliable dough.

2 Press the dough into a 23cm/9in loose-based fluted flan tin
(tart pan). Chill for 30 minutes.

3 Cream the butter and sugar with an electric whisk until light,
then use a wooden spoon to beat in the egg and egg yolks a
little at a time, alternating with the almonds. Beat in the pine nuts.

4 Preheat the oven to 160°C/325°F/Gas 3. Spread the jam
evenly over the pastry case (pie shell), then spoon in the filling.
Bake for 30–35 minutes until golden, or until a skewer inserted
in the centre of the tart comes out clean.

5 Transfer to a wire rack and leave to cool, then carefully
remove the side of the tin, leaving the tart on the tin base. Dust
with icing sugar and serve with whipped cream.

Greek Chocolate Mousse Tartlets

Irresistible Greek-style tartlets with a lightweight chocolate and yogurt filling.

Serves 6
175g/6oz/1½ cups plain
  (all-purpose) flour
30ml/2 tbsp cocoa powder
  (unsweetened)
30ml/2 tbsp icing
  (confectioners') sugar
115g/4oz/½ cup butter
60ml/4 tbsp water

melted dark (bittersweet)
  chocolate, to decorate

For the filling
200g/7oz white chocolate
120ml/4fl oz/½ cup milk
10ml/2 tsp powdered gelatine
25g/1oz/2 tbsp caster
  (superfine) sugar
5ml/1 tsp vanilla extract
2 eggs, separated
250g/9oz/generous 1 cup Greek
  (US strained plain) yogurt

1 Preheat the oven to 190°C/375°F/Gas 5. Sift the flour, cocoa and icing sugar into a large bowl.

2 Place the butter in a pan with the water and heat gently until just melted. Cool, then stir into the flour to make a smooth dough. Chill until firm.

3 Roll out the pastry and line six deep 10cm/4in loose-based flan tins (tart pans). Prick the base of the pastry cases (pie shells), cover with baking parchment, weigh down with baking beans and bake blind for 10 minutes. Remove the beans and paper, return to the oven and bake for 15 minutes until firm. Leave to cool.

4 Make the filling. Melt the broken-up chocolate in a heatproof bowl over hot water. Pour the milk into a pan, sprinkle over the gelatine and heat gently, stirring, until the gelatine has dissolved. Remove from the heat and stir in the chocolate.

5 Whisk the sugar, vanilla and egg yolks in a large bowl, then beat in the chocolate mixture. Beat in the yogurt until mixed.

6 Whisk the egg whites in a clean, grease-free bowl until stiff, then fold into the chocolate mixture. Spoon into the pastry cases and leave to set. Drizzle with melted chocolate to serve.

Alsace Plum Tart

Fruit tarts are typical of the Alsace region of France.

Serves 6–8
450g/1lb ripe plums, halved
  and stoned (pitted)
30ml/2 tbsp Kirsch or plum brandy
30ml/2 tbsp seedless raspberry
  jam
2 eggs
50g/2oz/¼ cup caster
  (superfine) sugar
175ml/6fl oz/¾ cup double
  (heavy) cream

grated rind of ½ lemon
1.5ml/¼ tsp vanilla extract

For the pastry
200g/7oz/1¾ cups plain
  (all-purpose) flour
pinch of salt
25g/1oz/¼ cup icing
  (confectioners') sugar
90g/3½oz/scant ½ cup butter,
  diced
2 egg yolks
15ml/1 tbsp chilled water

1 Make the pastry. Sift the flour, salt and sugar into a bowl. Rub or cut in the butter until the mixture resembles fine breadcrumbs. Mix the egg yolks and water together, sprinkle over the dry ingredients and mix to a soft dough.

2 Lightly knead for a few seconds until smooth. Wrap in clear film (plastic wrap) and chill for 30 minutes. Preheat the oven to 200°C/400°F/Gas 6. Mix the plums with the Kirsch or plum brandy in a bowl. Set aside for 30 minutes.

3 Roll out the pastry thinly and use to line a 23cm/9in flan tin (tart pan). Cover and chill for 30 minutes. Prick the base and line with foil. Add baking beans and bake for 15 minutes until slightly dry and set. Remove the foil and beans. Lightly brush the base of the pastry case (pie shell) with a thin layer of jam, bake for 5 minutes more, then transfer to a wire rack to cool.

4 Lower the oven temperature to 180°C/350°F/Gas 4. Beat the eggs and sugar until well combined, then beat in the cream, lemon rind, vanilla and any juice from the plums. Arrange the plums, cut side down, in the pastry case, then pour over the custard. Bake for 30 minutes, or until a knife inserted in the centre comes out clean. Serve the tart warm.

Mousse Tartlets Energy 555Kcal/2320kJ; Protein 11.9g; Carbohydrate 55g, of which sugars 32.2g; Fat 34g, of which saturates 19.7g; Cholesterol 105mg; Calcium 242mg; Fibre 1.5g; Sodium 263mg.
Alsace Plum Tart Energy 396Kcal/1652kJ; Protein 5.5g; Carbohydrate 37.2g, of which sugars 18.2g; Fat 25.2g, of which saturates 14.7g; Cholesterol 155mg; Calcium 74mg; Fibre 1.7g; Sodium 104mg.

Mango & Amaretti Strudel

Fresh mango and crushed amaretti wrapped in wafer-thin filo pastry make a special treat. The dessert looks impressive, but takes very little time to make.

Serves 4
1 large mango
grated rind of 1 lemon
2 amaretti
25g/1oz/2 tbsp demerara
    (raw) sugar
60ml/4 tbsp wholemeal
    (whole-wheat) breadcrumbs
2 sheets of filo pastry, each
    measuring 48 x 28cm/
    19 x 11in
25g/1oz/2 tbsp butter or
    20g/³⁄₄oz/4 tsp soft margarine,
    melted
15ml/1 tbsp chopped almonds
icing (confectioners') sugar,
    for dusting

1 Preheat the oven to 190°C/375°F/Gas 5. Lightly grease a baking sheet. Cut the flesh from the mango and chop into small cubes. Place in a bowl and sprinkle with the grated lemon rind.

2 Crush the amaretti and mix them with the sugar and breadcrumbs in a bowl.

3 Lay one sheet of filo pastry on a flat surface and brush with a quarter of the melted butter or margarine. Top with the second sheet, brush with one-third of the remaining fat, then fold both sheets over, if necessary, to make a rectangle measuring 28 x 24cm/11 x 9½in. Brush with half the remaining fat.

4 Sprinkle the filo with the amaretti mixture, leaving a border on each long side. Arrange the mango over the top.

5 Carefully roll up the filo from one long side, Swiss-roll (jelly-roll) fashion, to enclose the amaretti mixture. Lift the strudel on to the baking sheet, seam side down. Brush with the remaining melted fat and sprinkle with the chopped almonds.

6 Bake the strudel for 20–25 minutes until light golden brown, then transfer to a board. Dust with the icing sugar, slice diagonally and serve.

Fresh Cherry & Hazelnut Strudel

Serve this wonderful old-world treat as a warm dessert with crème fraîche.

Serves 6–8
75g/3oz/6 tbsp butter
75g/3oz/6 tbsp light muscovado
    (brown) sugar
3 egg yolks
grated rind of 1 lemon
1.5ml/¼ tsp grated nutmeg
250g/9oz/generous 1 cup
    ricotta cheese
8 large sheets of filo pastry,
    thawed if frozen
75g/3oz ratafia biscuits (almond
    macaroons), crushed
450g/1lb/2½ cups cherries, pitted
30ml/2 tbsp chopped hazelnuts
icing (confectioners') sugar,
    for dusting

1 Preheat the oven to 190°C/375°F/Gas 5. Beat 15g/½oz/1 tbsp of the butter with the sugar and egg yolks in a mixing bowl until light and fluffy. Beat in the lemon rind, grated nutmeg and ricotta cheese.

2 Melt the remaining butter in a small pan. Place a sheet of filo on a clean dish towel and brush it generously with melted butter. Place a second sheet on top and repeat the process. Continue until all the sheets of filo have been used, reserving some of the butter.

3 Sprinkle the crushed ratafias over the top of the filo, leaving a 5cm/2in border all round. Spoon the ricotta mixture over the ratafia biscuits, spreading it lightly, then sprinkle over the cherries.

4 Fold in the filo pastry border on all four sides, then, using the dish towel to help you, roll up the strudel, Swiss-roll (jelly-roll) style, beginning from one of the long sides of the pastry. Grease a large baking sheet with a little of the remaining melted butter.

5 Place the strudel, seam side down, on the baking sheet, brush with the remaining melted butter, and sprinkle the chopped hazelnuts over the surface.

6 Bake for 35–40 minutes, or until the strudel is golden and crisp. Dust with icing sugar and serve.

Cherry & Hazelnut Energy 317Kcal/1326kJ; Protein 6.5g; Carbohydrate 34.2g, of which sugars 22.9g; Fat 18.1g, of which saturates 9.1g; Cholesterol 109mg; Calcium 54mg; Fibre 1.2g; Sodium 93mg.
Strudel Energy 222Kcal/937kJ; Protein 4.2g; Carbohydrate 35.4g, of which sugars 13.4g; Fat 8.1g, of which saturates 3.6g; Cholesterol 13mg; Calcium 58mg; Fibre 2g; Sodium 162mg.

Chocolate, Date & Almond Filo Coil

Experience the allure of the Middle East with this delectable dessert. Crisp filo pastry conceals a chocolate and rose water filling studded with dates and almonds.

Serves 6

275g/10oz filo pastry, thawed
  if frozen
50g/2oz/¼ cup butter, melted
icing (confectioners') sugar, cocoa
  powder (unsweetened) and
  ground cinnamon, for dusting

For the filling
75g/3oz/6 tbsp butter
115g/4oz dark (bittersweet)
  chocolate, broken up into pieces
115g/4oz/1⅓ cup ground
  almonds
115g/4oz/⅔ cup chopped dates
75g/3oz/⅔ cup icing
  (confectioners') sugar
10ml/2 tsp rose water
2.5ml/½ tsp ground cinnamon

1 Preheat the oven to 180°C/350°F/Gas 4. Grease a 22cm/8½in round cake tin (pan). To make the filling, melt the butter with the chocolate in a heatproof bowl set over a pan of barely simmering water, then remove from the heat and stir in the remaining ingredients to make a thick paste. Leave to cool.

2 Lay one sheet of filo on a clean, flat surface. Brush with melted butter, then lay a second sheet on top and brush with more butter.

3 Roll a handful of the chocolate and almond mixture into a long sausage shape and place along one long edge of the layered filo. Roll up the pastry tightly around the filling to make a roll.

4 Fit the filo roll in the cake tin, in such a way that it sits snugly against the outer edge. Make more filo rolls in the same way, adding them to the tin from the outside towards the centre, until the coil fills the tin.

5 Brush the coil with the remaining melted butter. Bake for 30–35 minutes until the pastry is golden brown and crisp. Transfer the coil to a serving plate. Serve warm, dusted with icing sugar, cocoa and cinnamon.

Moroccan Serpent Cake

This famous Moroccan pastry is filled with lightly fragrant almond paste.

Serves 8

8 sheets of filo pastry
50g/2oz/¼ cup butter, melted
1 egg, beaten
5ml/1 tsp ground cinnamon
icing (confectioners') sugar,
  for dusting

For the almond paste
about 50g/2oz/¼ cup butter,
  melted
225g/8oz/2⅔ cups ground
  almonds
2.5ml/½ tsp almond extract
50g/2oz/½ cup icing
  (confectioners') sugar
1 egg yolk, beaten
15ml/1 tbsp rose water or orange
  flower water

1 Make the almond paste. Mix the melted butter with the ground almonds and almond extract in a bowl. Add the sugar, egg yolk and rose or orange flower water, mix well and knead until soft and pliable. Chill for 10 minutes.

2 Break the paste into 10 even-size balls and, with your hands, roll them into 10cm/4in sausages. Chill again.

3 Preheat the oven to 180°C/350°F/Gas 4. Place two sheets of filo pastry on the work surface so that they overlap slightly to form an 18 x 56cm/7 x 22in rectangle. Brush the overlapping edges with butter to secure and then lightly brush all over. Cover with another two sheets of filo in the same way.

4 Place five almond paste sausages along the lower edge of the filo sheet and roll up tightly, tucking in the ends. Repeat with the remaining filo and almond paste, so that you have two rolls. Shape the first roll into a loose coil, then transfer to a baking sheet brushed with butter. Attach the second roll and continue coiling the filo to make a snake. Tuck the end under.

5 Beat the egg with half the cinnamon; brush over the pastry. Bake in the oven for 25 minutes until golden. Carefully invert the snake on to another baking sheet and return to the oven for 5–10 minutes more. Transfer to a serving plate, dust with icing sugar, then sprinkle with the remaining cinnamon.

Filo Coil Energy 543Kcal/2267kJ; Protein 8.2g; Carbohydrate 55.4g, of which sugars 32.4g; Fat 33.6g, of which saturates 15g; Cholesterol 46mg; Calcium 108mg; Fibre 3.2g; Sodium 133mg.
Serpent Cake Energy 341Kcal/1417kJ; Protein 7.7g; Carbohydrate 18.3g, of which sugars 8g; Fat 26.9g, of which saturates 8g; Cholesterol 54mg; Calcium 94mg; Fibre 2.5g; Sodium 83mg.

Gâteau Saint-Honoré

This is named after the patron saint of bakers.

Serves 10
175g/6oz puff pastry

For the choux pastry
300ml/½ pint/1¼ cups water
115g/4oz/½ cup butter, diced
130g/4½oz/generous 1 cup plain
 (all-purpose) flour, sifted
2.5ml/½ tsp salt
4 eggs, lightly beaten
beaten egg, to glaze

For the filling
3 egg yolks
50g/2oz/¼ cup caster (superfine)
 sugar
30ml/2 tbsp plain (all-purpose) flour
30ml/2 tbsp cornflour (cornstarch)
300ml/½ pint/1¼ cups milk
150ml/¼ pint/⅔ cup double
 (heavy) cream
30ml/2 tbsp orange liqueur

For the caramel
225g/8oz/1 cup granulated sugar
120ml/4fl oz/½ cup water

1 Roll out the puff pastry, cut out a 20cm/8in circle, place on a lined baking sheet, prick all over and chill. Make the choux pastry. Heat the water and butter until the butter melts, bring to the boil, add the flour and salt, remove from the heat and beat until the mixture forms a ball. Beat in the eggs to form a paste.

2 Preheat the oven to 200°C/400°F/Gas 6. Using a piping (pastry) bag with a 1cm/½in nozzle, pipe a choux spiral on the puff pastry base. Pipe 16 choux buns on to a lined baking sheet. Brush with egg. Bake for 20 minutes and the base on the shelf below for 35 minutes. Pierce holes in the spiral, and one in the side of each bun. Return to the oven for 5 minutes to dry out. Cool on a rack.

3 Make the filling. Whisk the yolks and sugar until creamy. Whisk in the flours, then boil the milk and whisk that in. Return to the cleaned pan. Cook for 3 minutes, until thick, cover with damp parchment and cool. Whip the cream, fold in to the crème pâtissière with the liqueur and pipe into the buns. Make the caramel. Simmer the sugar and water until dissolved and golden. Transfer to a bowl of hot water to keep it liquid. Dip the bun bases in the caramel, put around the edge of the pastry case and pipe the remaining crème pâtissière into the centre. Drizzle the buns with the remaining caramel and leave to set for 2 hours.

Exotic Fruit Tranche

This is a good way to make the most of a small selection of exotic fruit.

Serves 8
175g/6oz/1½ cups plain
 (all-purpose) flour
50g/2oz/¼ cup unsalted
 (sweet) butter
25g/1oz/2 tbsp white vegetable fat
50g/2oz/¼ cup caster
 (superfine) sugar
2 egg yolks
about 15ml/1 tbsp water
115g/4oz/scant ½ cup apricot
 jam, strained and warmed

For the filling
150ml/¼ pint/⅔ cup double
 (heavy) cream, plus extra
 to serve
250g/9oz/generous 1 cup
 mascarpone
25g/1oz/2 tbsp icing
 (confectioners') sugar, sifted
grated rind of 1 orange
450g/1lb/3 cups mixed prepared
 fruits, such as mango, papaya,
 star fruit, kiwi fruit and
 blackberries
90ml/6 tbsp apricot jam,
 strained
15ml/1 tbsp white or coconut rum

1 Sift the flour into a bowl and rub in the butter and white vegetable fat until the mixture resembles fine breadcrumbs. Stir in the caster sugar. Add the egg yolks and enough cold water to make a soft dough. Thinly roll out the pastry between two sheets of clear film (plastic wrap) and use the pastry to line a 35 x 12cm/14 x 4½in fluted tranche tin or a 23cm/9in flan tin (tart pan). Allow the excess pastry to hang over the edge of the tin, and chill for 30 minutes.

2 Preheat the oven to 200°C/400°F/Gas 6. Prick the base of the pastry case and line with baking parchment and baking beans. Bake for 10–12 minutes. Lift out the paper and beans and return the pastry case to the oven for 5 minutes. Trim off the excess pastry and brush the inside of the case with the warmed apricot jam to form a seal. Cool on a wire rack.

3 Make the filling. Whip the cream to soft peaks, then stir it into the mascarpone with the icing sugar and orange rind. Spread in the cooled pastry case and top with the prepared fruits. Warm the apricot jam with the rum and drizzle or brush over the fruits to make a glaze. Serve with extra cream.

Gâteau Saint-Honoré Energy 466Kcal/1952kJ; Protein 7.3g; Carbohydrate 51.9g, of which sugars 30.9g; Fat 26.5g, of which saturates 12.5g; Cholesterol 186mg; Calcium 139mg; Fibre 0.5g; Sodium 221mg.
Fruit Tranche Energy 429Kcal/1801kJ; Protein 6.4g; Carbohydrate 53.3g, of which sugars 36.9g; Fat 22.2g, of which saturates 12.7g; Cholesterol 99mg; Calcium 105mg; Fibre 2.1g; Sodium 136mg.

Chocolate Eclairs

A delicious version of a popular French dessert.

Makes 12
300ml/½ pint/1¼ cups double
   (heavy) cream
10ml/2 tsp icing (confectioners')
   sugar, sifted
1.5ml/¼ tsp vanilla extract
115g/4oz plain (semisweet)
   chocolate

30ml/2 tbsp water
25g/1oz/2 tbsp butter

For the pastry
65g/2½oz/9 tbsp plain
   (all-purpose) flour
pinch of salt
50g/2oz/¼ cup butter, diced
150ml/¼ pint/⅔ cup water
2 eggs, lightly beaten

1 Preheat the oven to 200°C/400°F/Gas 6. Grease a large baking sheet and line with baking parchment. Make the pastry. Sift the flour and salt on to a sheet of parchment. Heat the butter and water in a pan until the butter melts. Increase the heat to a rolling boil. Remove from the heat and beat in the flour with a wooden spoon. Return to a low heat, then beat the mixture until it forms a ball. Set the pan aside and allow to cool for 2–3 minutes.

2 Gradually beat in the beaten eggs until you have a smooth paste thick enough to hold its shape. Spoon the pastry into a piping (pastry) bag with a 2.5cm/1in plain nozzle. Pipe 10cm/4in lengths on to the prepared baking sheet. Bake for 25–30 minutes, until the pastries are well risen and golden brown. Remove from the oven and make a slit along the side of each to release steam. Lower the heat to 180°C/350°F/Gas 4 and bake for 5 minutes. Cool on a wire rack.

3 Make the filling. Whip the cream with the icing sugar and vanilla extract until it just holds its shape. Spoon into a piping bag fitted with a 1cm/½in plain nozzle and use to fill the éclairs.

4 Place the chocolate and water in a small bowl set over a pan of hot water. Melt, stirring until smooth. Remove from the heat and gradually stir in the butter. Dip the top of each éclair in the melted chocolate, place on a wire rack and leave in a cool place to set. Ideally, serve within 2 hours of making.

Mince Pies with Orange Cinnamon Pastry

Home-made mince pies are so much nicer than shop bought ones, especially with this tasty pastry. Serve with whipped cream, flavoured with liqueur, for a special festive treat.

Makes 18
225g/8oz/2 cups plain
   (all-purpose) flour
40g/1½oz/⅓ cup icing
   (confectioners') sugar

10ml/2 tsp ground cinnamon
150g/5oz/10 tbsp butter
grated rind of 1 orange
60ml/4 tbsp chilled water
225g/8oz/⅔ cup mincemeat
1 beaten egg, to glaze
icing (confectioners') sugar,
   for dusting

1 Make the pastry. Sift together the flour, icing sugar and cinnamon in a mixing bowl, then rub in the butter until it resembles breadcrumbs. (This can be done in a food processor.) Stir in the grated orange rind.

2 Mix to a firm dough with the chilled water. Knead lightly, then roll out to 5mm/¼in thick.

3 Using a 6cm/2½in round cutter, cut out 18 circles, re-rolling as necessary. Then cut out 18 smaller 5cm/2in circles.

4 Line two bun tins (muffin pans) with the 18 larger circles – they will fill one and a half tins. Spoon a small spoonful of mincemeat into each and top with the smaller pastry circles, pressing the edges lightly together to seal.

5 Glaze the tops of the pies with egg and chill for 30 minutes. Preheat the oven to 200°C/400°F/Gas 6.

6 Bake the pies for 15–20 minutes until they are golden brown. Transfer them to wire racks to cool. Serve just warm and dusted with icing sugar.

Eclairs Energy 253Kcal/1050kJ; Protein 2.5g; Carbohydrate 11.6g, of which sugars 7.4g; Fat 22.2g, of which saturates 13.5g; Cholesterol 80mg; Calcium 29mg; Fibre 0.4g; Sodium 56mg.
Mince Pies Energy 148Kcal/619kJ; Protein 1.3g; Carbohydrate 19.9g, of which sugars 10.3g; Fat 7.6g, of which saturates 4.4g; Cholesterol 18mg; Calcium 25mg; Fibre 0.6g; Sodium 53mg

Luxury Mince Pies

A luxury version of the festive favourite.

Makes 12–15
225g/8oz/²⁄₃ cup mincemeat
50g/2oz/¹⁄₃ mixed chopped
    (candied) peel
50g/2oz/¹⁄₄ cup glacé (candied)
    cherries, chopped
30ml/2 tbsp whisky
1 egg, beaten or a little milk

icing (confectioners') sugar,
    for dusting
double (heavy) cream, to serve

For the pastry
1 egg yolk
5ml/1 tsp grated orange rind
15ml/1 tbsp caster (superfine)
    sugar
10ml/2 tsp chilled water
225g/8oz/2 cups plain
    (all-purpose) flour
150g/5oz/10 tbsp butter, diced

1 Make the pastry. Lightly beat the egg yolk in a bowl, then add the grated orange rind, caster sugar and water and mix together. Cover and set aside. Sift the flour into a separate mixing bowl.

2 Rub the butter into the flour until the mixture resembles fine breadcrumbs. Stir in the egg mixture and mix to a dough. Wrap in clear film (plastic wrap) and chill for 30 minutes.

3 Mix together the mincemeat, mixed peel and glacé cherries, then add the whisky.

4 Roll out three-quarters of the pastry. With a fluted pastry (cookie) cutter, stamp out rounds and line 12–15 patty tin (muffin pan) holes. Re-roll the trimmings and stamp out star shapes.

5 Preheat the oven to 200°C/400°F/Gas 6. Spoon a little filling into each pastry case (pie shell) and top with a star shape. Brush with a little beaten egg or milk and bake for 20–25 minutes, or until golden. Leave to cool.

6 If you like, lift the pastry star off each mince pie and place a dollop of thick cream on top of the filling before replacing the star. Lightly dust the mince pies with a little icing sugar.

Mango & Tamarillo Pastries

These fruit-topped little pastries go down a treat at the end of a spicy meal. Exotic mango and tamarillos provide a refreshing taste, while the marzipan adds a delectable sweetness to the pastry and fruit.

Makes 8
225g/8oz ready-rolled puff pastry
    (30 x 25cm/12 x 10in
    rectangle)
1 egg yolk, lightly beaten
115g/4oz/¹⁄₂ cup white marzipan
40ml/8 tsp ginger or apricot
    conserve
1 mango, peeled and thinly sliced
    off the stone (pit)
2 tamarillos, halved and sliced
caster (superfine) sugar, for
    sprinkling

1 Preheat the oven to 200°C/400°F/Gas 6. Unroll the pastry and cut it into 8 rectangles. Carefully transfer to a couple of baking sheets.

2 Using a sharp knife, score the surface of each piece of pastry into a diamond pattern, then brush with the egg yolk to glaze.

3 Cut eight thin slices of marzipan and lay one slice on each pastry rectangle. Top each with a teaspoon of the ginger or apricot conserve and spread over evenly.

4 Top each pastry rectangle with alternate slices of mango and tamarillo. Sprinkle the fruit with some of the caster sugar, then bake in the preheated oven for 15–20 minutes until the pastry is well puffed up and golden.

5 Transfer the pastries to a wire rack to cool. Sprinkle with more caster sugar before serving.

Variation
If you have difficulty finding tamarillos, use apricot slices instead or try a mix of plums and peaches.

Mince Pies Energy 195Kcal/818kJ; Protein 1.8g; Carbohydrate 26.3g, of which sugars 14.8g; Fat 9.5g, of which saturates 5.3g; Cholesterol 35mg; Calcium 36mg; Fibre 0.9g; Sodium 75mg.
Mango Pastries Energy 202Kcal/847kJ; Protein 3.2g; Carbohydrate 28.4g, of which sugars 18.3g; Fat 9.5g, of which saturates 0.4g; Cholesterol 25mg; Calcium 43mg; Fibre 1.2g; Sodium 95mg.

Fruit-Filled Empanadas

Imagine biting through crisp buttery pastry to discover a rich fruity filling flavoured with oranges and cinnamon. These are the stuff that dreams are made of.

Makes 12
275g/10oz/2½ cups plain (all-purpose) flour
30ml/2 tbsp sugar
75g/3oz/6 tbsp chilled butter, cubed
I egg yolk

iced water
milk, to glaze
sugar, for sprinkling
whole almonds and orange wedges, to serve

For the filling
30ml/2 tbsp butter
3 ripe plantains, peeled and mashed
2.5ml/½ tsp ground cloves
5ml/1 tsp ground cinnamon
200g/7oz/1⅓ cups raisins
grated rind and juice of 2 oranges

1 Make the pastry. Combine the flour and sugar in a mixing bowl. Rub in the chilled cubes of butter until the mixture resembles fine breadcrumbs.

2 Beat the egg yolk and add to the flour mixture. Add enough iced water to make a smooth dough, then shape into a ball.

3 Make the filling. Melt the butter in a pan. Add the plantains, cloves and cinnamon and cook over medium heat for 2–3 minutes. Stir in the raisins with the orange rind and juice. Lower the heat so that the mixture barely simmers. Cook for about 15 minutes, until the raisins are plump and the juice has evaporated. Set the mixture aside to cool.

4 Preheat the oven to 200°C/400°F/Gas 6. Roll out the pastry on a lightly floured surface. Cut it into 10cm/4in rounds. Place the rounds on a baking sheet and spoon on a little of the filling. Dampen the rim of the pastry rounds with water; fold the pastry over the filling and crimp the edges to seal.

5 Brush the empanadas with milk. Bake in batches for about 15 minutes or until golden. Allow to cool a little, sprinkle with sugar and serve warm, with almonds and orange wedges.

Baked Sweet Ravioli

These sweet ravioli have a wonderful ricotta filling.

Serves 4
175g/6oz/¾ cup ricotta cheese
50g/2oz/¼ cup caster (superfine) sugar
4ml/¾ tsp vanilla extract
small egg, beaten, plus 1 egg yolk
15ml/1 tbsp mixed glacé (candied) fruits

25g/1oz dark (bittersweet) chocolate, finely chopped

For the pastry
225g/8oz/2 cups plain (all-purpose) flour
65g/2½oz/5 tbsp caster (superfine) sugar
90g/3½oz/scant ½ cup butter, diced
1 egg
5ml/1 tsp finely grated lemon rind

1 Make the pastry. Place the flour and sugar in a food processor and gradually process in the butter. Keep the motor running while you add the egg and lemon rind to make a dough.

2 Transfer the dough to a sheet of clear film (plastic wrap), cover with another sheet of film and flatten into a round. Chill.

3 Press the ricotta through a sieve (strainer) into a bowl. Stir in the sugar, vanilla, egg yolk, glacé fruits and dark chocolate.

4 Bring the pastry back to room temperature. Divide in half and roll each between clear film to make rectangles measuring 15 x 56cm/6 x 22in. Preheat the oven to 180°C/350°F/Gas 4.

5 Arrange heaped tablespoonfuls of the filling in two rows along one of the pastry strips, leaving a 2.5cm/1in margin around each. Brush the pastry between the mounds of filling with beaten egg. Place the second strip of pastry on top and press down between each mound of filling to seal.

6 Use a 6cm/2½in plain pastry (cookie) cutter to cut around each mound of filling to make small circular ravioli. Gently pinch each ravioli with your fingertips to seal the edges. Place on a greased baking sheet and bake for 15 minutes until golden brown. Serve warm, sprinkled with lemon rind, if you wish.

Empanadas Energy 235Kcal/990kJ; Protein 3.2g; Carbohydrate 39.7g, of which sugars 21.6g; Fat 8.1g, of which saturates 4.8g; Cholesterol 35mg; Calcium 47mg; Fibre 1.4g; Sodium 66mg.
Ravioli Energy 628Kcal/2636kJ; Protein 13.1g; Carbohydrate 81.4g, of which sugars 38.5g; Fat 30.1g, of which saturates 17.7g; Cholesterol 162mg; Calcium 119mg; Fibre 2.1g; Sodium 186mg.

Ginger Thins

As delicate as fine glass, these elegant ginger biscuits (cookies) are ideal served with creamy desserts, syllabubs, sorbets and luxury ice creams.

Makes about 18

50g/2oz/¼ cup unsalted (sweet) butter, diced
40g/1½oz/3 tbsp liquid glucose (clear corn syrup)
90g/3½oz/½ cup caster (superfine) sugar
40g/1½oz/⅓ cup plain (all-purpose) flour
5ml/1 tsp ground ginger

1 Put the butter and liquid glucose in a heatproof bowl and place over a pan of simmering water. Stir until melted. Set aside.

2 Put the sugar in a bowl and sift over the flour and ginger. Stir into the butter mixture, then beat well until combined. Cover with clear film (plastic wrap) and chill for about 25 minutes, until firm. Meanwhile, preheat the oven to 180°C/350°F/Gas 4 and line two or three baking sheets with baking parchment.

3 Roll teaspoonfuls of the biscuit mixture into balls between your hands and place on the prepared baking sheets, spacing them well apart to allow room for spreading.

4 Place a second piece of baking parchment on top of the dough balls and roll them as thinly as possible. Peel off the top sheet, then stamp each rolled-out biscuit with a 7.5 or 9cm/3 or 3½in plain round cutter. Remove the trimmings.

5 Bake for 5–6 minutes, or until golden. Leave for a few seconds on the baking sheets to firm up slightly, then either leave flat or curl over in half. Leave to cool completely.

> **Cook's Tip**
> Use unlipped baking sheets, so that you can roll the biscuits (cookies) thinly.

Butterfly Pastries

Melt-in-the-mouth puff pastry interleaved with sugar, nuts and cinnamon produces an eye-catching accompaniment that teams well with ice creams, baked custards or fruit salads.

Makes about 12

500g/1¼lb packet ready-made puff pastry
1 egg, beaten
115g/4oz/generous ½ cup granulated sugar
25g/1oz/¼ cup chopped mixed nuts
5ml/1 tsp ground cinnamon

1 Preheat the oven to 200°C/400°F/Gas 6. Roll out the pastry on a lightly floured surface to a rectangle measuring 50 x 17cm/20 x 6½in. Cut widthways into four pieces. Brush each piece with beaten egg.

2 Mix 75g/3oz/6 tbsp of the sugar with the nuts and cinnamon in a bowl. Sprinkle this mixture evenly over three of the pieces of pastry. Place the pieces one on top of the other, ending with the uncoated piece, placing this one egg side down on the top. Press lightly together with the rolling pin.

3 Cut the stack of pastry sheets widthways into 5mm/¼in slices. Carefully place one strip on a non-stick baking sheet and place the next strip over it at an angle. Place a third strip on top at another angle so that it looks like a butterfly. Don't worry if the strips separate slightly when you move them.

4 Press the centre very flat. Sprinkle with a little of the reserved sugar. Continue in this way with the rest of the pastry.

5 Bake for 10–15 minutes, or until golden brown all over. Cool completely on the baking sheet before serving.

> **Cook's Tip**
> If using frozen puff pastry, thaw it first, but keep it chilled. Handle the dough lightly so it doesn't toughen.

Butterfly Pastries Energy 212Kcal/889kJ; Protein 3.4g; Carbohydrate 25.6g, of which sugars 10.6g; Fat 11.8g, of which saturates 0.2g; Cholesterol 16mg; Calcium 37mg; Fibre 0.2g; Sodium 136mg.
Ginger Thins Energy 55Kcal/229kJ; Protein 0.3g; Carbohydrate 8.7g, of which sugars 7g; Fat 2.3g, of which saturates 1.5g; Cholesterol 6mg; Calcium 7mg; Fibre 0.1g; Sodium 23mg.

Almond & Vanilla Biscuits with Praline Coating

These short-textured almond biscuits (cookies), filled with vanilla cream and coated in praline, are just the thing to serve with a light sorbet or fresh fruit salad. They're also great served alone, simply with a cup of strong coffee.

Makes 17–18
150g/5oz/1¼ cups plain (all-purpose) flour
75g/3oz/¾ cup ground almonds
75g/3oz/6 tbsp unsalted (sweet) butter, at room temperature, diced
1 egg yolk

5ml/1 tsp vanilla extract
icing (confectioners') sugar, sifted, for dusting

For the praline
oil, for greasing
25g/1oz/¼ cup whole blanched almonds
50g/2oz/¼ cup caster (superfine) sugar

For the filling
150g/5oz/1¼ cups icing (confectioners') sugar, sifted
75g/3oz/6 tbsp unsalted (sweet) butter, at room temperature, diced
5ml/1 tsp vanilla extract

1 Make the praline. Lightly oil a baking sheet and place the almonds on it, fairly close together. Melt the sugar in a small non-stick pan over a very low heat. Continue heating until it turns dark golden brown and pour immediately over the almonds. Set aside to cool. Crush the praline finely in a food processor.

2 Preheat the oven to 160°C/325°F/Gas 3. Line three baking sheets with baking parchment.

3 Put the flour, ground almonds and butter in a bowl. Rub together until the mixture starts to cling together. Add the egg and vanilla and work together using your hands to make a soft but not sticky dough. Roll out to a thickness of about 5mm/¼in on baking parchment. Using a 5cm/2in round biscuit (cookie) cutter, stamp out rounds and carefully transfer them to the prepared baking sheets.

4 Bake the biscuits for about 15–20 minutes, or until light golden brown. Leave on the baking sheets for 5 minutes to firm up slightly, then transfer to a wire rack to cool.

5 Make the filling. Beat together the icing sugar, butter and vanilla until light and creamy. Use this mixture to sandwich the biscuits in pairs. Be generous with the filling, spreading right to the edges. Press the biscuits gently so the filling oozes out of the sides and, using your finger, smooth around the sides of the biscuit.

6 Put the praline on a plate and roll the edges of each biscuit in the praline until thickly coated. Dust the tops of the biscuits with icing sugar and serve.

> **Cook's Tip**
> Serve these biscuits (cookies) on the day they are made. Left longer, the filling makes them soggy and unpleasant.

Tiramisu Biscuits

These sophisticated biscuits (cookies) taste like the famed Italian dessert, with its flavours of coffee, chocolate and rum. A perfect luxurious accompaniment to ices, fools or other light dishes.

Makes 14
50g/2oz/¼ cup butter, at room temperature, diced
90g/3½oz/½ cup caster (superfine) sugar
1 egg, beaten
50g/2oz/½ cup plain (all-purpose) flour

For the filling
150g/5oz/⅔ cup mascarpone
15ml/1 tbsp dark rum
2.5ml/½ tsp instant coffee powder
15ml/1 tbsp light muscovado (brown) sugar

For the topping
75g/3oz white chocolate
15ml/1 tbsp milk
30ml/2 tbsp crushed chocolate flake

1 Make the filling. Put the mascarpone in a bowl. Mix together the rum and coffee powder until the coffee has dissolved. Add to the cheese, with the sugar, and mix together well. Cover with clear film (plastic wrap) and chill until required.

2 Preheat the oven to 200°C/400°F/Gas 6. Line two or three baking sheets with baking parchment. Make the biscuits. Cream together the butter and sugar in a bowl until light and fluffy. Add the egg and mix well. Stir in the flour and mix thoroughly.

3 Put the mixture into a piping (pastry) bag fitted with a 1.5cm/½in plain nozzle and pipe 28 small blobs on to the baking sheets, spaced slightly apart. Cook for 6–8 minutes until firm in the centre and just beginning to brown on the edges. Remove from the oven and set aside to cool.

4 To assemble, spread a little of the filling on to half the biscuits and place the other halves on top. Put the chocolate and milk in a heatproof bowl and melt over a pan of hot water. When melted, stir vigorously until spreadable. Spread the chocolate evenly over the biscuits, then top with crushed chocolate flake.

Almond & Vanilla Biscuits Energy 172Kcal/717kJ; Protein 2.2g; Carbohydrate 18.5g, of which sugars 12g; Fat 10.4g, of which saturates 4.7g; Cholesterol 29mg; Calcium 34mg; Fibre 0.7g; Sodium 53mg. **Tiramisu Biscuits** Energy 178Kcal/742kJ; Protein 2.4g; Carbohydrate 15.5g, of which sugars 12.8g; Fat 7.2g, of which saturates 4.3g; Cholesterol 26mg; Calcium 28mg; Fibre 0.2g; Sodium 34mg.

Mini Fudge Bites

These cute little treats have the flavour of butterscotch and fudge and are topped with chopped pecan nuts for a delicious crunch – ideal as a contrast to smooth, creamy desserts.

Makes 30
200g/7oz/1¾ cups self-raising (self-rising) flour
115g/4oz/½ cup butter, at room temperature, diced
115g/4oz/scant ½ cup dark muscovado (molasses) sugar
75g/3oz vanilla cream fudge, diced
1 egg, beaten
25g/1oz/¼ cup pecan nut halves, sliced widthways

1 Preheat the oven to 190°C/375°F/Gas 5. Line two or three baking sheets with baking parchment. Put the flour in a bowl and rub in the diced butter, with your fingertips, until the mixture resembles fine breadcrumbs.

2 Add the sugar and diced vanilla cream fudge to the flour mixture and stir well until combined. Add the beaten egg and mix in well. Bring the dough together with your hands, then knead gently on a lightly floured surface. It will be soft yet firm.

3 Roll the dough into two cylinders, 23cm/9in long. Cut into 1cm/½in slices and place on the baking sheets. Sprinkle over the pecan nuts and press in lightly. Bake for about 12 minutes until browned at the edges. Transfer to a wire rack to cool.

Rosemary-Scented Citrus Tuiles

These elegant, crisp biscuits (cookies) are flavoured with tangy citrus rind, and made beautifully fragrant with fresh rosemary – an unusual but winning combination.

Makes 18–20
50g/2oz/¼ cup unsalted (sweet) butter, diced
2 egg whites

115g/4oz/generous ½ cup caster (superfine) sugar
finely grated rind of ½ lemon
finely grated rind of ½ orange
10ml/2 tsp finely chopped fresh rosemary
50g/2oz/½ cup plain (all-purpose) flour

1 Preheat the oven to 190°C/375°F/Gas 5. Line a baking sheet with baking parchment. Melt the butter in a pan over a low heat. Leave to cool. Whisk the egg whites until stiff, then gradually whisk in the sugar.

2 Fold in the lemon and orange rinds, rosemary and flour and then the melted butter. Place 2 large tablespoonfuls of the mixture on the baking sheet. Spread each to a thin disc about 9cm/3½in in diameter. Bake for 5–6 minutes until golden.

3 Remove from the oven and lift the tuiles using a palette knife (metal spatula) and drape over a rolling pin. Transfer to a wire rack when set in a curved shape. Continue baking the rest of the mixture in the same way.

Lace Biscuits

Very pretty, delicate and crisp, these lacy biscuits (cookies) are ideal for serving with elegant creamy or iced desserts at the end of a dinner party. Don't be tempted to bake more than four on a sheet.

Makes about 14
75g/3oz/6 tbsp butter, diced
75g/3oz/¾ cup rolled oats
115g/4oz/generous ½ cup golden caster (superfine) sugar
1 egg, beaten
10ml/2 tsp plain (all-purpose) flour
5ml/1 tsp baking powder
2.5ml/½ tsp mixed spice (apple pie spice)

1 Preheat the oven to 180°C/350°F/Gas 4. Line three or four baking sheets with baking parchment. Put the butter in a pan and place over a low heat until just melted. Remove the pan from the heat.

2 Stir the rolled oats into the melted butter. Add the remaining ingredients and mix well.

3 Place only 3 or 4 heaped teaspoonfuls of the mixture, spaced well apart, on each of the lined baking sheets.

4 Bake for 5–7 minutes, or until they have turned a deepish golden brown all over. Leave the biscuits (cookies) on the baking sheets for a few minutes.

5 Carefully cut the baking parchment so that you can lift each biscuit singly. Invert on to a wire rack and carefully remove the parchment lining. Leave to cool before serving.

Cook's Tip
Do not try to prise the biscuits (cookies) off the baking parchment while they are still upright, as you will damage their shape. It is much easier and neater to gently peel off the parchment once the biscuits are upside down on the wire rack.

Mini Fudge Bites Energy 85Kcal/356kJ; Protein 1g; Carbohydrate 11.1g, of which sugars 6.2g; Fat 4.3g, of which saturates 2.3g; Cholesterol 15mg; Calcium 31mg; Fibre 0.2g; Sodium 53mg.
Citrus Tuiles Energy 51Kcal/214kJ; Protein 0.6g; Carbohydrate 8g, of which sugars 6.1g; Fat 2.1g, of which saturates 1.3g; Cholesterol 5mg; Calcium 7mg; Fibre 0.1g; Sodium 22mg.
Lace Biscuits Energy 94Kcal/391kJ; Protein 1.2g; Carbohydrate 11g, of which sugars 6.5g; Fat 5.3g, of which saturates 2.9g; Cholesterol 25mg; Calcium 8mg; Fibre 0.4g; Sodium 61mg.

Dark Chocolate Fingers

With their understated elegance and distinctly grown-up flavour, these deliciously decadent chocolate fingers add a touch of luxury to compotes and other fruity desserts.

Makes about 26

115g/4oz/1 cup plain (all-purpose) flour
2.5ml/½ tsp baking powder
30ml/2 tbsp (unsweetened) cocoa powder
50g/2oz/¼ cup unsalted (sweet) butter, softened
50g/2oz/¼ cup caster (superfine) sugar
20ml/4 tsp golden (light corn) syrup
150g/5oz dark (bittersweet) chocolate
chocolate flake, broken up, for sprinkling

1 Preheat the oven to 160°C/325°F/Gas 3. Line two baking sheets with baking parchment. Put the flour, baking powder, cocoa powder, butter, sugar and syrup in a large mixing bowl.

2 Work the ingredients together with your hands to combine and form into a dough.

3 Roll the dough out between sheets of baking parchment to an 18 × 24cm/7 × 9½in rectangle. Remove the top sheet. Cut in half lengthways, then into bars 2cm/¾in wide. Transfer to the baking sheets.

4 Bake for about 15 minutes, taking care not to allow the bars to brown or they will taste bitter. Transfer to a wire rack to cool.

5 Melt the chocolate in a heatproof bowl set over a pan of hot water. Half-dip the biscuits into the chocolate, then carefully place on a sheet of baking parchment. Sprinkle with chocolate flake, then leave to set.

Chocolate & Pistachio Wedges

These are rich and grainy in texture, with a delicious bitter chocolate flavour. They go extremely well with vanilla ice cream and are especially good with bananas and custard.

Makes 16

200g/7oz/scant 1 cup unsalted (sweet) butter, at room temperature, diced
90g/3½oz/½ cup golden caster (superfine) sugar
250g/9oz/2¼ cups plain (all-purpose) flour
50g/2oz/½ cup cocoa powder (unsweetened)
25g/1oz/¼ cup shelled pistachio nuts, finely chopped
cocoa powder (unsweetened) for dusting

1 Preheat the oven to 180°C/350°F/Gas 4 and line a 23cm/9in round sandwich tin (layer pan) with baking parchment.

2 Beat the butter and sugar until light and creamy. Sift the flour and cocoa powder, then add the flour mixture to the butter and work in with your hands until the mixture is smooth. Knead until soft and pliable then press into the prepared tin.

3 Using the back of a tablespoon, spread the mixture evenly in the tin. Sprinkle the pistachio nuts over the top and press in gently. Prick with a fork, then mark into 16 segments using a round-bladed knife.

4 Bake for 15–20 minutes. Do not allow to brown at all or the biscuits (cookies) will taste bitter.

5 Remove the tin from the oven and dust the biscuits with cocoa powder. Cut through the marked sections with a round-bladed knife and leave to cool completely before removing from the tin and serving.

Variation
Try using almonds or hazelnuts instead of pistachio nuts.

Variation
For an extra touch of sophistication, add a dash of orange-flavoured liqueur to the chocolate.

Choc. & Pistachio Wedges Energy 188Kcal/783kJ; Protein 2.4g; Carbohydrate 18.6g, of which sugars 6.3g; Fat 12g, of which saturates 7.1g; Cholesterol 27mg; Calcium 33mg; Fibre 1g; Sodium 115mg. **Dark Choc. Fingers** Energy 72Kcal/303kJ; Protein 0.9g; Carbohydrate 9.9g, of which sugars 6.3g; Fat 3.5g, of which saturates 2.1g; Cholesterol 4mg; Calcium 11mg; Fibre 0.4g; Sodium 25mg.

Chocolate-Dipped Cinnamon & Orange Tuiles

These lightweight chocolate-dipped tuiles are a divine accompaniment to fruit or creamy desserts.

Makes 12-15
2 egg whites
90g/3½oz/½ cup caster
    (superfine) sugar
7.5ml/1½ tsp ground cinnamon
finely grated rind of 1 orange

50g/2oz/½ cup plain
    (all-purpose) flour
75g/3oz/6 tbsp butter, melted
15ml/1 tbsp recently boiled water

For the dipping chocolate
75g/3oz Belgian plain
    (semisweet) chocolate
45ml/3 tbsp milk
75–90ml/5–6 tbsp double
    (heavy) or whipping cream

1 Preheat the oven to 200°C/400°F/Gas 6. Line three large baking trays with baking parchment.

2 Whisk the egg whites until softly peaking, then whisk in the sugar until smooth and glossy. Add the cinnamon and orange rind, sift over the flour and fold in with the melted butter. When well blended, add water to thin the mixture.

3 Place 4–5 teaspoons of the mixture on each tray, well apart. Flatten out and bake, one tray at a time, for 7 minutes until just turning golden. Cool for a few seconds then remove from the tray with a metal spatula and immediately roll around the handle of a wooden spoon. Place on a rack to cool.

4 Melt the chocolate in the milk until smooth; stir in the cream. Dip one or both ends of the tuiles in the chocolate, then cool.

Cook's Tip
If you haven't made these before, cook only one or two at a time until you get the hang of it. If they harden too quickly to allow you time to roll them, return the baking sheet to the oven for a few seconds, then try rolling them again.

Chocolate Truffles

Gloriously rich chocolate truffles are given a really wicked twist in this recipe simply by the addition of a small quantity of cherry brandy – the perfect indulgent way to end a special dinner party. Instead of adding cherry brandy, experiment with using some other favourite alcoholic tipples.

Makes 18
50g/2oz/½ cup plain
    (all-purpose) flour
25g/1oz/¼ cup cocoa powder
    (unsweetened)
2.5ml/½ tsp baking powder
90g/3½oz/½ cup caster
    (superfine) sugar
25g/1oz/2 tbsp butter, diced
1 egg, beaten
5ml/1 tsp cherry brandy
50g/2oz/½ cup icing
    (confectioners') sugar

1 Preheat the oven to 200°C/400°F/Gas 6. Line two baking sheets with baking parchment.

2 Sift the flour, cocoa and baking powder into a bowl and stir in the sugar.

3 Rub the butter into the flour mixture with your fingertips until the mixture resembles coarse breadcrumbs.

4 Mix together the beaten egg and cherry brandy and stir thoroughly into the flour mixture. Cover with clear film (plastic wrap) and chill for approximately 30 minutes.

5 Put the icing sugar in a bowl. Shape walnut-size pieces of dough roughly into a ball and drop into the icing sugar. Toss until thickly coated then place on the baking sheets.

6 Bake for about 10 minutes, or until just set. Transfer to a wire rack to cool completely.

Variation
Try using fresh orange juice instead of cherry brandy.

Cinnamon & Orange Tuiles Energy 125Kcal/523kJ; Protein 1.2g; Carbohydrate 12.3g, of which sugars 9.7g; Fat 8.3g, of which saturates 5.2g; Cholesterol 18mg; Calcium 17mg; Fibre 0.2g; Sodium 42mg. **Choc. Truffles** Energy 60Kcal/251kJ; Protein 0.9g; Carbohydrate 10.5g, of which sugars 8.2g; Fat 1.8g, of which saturates 1g; Cholesterol 14mg; Calcium 12mg; Fibre 0.3g; Sodium 26mg.

Florentine Bites

Extremely sweet and rich, these little mouthfuls – based on a classic Italian biscuit (cookie) – are really delicious when served with after-dinner coffee and liqueurs. Nicely wrapped, they would also make a very special gift for anyone – your dinner party host for example.

Makes 36

200g/7oz good quality plain (semisweet) chocolate (minimum 70 per cent cocoa solids)
50g/2oz/2½ cups cornflakes
50g/2oz/scant ½ cup sultanas (golden raisins)
115g/4oz/1 cup toasted flaked (sliced) almonds
115g/4oz/½ cup glacé (candied) cherries, halved
50g/2oz/⅓ cup mixed (candied) peel
200ml/7fl oz/scant 1 cup can sweetened condensed milk

1 Preheat the oven to 180°C/350°F/Gas 4. Line the base of a shallow 20cm/8in cake tin (pan) with baking parchment. Lightly grease the sides.

2 Melt the chocolate in a heatproof bowl over a pan of hot water. Spread over the base of the tin. Chill until set.

3 Meanwhile, put the cornflakes, sultanas, almonds, cherries and mixed peel in a large bowl.

4 Pour the condensed milk over the cornflake mixture and toss the mix gently, using a fork.

5 Spread the mixture evenly over the chocolate base and bake for 12–15 minutes or until golden brown.

6 Put the cooked Florentine mixture aside in the tin until completely cooled, then chill for 20 minutes.

7 Cut into tiny squares and serve.

Tunisian Almond Cigars

These delicate rolled pastries are a great favourite in North Africa. Wonderful with all manner of desserts, they are also excellent served on their own, with a small cup of fragrant mint tea or strong, dark coffee, at the end of a meal.

Makes 8–12

250g/9oz marzipan
1 egg, lightly beaten
15ml/1 tbsp rose water or orange flower water
5ml/1 tsp ground cinnamon
1.5ml/¼ tsp almond extract
8–12 sheets filo pastry
melted butter, for brushing
icing (confectioners') sugar and ground cinnamon, for dusting

1 Knead the marzipan until it is soft, then put in a bowl, and mix in the egg, rose water, cinnamon and almond extract. Chill for 1–2 hours.

2 Preheat the oven to 190°C/375°F/Gas 5. Lightly grease a baking sheet. Place a sheet of filo pastry on a piece of baking parchment, keeping the remaining pastry covered with a damp cloth, and brush with the melted butter.

3 Shape 30–45ml/2–3 tbsp of the filling mixture into a cylinder and place at one end of the pastry. Fold the pastry over to enclose the ends of the filling, then roll up to form a cigar shape. Place on the baking sheet and make 7–11 more cigars in the same way.

4 Bake the pastries for about 15 minutes, or until golden. Leave to cool, then serve, dusted with sugar and cinnamon.

Variation
Instead of dusting with sugar, drench the pastries in syrup. In a pan, dissolve 250g/9oz/1¼ cups sugar in 250ml/8fl oz/1 cup water and boil until thickened. Stir in a squeeze of lemon juice and a few drops of rose water and pour over the pastries. Allow the syrup to soak in before serving.

Florentine Bites Energy 87Kcal/364kJ; Protein 1.6g; Carbohydrate 12g, of which sugars 10.7g; Fat 3.9g, of which saturates 1.4g; Cholesterol 2mg; Calcium 30mg; Fibre 0.5g; Sodium 28mg.
Tunisian Almond Cigars Energy 101Kcal/428kJ; Protein 2g; Carbohydrate 17.3g, of which sugars 14.2g; Fat 3.2g, of which saturates 0.4g; Cholesterol 16mg; Calcium 22mg; Fibre 0.5g; Sodium 10mg.

Greek Fruit & Nut Pastries

Packed with candied citrus peel and walnuts, and soaked in a coffee syrup, these aromatic pastries make a different way to end a meal with coffee.

Makes 16
60ml/4 tbsp clear honey
60ml/4 tbsp strong brewed coffee
75g/3oz/½ cup mixed (candied) citrus peel, finely chopped
175g/6oz/1 cup walnuts, chopped
1.5ml/¼ tsp freshly grated nutmeg

milk, to glaze
caster (superfine) sugar, for sprinkling

For the pastry
450g/1lb/4 cups plain (all-purpose) flour
2.5ml/½ tsp ground cinnamon
2.5ml/½ tsp baking powder
pinch of salt
150g/5oz/10 tbsp butter
30ml/2 tbsp caster (superfine) sugar
1 egg
120ml/4fl oz/½ cup chilled milk

1 Preheat the oven to 180°C/350°F/Gas 4. Make the pastry. Sift the flour, cinnamon, baking powder and salt into a bowl. Rub or cut in the butter until the mixture resembles breadcrumbs. Stir in the sugar. Make a well.

2 Beat the egg and milk together and pour into the well. Mix to a soft dough. Divide the dough into two and wrap each piece in clear film (plastic wrap). Chill for 30 minutes.

3 Mix the honey and coffee in a mixing bowl. Stir in the mixed peel, walnuts and nutmeg. Cover and leave for 20 minutes.

4 Roll out one portion of the dough on a lightly floured surface to 3mm/⅛in thick. Stamp out rounds, using a 10cm/4in cutter.

5 Place a heaped teaspoonful of filling on one side of each round. Brush the edges with a little milk, then fold over and press together to seal. Repeat with the second piece of pastry.

6 Place the pastries on greased baking sheets, brush with a little milk and sprinkle with sugar. Make a steam hole in each with a skewer. Bake for 35 minutes until golden. Cool on a wire rack.

Gazelles' Horns

These Moroccan pastries are a stylish accompaniment to light fruit dishes.

Makes about 16
200g/7oz/scant 2 cups ground almonds
115g/4oz/1 cup icing (confectioners') sugar, plus extra for dusting
30ml/2 tbsp orange flower water
25g/1oz/2 tbsp butter, melted

2 egg yolks, beaten
2.5ml/½ tsp ground cinnamon

For the pastry
200g/7oz/1¾ cups plain (all-purpose) flour
pinch of salt
25g/1oz/2 tbsp butter, melted
about 30ml/2 tbsp orange flower water
1 egg yolk, beaten
60–90ml/4–6 tbsp chilled water

1 Mix the almonds, icing sugar, orange flower water, butter, egg yolks and cinnamon in a mixing bowl to make a smooth paste.

2 Make the pastry. Sift the flour and salt into a large bowl, then stir in the melted butter, orange flower water and about three-quarters of the egg yolk. Stir in enough chilled water to make a fairly soft dough.

3 Quickly and lightly, knead the pastry until it is smooth and elastic, then place on a lightly floured surface and roll out as thinly as possible. With a sharp knife, cut the dough into long strips about 7.5cm/3in wide.

4 Preheat the oven to 180°C/350°F/Gas 4. Roll small pieces of the almond paste into thin sausages about 7.5cm/3in long with tapering ends. Place these in a line along one side of the strips of pastry, about 3cm/1¼in apart. Dampen the pastry edges with water, then fold the other half of the strip over the filling and press the edges together firmly.

5 Using a pastry wheel, cut around each pastry sausage to make a crescent shape. Pinch the edges firmly together. Prick the crescents with a fork and place on a buttered baking sheet. Brush with the remaining egg yolk and bake for 12–16 minutes until lightly coloured. Allow to cool, then dust with icing sugar.

Fruit & Nut Pastries Energy 278Kcal/1162kJ; Protein 5g; Carbohydrate 30.2g, of which sugars 8.7g; Fat 16.1g, of which saturates 5.7g; Cholesterol 32mg; Calcium 69mg; Fibre 1.5g; Sodium 80mg.
Gazelles' Horns Energy 182Kcal/762kJ; Protein 4.4g; Carbohydrate 18.1g, of which sugars 8.2g; Fat 10.7g, of which saturates 2.5g; Cholesterol 44mg; Calcium 56mg; Fibre 1.3g; Sodium 23mg.

Baklava

Serve wedges of this luxuriously sweet Greek treat with fresh fruit or lots of strong coffee to round off a meal with panache.

Makes 16
50g/2oz/½ cup blanched almonds, chopped
50g/2oz/½ cup pistachio nuts, chopped
75g/3oz/6 tbsp caster (superfine) sugar
75g/3oz/6 tbsp butter, melted
6 sheets of filo pastry, thawed if frozen

For the syrup
115g/4oz/generous ½ cup caster (superfine) sugar
7.5cm/3in piece cinnamon stick
1 whole clove
2 green cardamom pods, crushed
75ml/5 tbsp very strong brewed coffee

1 Preheat the oven to 180°C/350°F/Gas 4. Add the almonds, pistachio nuts and sugar to a small bowl and mix well, stirring to coat the nuts in sugar. Brush a shallow 18 x 28cm/7 x 11in baking tin (pan) with a little of the melted butter.

2 Using the tin as a guide, cut the six sheets of filo pastry with a very sharp knife so that they fit the tin exactly. It is easiest to cut through all the sheets in one go, rather than working through them singly. Lay a sheet of pastry in the tin and brush it all over with some of the melted butter.

3 Lay a second sheet of filo in the tin and brush with butter. Add a third sheet, brushing with a little butter. Sprinkle the filo with half of the nut mixture, making sure it is evenly distributed.

4 Layer three more sheets of filo pastry on top of the nut mixture, brushing each layer with butter as you go. Then spread the remaining nut mixture over the pastry, smoothing it evenly over the entire surface. Top with the remaining sheets of pastry, brushing with butter as before, and liberally brushing the top layer too. Gently press down all around the edges to seal.

5 Using a very sharp knife, mark the top of the baklava into diamonds. Place in the preheated oven and bake for 20–25 minutes, or until golden brown and crisp all over.

6 Meanwhile, make the syrup. Put the sugar, spices and coffee in a small pan and heat gently until the sugar has dissolved – be careful not to burn the sugar as there is a high proportion of it to the liquid. Cover the pan and set aside for 20 minutes, to give the spices time to flavour the syrup.

7 Remove the baklava from the oven. Reheat the syrup over a gentle heat, then strain it evenly over the pastry. Leave to cool in the tin. Set aside for 6 hours or preferably overnight to allow the flavours to mingle. To serve, cut the baklava into diamonds, following the lines scored prior to baking.

> **Variation**
> Try different nuts in the baklava filling if you prefer. Walnuts, pecan nuts and hazelnuts can all be used to great effect.

Rugelach

Thought to hail from Poland, these crisp, flaky pastries, with a sweet filling, resemble a snake or croissant. Memorable little bites to serve with coffee.

Makes 48–60
115g/4oz/½ cup unsalted (sweet) butter
115g/4oz/½ cup full-fat soft white (farmer's) cheese
15ml/1 tbsp sugar
1 egg
2.5ml/½ tsp salt
about 250g/9oz/2¼ cups plain (all-purpose) flour
about 250g/9oz/generous 1 cup butter, melted
250g/9oz/scant 2 cups sultanas (golden raisins)
130g/4½oz/generous 1 cup chopped walnuts or walnut pieces
about 225g/8oz/1 cup caster (superfine) sugar
10–15ml/1–2 tsp ground cinnamon

1 Make the pastry. Put the butter and soft cheese in a bowl and beat with an electric whisk until creamy. Beat in the sugar, egg and salt.

2 Fold the flour into the creamed mixture, a little at a time, until the dough can be worked with the hands. Continue adding the flour, kneading, until it is a consistency that can be rolled out. (Add only as much flour as needed.) Shape the dough into a ball, cover and chill for at least 2 hours or overnight. (The dough will be too soft if not chilled properly.)

3 Preheat the oven to 180°C/350°F/Gas 4. Divide the dough into six equal pieces. On a lightly floured surface, roll out each piece into a round about 3mm/⅛in thick, then brush with a little of the melted butter and sprinkle over the sultanas, chopped walnuts, a little sugar and the cinnamon.

4 Cut the rounds into eight to ten wedges and carefully roll the large side of each wedge towards the tip. (Some of the filling will fall out.) Arrange the rugelach on baking sheets, brush with a little butter and sprinkle with the sugar. Bake for 15–30 minutes until lightly browned. Leave to cool before serving.

Baklava Energy 130Kcal/545kJ; Protein 1.6g; Carbohydrate 15.3g, of which sugars 12.8g; Fat 7.4g, of which saturates 2.8g; Cholesterol 10mg; Calcium 22mg; Fibre 0.5g; Sodium 46mg.
Rugelach Energy 111Kcal/463kJ; Protein 1g; Carbohydrate 10.4g, of which sugars 7.2g; Fat 7.6g, of which saturates 3.9g; Cholesterol 18mg; Calcium 15mg; Fibre 0.3g; Sodium 47mg.

Index